1,000,000 Books

are available to read at

Forgotten Books

www.ForgottenBooks.com

Read online
Download PDF
Purchase in print

ISBN 978-0-428-59624-8
PIBN 10199203

This book is a reproduction of an important historical work. Forgotten Books uses state-of-the-art technology to digitally reconstruct the work, preserving the original format whilst repairing imperfections present in the aged copy. In rare cases, an imperfection in the original, such as a blemish or missing page, may be replicated in our edition. We do, however, repair the vast majority of imperfections successfully; any imperfections that remain are intentionally left to preserve the state of such historical works.

Forgotten Books is a registered trademark of FB &c Ltd.
Copyright © 2018 FB &c Ltd.
FB &c Ltd, Dalton House, 60 Windsor Avenue, London, SW19 2RR.
Company number 08720141. Registered in England and Wales.

For support please visit www.forgottenbooks.com

1 MONTH OF FREE READING

at
www.ForgottenBooks.com

By purchasing this book you are eligible for one month membership to ForgottenBooks.com, giving you unlimited access to our entire collection of over 1,000,000 titles via our web site and mobile apps.

To claim your free month visit:
www.forgottenbooks.com/free199203

* Offer is valid for 45 days from date of purchase. Terms and conditions apply.

English
Français
Deutsche
Italiano
Español
Português

www.forgottenbooks.com

Mythology Photography **Fiction**
Fishing Christianity **Art** Cooking
Essays Buddhism Freemasonry
Medicine **Biology** Music **Ancient
Egypt** Evolution Carpentry Physics
Dance Geology **Mathematics** Fitness
Shakespeare **Folklore** Yoga Marketing
Confidence Immortality Biographies
Poetry **Psychology** Witchcraft
Electronics Chemistry History **Law**
Accounting **Philosophy** Anthropology
Alchemy Drama Quantum Mechanics
Atheism Sexual Health **Ancient History**
Entrepreneurship Languages Sport
Paleontology Needlework Islam
Metaphysics Investment Archaeology
Parenting Statistics Criminology
Motivational

History

OF THE

Parish of Ryton,

INCLUDING THE

PARISHES OF WINLATON, STELLA,
AND GREENSIDE.

BY

WILLIAM BOURN,

AUTHOR OF THE "HISTORY OF THE PARISH
OF WHICKHAM," ETC.

CARLISLE:
G. & T. COWARD, PRINTERS, THE WORDSWORTH PRESS.
MDCCCXCVI.

Br 5229.150

HARVARD COLLEGE LIBRARY
NOV 6 1920
GIFT OF
WILLIAM ENDICOTT, JR.

THIS WORK

IS RESPECTFULLY DEDICATED

TO

JOSEPH COWEN, ESQ.,

OF STELLA HALL,

BY THE AUTHOR.

ERRATA.

Page 31, for Lambly read Lambley.
,, 50, for Wallace read Wallis.
,, 78, last line, for Potter read Porter.
,, 139, for 1888 read 1838.

PREFACE.

SEVERAL of the chapters in this work were contributed to the *Newcastle Weekly Chronicle*, while others formed parts of Lectures delivered before local societies by the Author. Several of the literary friends of the Author, whose opinions are highly esteemed, recommended their re-publication in book form; hence the present volume.

No apology need be offered for its appearance, as no account of the Parish exists in a popular and convenient form.

The facts embodied in this work have been secured after no inconsiderable labour on the part of the Author, who has drawn from all sources available to him. Having visited every part of the Parish about which he writes, he now offers all the facts relating to its history, antiquities, traditions and folk-lore which he collected, to the public, and hopes thereby to enable those who live in the neighbourhood to appreciate the rich stores of historical remains around them, and to find their way to such places of interest as they may wish to inspect.

The writer desires to express his thanks to the Editor of the *Newcastle Weekly Chronicle* for nine of the illustrations; to Mr. Robert Barrass, Rembrandt Studio, 180 Westgate Road, for Photo of Sir Henry Augustus Clavering, Bart.; to Canon Baily, Rector of Ryton, for the use of the Parish Register, and for assisting him in other ways; to Mr. W. W. Thomlinson, and to Mr. G. R. Ramsay.

In conclusion, the Author will gratefully receive any suggestions that may tend to the improvement of the present work, and the correction in a future edition of any errors that may perchance have found their way into its pages.

WILLIAM BOURN.

WHICKHAM,
    March 17th, 1896.

CONTENTS.

	Page
Ryton	1
The Church	3
The Rectory	17
The Churchyard	26
Bequests to the Poor	30
Ryton Burnt by the Scots	31
The Scots again at Ryton	32
The Market Cross	33
Ryton in 1895	35
Bar (Bare) Moor	43
Crawcrook	45
Pethhead	52
Greenside	54
Coalburns	57
Ryton Woodside	60
Stella	63
Stella Hall	71
Battle of Stella Haughs	74
Cromwell at Stella	80
Stella House	81
The Coal Trade	83
The Staiths	85
The Catholic Chapel	87
The Cowen Family	90
Blaydon	99

	Page
Blaydon Church	103
Blaydon and District Co-operative Literary Institute	106
Blaydon Co-operative Society	106
Winlaton	111
Freemasonry at Winlaton	127
Winlaton Subscription Library	128
Winlaton in 1895	130
Church (St. Paul's)	138
Park Head Hall	143
Winlaton Mill	147
Blaydon Burn	152
Thornley	156
Barlow	159
Spen (High)	161
Spen (Low)	162
Chopwell Township	164
Blackhall Mill	168
Axwell Park	171
The Claverings	175

LIST OF ILLUSTRATIONS.

Frontispiece—RYTON GREEN.	
RYTON CHURCH	4
RYTON FERRY	41
STELLA HALL	72
STELLA CHAPEL	86
OLD HOUSE IN BACK STREET, WINLATON	110
A BIT OF WINLATON	130
WINLATON MILL	146
AXWELL PARK	170
SIR HENRY A. CLAVERING	176

History of the Parish of Ryton.

RYTON.

THE village of Ryton gives name to this Parish and the township in which it is situated. The village occupies a lofty and beautiful situation on the south banks of the Tyne, seven miles west of Newcastle. The Newcastle and Carlisle Railway runs along the foot of the hill on the north side of the village, where there is a railway station. The name Ryton is probably derived from *rye* = water, and *ton* = a settlement hedged in and protected from intruders.

The Parish of Ryton was anciently very extensive. It was bounded on the north and north-east by the river Tyne, till its junction with the Derwent at Derwenthaugh, which divided Ryton from Whickham, and from the chapelries of Tanfield and Medomsley on the south, till the junction of the Milkwell Burn and Derwent on the south-west; the Milkwell Burn, a short imaginary line, and the Stanley Burn, flowing northwards, and falling into the Tyne near Bradley Mill, completed the western boundary. The Parish, which formed almost a triangle, was originally subdivided into six constableries, viz: 1, Ryton; 2, Ryton Woodside; 3, Crawcrook (including Bradley); 4, Stella; 5, Winlaton (including Blaydon, Thornley, Spen, and Axwell); '6' Chopwell (which includes Blackhall Mill, Milkwell Burn, Ravenside, Armondside, Hugergate, and other tenements). Winlaton parish was formed from Ryton on November 6th, 1832; Stella parish in August,

1844; and Greenside parish on May 6th, 1886. Ryton Parish now comprises the township of Ryton, with the villages of Ryton, Addison, and Stargate.

Population of the township of Ryton: 1801, 432; 1811, 462; 1821, 445; 1831, 590; 1841, 677; 1851, 739; 1861, 1140; 1871, 1939; 1881, 3036; 1891, 3393.

Area, 1200 acres. Rateable value in 1821, £1,882; and in 1894, £16,452. The principal proprietors of land are Sir Alexander Kinlock; Joseph Cowen, Esq.; James Hindmarsh, Esq.; William R. Lamb, Esq.; the Rector of Ryton; Archibald M. Dunn, Esq.; Townely Trustees; Mrs. Thorp; John B. Simpson, Esq.; and the Stella Coal Company.

The manor of Ryton formerly belonged to the See of Durham, under which the greater part of the lands were held by lease or copy of court-roll. Under Boldon Book, 1183, "the men of Ryton held the vill on lease, with the demesne, the assize rent, the mill, and the service due (from the villeins), with a stock of one draught and two harrows, and twenty chalder of oats of the bishop's measure, and the fisheries; they pay fourteen pounds rent, make ladings like the men of Whickham, and, jointly with Crawcrook, provide the carriage of one ton of wine. The punder (keeper of the pinfold) has five acres and the thraves like other punders, and renders thirty hens and two hundred eggs. The villeins pay twenty-four hens and two hundred eggs."

In a Roll of Bishop Bek, 1283—1310, there is an entry of 10s. for "repairing mill" at Ryton.

Hatfield's Survey, 1345—1381, mentions three free tenements, held by the Rector of Ryton, Thomas Gategang, and John Stepyng. An inquisition was taken at Gateshead in 1344, stating that from time beyond the memory of man there existed a fishery near Ryton called the Blaklough, to the westward of Tyne bridge, belonging to the Bishop of Durham.

The Common, belonging to the manor of Ryton, was extremely extensive, and its boundaries towards Chopwell were the subject of litigation as early as 1562. A division of Ryton Moor bears date 16th September, 1638; the whole of the allotments are stated to be held of the See by copy of court roll under fourpence an acre rent; the mines were reserved to the See, with the usual clauses of compensation for damage to the tenant of the soil in working;

and twenty acres were allotted to the manor mill, to provide horses for fetching the corn.

In 1699, the division of Ryton Broomfields and High Hedgefield took place. The Broomfields contained 100 acres, and High Hedgefields 61 a. 1 r. 5 p. Both were copyhold lands, were held in common, and divided by twenty-one tenants. The acres allowed to each varied from 25 acres assigned to William Jolly, down to 3 roods 25 perches to John Humble.

In 1690, Ryton West Field, West Crofts, East Field, and Low Hedgefield, in all 400 acres, were divided. These lands were held in common, and divided by thirty-six people whose names are set down in the award, and who are all described as owners by copy of Court Roll, according to the custom of the manor of Ryton. 107 acres fell to Sir Thomas Tempest, and other portions varying from 34 acres to an acre, to other owners.

The Church.

"Ye holy walls, that still sublime,
Resist the crumbling touch of time."

RYTON CHURCH (Holy Cross) stands at the western extremity of the village, and its situation is extremely picturesque and attractive. The edifice consists of chancel, nave with north and south aisles, south porch, and a western tower surmounted by an octangular spire, covered with lead. The chancel is forty-four feet long by eighteen feet three inches wide, and is entered on the south side by an old square-headed doorway, with curious carvings on the angles. There is within the altar-rails, on the south side, a square-headed piscina with a projecting basin. At the west end of the chancel, on the south side, is a low side window, built up on the outside. These windows are sometimes called "leper" windows, it being the opinion of some authorities that they were used for administering the holy sacrament to lepers. Between the door and the low side window, there is a slab inserted in the wall with the following inscription:—

BERNARD	OBIITQVA
GILPINRE	RTODIEM
CTORHV	ARTIIAN
IVSECCLLIÆ	DOM. 1583

The Church from the Vicarage Garden

"Bernard Gilpin, rector of this (Houghton) Church, who died 4th day of March, 1583." There is inscribed underneath the above:—"From Bernard Gilpin's monument in Houghton-le-Spring Church, dated A.D. 1583. Charles Thorp. 1828."

Within the altar rails, on the north side, there is a fine effigy in Stanhope marble. The length of the figure is five feet nine inches. The effigy is described by Surtees as that of a Benedictine monk; but Mr. J. R. Boyle, in describing it, says :—"He wears the alb, and over this the dalmatic. The sleeves of the former (monk) are close-fitting, whilst those of the latter (deacon) are loose. On the right side, beneath the dalmatic, are the extremities of the stole. From the left wrist hangs the maniple. The head, which rests on a cushion, and is further supported by two small figures of angels, is tonsured. The hands hold a book, on the back of which a bird, possibly a dove, is carved. The feet rest on a lion. This effigy is of especial interest from the extreme rarity of effigies of ecclesiastics who had not attained the order of the priesthood. The effigy is probably of late thirteenth century date." There is an aumbrey within the altar-rails, in the north wall. The handsome altar table is of oak; on the front of it is inscribed:—"The offering of Charles Thorp, Rector, A.D. 1849." In the north wall of the chancel, opposite the priest's door, is the entrance to the vestry, which formerly consisted of two apartments; but, in 1888 part of the old vestry was converted into an organ chamber, and by means of a pointed arch in the north wall, the organ faces the chancel. The chancel is stalled with oak; on the end of one o the stalls is carved a dolphin embowered inter three crosses repeated, supposed to be the arms of the Rev. William James, rector of Ryton from 1617 till the usurpation. There is on the left side of the vestry door a quaint carving of the Nativity, with the inscription, "C. Thorp, 1826." A fine old chair stands within the altar rails, on which is inscribed "T.T. 1662." The initials are probably those of Sir Thomas Tempest, and the chair a gift to the church. Previous to 1844 the east window was a square of five lights, but in that year the old window was removed, and a pointed window of three lights was inserted.

Underneath the window, and above the communion table, is a handsome reredos, carved in oak. In the centre is represented The Descent from the Cross; on the left side, Christ bearing the

Cross; and on the right, Christ on Calvary. At the extreme right is Moses, pointing to the Brazen Serpent in the Wilderness; and at the extreme left Abraham and Isaac, journeying to Mount Moriah. Formerly there were in the south wall of the chancel six pointed lights; afterwards, the window at the east end was altered into one of two lights, with central shaft, and round-headed. The chancel arch, which rests on corbels, is pointed, and plain in design. A screen of old oak, carved in open tracery, roses, quatrefoils, and foliage, encloses the chancel. The nave is forty-five feet by nineteen feet; the tower at the west end seventeen feet by seventeen feet; and the north and south aisles each eleven feet wide, including the pillars, and extending the full length of the nave and tower, viz., sixty-eight feet. Each aisle is formed by two pillars supporting pointed arches, the groins of which are ornamented with sculptured heads. The western pillars are plain cylinders, those to the east octagonal. The walls of the aisles and porch have been raised several feet, and a parapet added, probably about the end of the fourteenth century. The body of the church would then present a different appearance to what it does now, as the high-pitched roof came down in one continuous slope over the aisles, as may be seen by examining the east gable of the nave.

Hutchinson states that the wall of the south aisle was rebuilt in 1627; but the historian is clearly mistaken, as the most casual observer may see. The tower is engaged, and of three stages. In the lowest stage there is a lancet twenty feet high, and two feet four inches wide, which is the only window in the body of the church which remains unaltered. In the second stage, which is twenty-two feet square, is the clock. A brass plate on the clock bears the inscription:—" Erected September, 1881, by Subscription by Parishioners and Friends, in Memory of William Webb, Rector of Ryton 1862—1878." This stage is lighted by a single lancet in the north, west, and south sides. The third stage contains the bells. In 1763 three new bells were ordered to replace three old bells. Two of the bells bear the inscription: "Lester and Pack of London, fecit 1763;" the third: "Recast by John Warner and Son, 1868;" and a fourth: "In loving Memory of Charles Baring. Cast by John Warner and Son, 1881." The entrance to the tower is by a door in the second stage, which is reached by a spiral staircase of oak, erected in 1886. This staircase replaced one probably erected in 1746, for on April 25th of that year, the "four-and-twenty agreed with Ralph Hawdon and William Waddle, for three pounds and ten shillings and the old ladder, to make a staircase to the belfry."

The spire of the church is formed of a complicated framework of oak timber, and is covered with sheets of lead, placed diagonally, and carefully overlapped. The spire underwent extensive repairs in 1751, and in 1877 was again substantially repaired, and much defective lead removed and renewed. The total height of the tower and spire is one hundred and twenty feet six inches, and not one hundred and eight feet, as stated by all the historians of Durham. The weather-cock bears the date 1835. The tower terminates with a corbel table. Several of the corbels are carved with conventional foliage of early character. On the east side of the tower is a large piece of sculpture representing St. George subduing the Dragon. The tower is open to the nave and aisles by pointed arches, each of two chamfered orders. All the arches rest on moulded corbels, in five out of the six of which the nail-head ornament appears. All the tower arches have hood mouldings. The label of the arch which opens to the nave terminates in carved heads, one of which has a barrel-shaped object in its mouth. There are half-straining arches from the east wall of the tower to the walls of the aisles. These are of two chamfered orders, and rest on corbels in the aisle walls. In both these corbels are found the nail-headed ornament.

The porch has a richly-moulded doorway; formerly the roof would slope down the same as the roof of the church. About the middle of the last century the roof of the nave was thatched with straw, which was burnt, and replaced by one of lower pitch, covered with lead; this roof was covered with slates in 1816. The nave and aisle roofs were restored and raised to their original pitch in 1877, and were covered with green Westmorland slates, except the north aisle roof, which was covered with the old slates from the nave roof. The roof of the chancel was restored to its original pitch by Archdeacon Thorp, and the flat ceiling allowed to remain. In 1886, the chancel was beautified by the present oak ceiling.

Formerly, the south wall of the church contained lancets, which were replaced by sash windows; in 1812 these were removed, and the present windows inserted.

About the year 1813, the nave and aisles were re-pewed; and in 1886, they were again filled with seats made of oak. On the south side of the chancel is a buttress on which grotesque heads are carved. Above the entrance of the porch is an old sun-dial, mutilated, and without any date. Only the word *Pereunt* remains on the stone. Originally the inscription was: "*Pereunt et imputantur.*" (The hours pass and are reckoned.)

The font is a large stone basin supported by a pedestal, and is described by Surtees as ancient. In the church books there is the following entry: "1662. Paid for the fonte and lading, and for drink for the men that helped to set it, £2 3s. 6d." If Surtees is correct as to the antiquity of the font—and we think he is—may it not be inferred from the above entry, that the font was removed at the time when John Weld (intruder,) became rector, and taken back to the church in the time of Ralph Blakiston, who became rector in 1660.

The pulpit is of oak, octagonal in form, artistically designed, and ornamented with carved tracery, and stands on a pedestal of Caen stone, adorned with marble shafts. At each angle, under a niche, is a sculptured figure, representing the Venerable Bede, St. Cuthbert, St. Aidan, St. Helena, and the Emperor Constantine. In design and execution the pulpit displays admirable workmanship.

In the year 1703, a gallery was erected at the west end of the nave, by Sir Ambrose Crowley, for the use of his workmen who attended Ryton church. There were other galleries—at the north-east end of the nave, and over the aisles—all of which were removed in 1846. Formerly a stall was enclosed on the south side of the church for the owners of Chopwell, and another on the north side for the house of Stella. At one time there was a door eight feet six inches high and five feet wide, on the north side of the church, which is now built up. The style of architecture is of one period, Early English or Lancet, and the date of the erection of the church may be ascribed to the early part of the thirteenth century (1220).

In early times there was a chantry in the church dedicated to the Virgin; its foundation is unknown. Ralph Eure, the bishop's escheater in 1425, mentions five shillings, the tenth of a messuage, and eighteen acres called St. Mary's Land, given by the Lord of Crawcrook to St. Mary's Altar, in Ryton Church, in mortmain without license.

On September 13th, 1498, John Saunders of Ryton granted a cottage, three acres and a plot of ground, to William Clark and his successors, chaplain of St. Mary's Altar, for the perpetual maintenance of a light before the image of the Virgin.

The church possesses several windows of stained glass. The altar window contains in the centre light the figure of Christ on the Cross; and those on the right and left, scenes connected with the Crucifixion. Underneath is the inscription: "Dedicated to the Glory of God, in loving Memory of Emma Easton, by her sister Emily." On the south side, at the east end of the chancel, there are two windows; one containing the figures of St. Luke and St. Matthew, and the other the Baptism of our Lord. Underneath is the inscription: "Mary Ann Thorp, died April 1st, 1839; Robert Thorp, died April 7th, 1847." There are other three memorial windows in the south side of the chancel to members of the Thorp family. In the south aisle are two: one containing the figures of St. Thomas and St. John; the other St. Bartholomew and St. Philip. Under the tower a high single light containing the figure of St. Paul, bears the inscription: "Church Offering at Christmas, Anno Domini, 1848."

In the north aisle there are two windows of stained glass, one of which represents Christ Blessing little Children; underneath is inscribed: "In Memory of Margaret Isabella, the beloved wife of Thomas Spencer of the Grove, Ryton, who died in Madeira, December 20th, 1865, aged twenty-two years." The other is a window of two lights, containing the figures of St. Mary and St. John, underneath which is the following inscription: "To the Glory of God, and in Memory of John Easton of Layton Manor, Yorkshire, who died 14th August, 1880, aged seventy-seven years. Erected by his sisters Emily and Matilda."

The walls of the church contain several mural tablets. In the north wall of the chancel are:—

1. White marble on black marble slab.

FRANCES WILKIE THORP,
Wife of Charles Thorp, M.A.,

Rector of this Parish.
The only child of
Henry Collingwood Selby, Esq.,
Died a few months after marriage,
the 21st of April, 1811, aged Twenty years.

2. White marble on black slab.
In the vault beneath are placed
the remains of
ROBERT THORP, D.D.,
Archdeacon of Northumberland,
And sometime rector of this Parish,
Who departed this life in the blessed
hope of immortality through Jesus Christ,
the xx. day April, 1812, in his 76 year.
GRACE THORP, wife of Robert Thorp,
Died 3 August, 1814, aged 70 years.

3. White marble.
Near to this place lies interred
the body of the Rev. JOHN LLOYD, A.M.,
late rector of this Parish. He departed
this life on the 15th day of September,
in the year of our Lord, 1765,
in the 56th year of his age.
Most justly lamented by his family and
friends, nor less by his parishioners,
whom he had endeared himself to,
by every act of affection and duty.
By his unlimited benevolence and charity,
and, by a constant attention to the duties
of his sacred function, through a course
of 27 years, during which he was their
Minister. He was the eldest son of the
Rev. WILLIAM LLOYD, D.D.,
Sometime since Chancellor of the
Diocese of Worcester, and grandson
of William Lloyd, the Bishop
of that Diocese. Distinguished in the
age he lived, for his extensive learning,

but more for his fervent zeal for the
Protestant Religion, and for the rights
and liberties of his Country, which he
supported with unshaken fidelity.
The deceased married Mary, the
daughter of the Rev. Robert Lightfoot, A.M.,
Rector of Deal, in the County of Kent,
by whom he left issue three daughters,
Elizabeth, Catherine, and Mary.

4.

Near this place lies interred
Mr. JOHN SIMPSON, of Bradley,
and JANE, his wife.
John died Dec. 31st, 1732, aged 52;
and by his will left to the poor
of Ryton £60, with interest of which
to be distributed by the Rector every
23rd of December; as also £50, to
All Saints Charity School, in
Newcastle. Jane, daughter of
Henry Anderson, Esq., died Nov. 23,
1748, aged 66 years.
He left issue two sons, John, and Francis.

5.

To the memory of
GEORGE THORP, R.N.,
Fourth Son of Robert Thorp, D.D.,
Who being First Lieutenant of the
Terpsichore Frigate of the Squadron
of Com: Wilson, fell with Captain
Bowen, and many men, upon the
Mole Battery of Santa Cruz,
Teneriffe, the XXIV. day of June, A.D. MDCCXCVII.
in his twentieth year, and was
buried in the deep.

6. White marble on black slab.
>
> In the family vault near
> this place lie the remains of
> JOHN SIMPSON, Esq., of Bradley Hall,
> who departed this life April 24th, 1786.
> And ANN, his wife, who departed Aug. 4th, 1783.
> She was the only child of Richard Clutterbuck,
> Esq., Warkworth, in Northumberland.
> By his second wife Eleanor Collyer,
> they had issue twelve children.
> This small tribute of filial affection
> to the best of parents is erected by their
> two surviving daughters, Eleanor, the
> wife of John Ord, Esq., and Ann Simpson.

7.
> This Tablet and the Clock in the tower
> of the Church, are erected by his friends
> and parishioners in affectionate
> Remembrance of Rev. WILLIAM WEBB, M.A.,
> for sixteen years rector of this Parish,
> who died April 15th, 1878, aged 74 years,
> And was interred in a vault in the Churchyard.
> "Blessed are the dead which die in
> the Lord."—Rev. XIX., ver. 10.

8. A brass plate.
>   A.M.   D.G.
> In the year of our Lord
>   MDCCCLXXXVI.
> The following works were carried out
> in this church. New vestries and organ
> chamber built. New organ set up. New
> hot heating apparatus. New staircase to
> Belfry. New Inner Porch. New Oak Ceiling
> to Chancel. New stained glass east window.
> New gas fittings. New Reredos, Pulpit, Litany
> Desk, and complete oak seating for the Nave
> and Aisles. Such of the old seating as was
> sound was worked up to form the inner

Porch and the panelling round the walls.
The whole cost of these works was defrayed by THOMAS SPENCER, Esquire, of the Grove, Ryton, and Miss EMILY M. EASTON, of Nest House, Gateshead, and Layton Manor, Yorkshire.

T. H. CHESTER, M.A., Rector.
C. E. BLACKETT ORD, M.A., Curate.
JOHN RICHARDSON,
WILLIAM RUTHERFORD LAMB, } Churchwardens.
ROBERT J. JOHNSTON, Architect.

Within the altar rails, and fixed to the north wall, are five small brass plates. Three of them are inscribed as follows:—

(1)

FRANC' THE THIRD SONNE OF RICHARD BVNNY OF NEWLAND NEERE WAKEFIELD ESQVIER, & OF BRIDGET RESTWOVLD OF YE VACH IN BVCKINGHASHIRE OF VERY WORLL PARENTAGE, WIFE TO THE SAIDE RICHARD BVNNY; WAS INDVCTED INTO THIS PSONAGE OF RYTON A^O 1578 SEPT. 13 AND HAD FIVE CHILDREN, ELIZABATH THE ELDEST BEING MARIED TO WILLM FENAY OF FENAY NEERE ALMONBVRY IN YORKSHIRE, DIED WTHOVT ISSVE & LYETH BVRIED IN YORK IN YE QVYER OF ALLHALLOWES CHVRCH; IOHN THE ELDEST SONNE, HENRY THE THIRD SONNE, MATHEW THE FOURTH SONNE, DIED VERY YOVNG & WER ALL BVRIED IN THIS QVIER OF RYTON CHVRCH WHER ALSO LYETH FRANCIS Y^E SECOND SONE OF FRANCIS AFORESAID WHOSE MONVMENT THIS IS: HE MARRIED MARY DAVGHTER & SOLE HEIRE OF IOHN WORTLEY SECOND BROTHER OF S^R RICHARD WORTLEY OF WORTLEY KNIGHT: HE DIED WTHOVT ISSVE FEB. 26 A^O 1610 BEING MORE THEN 26 YEARES OLDE. HE WAS BORNE A^O 1584 NOVEM: 9.

  I WAS SOMETIME BVT NOW I AM
   AND SHALL LIVE THYS FOR AYE
  I AM I SAY IN IOY THAT LASTS
   AND NEVER SHALL DECAY.
  I WAS; BVT THEN I DID BVT DREAM
   MY PLEASVRES WERE BVT PAINE
  MY IOYES WERE SHORT AND MIXT WITH GREIF
   ADEW THEN LIFE SO VAINE.

(2)

FRANCIS BVNNY BORNE MAY THE 8TH AO 1543
BEGAN TO PREACH GOD'S WORD NOVEMBR THE
FIRST ANO 1567, INDVCTED INTO A P'BEND
AT DYRHAM THE 9TH OF MAY ANNO 1572,
MADE ARCHDEACON OF NORTHVMBERLAND
AO 1573 OCTR YE 20 AND THE XITH OF SEPT: AO
1578 MADE RECTOR OF RYTON; HAVING BVRIED
HERE HIS 4 SONES, AND HIS DAVGHTER AT YORKE
HASTENETH TO HEAVEN AFTER THEM AND TRIVM—
PHING FOR HOPE OF IMMORTALITIE SAITH, THYS—

MY BARKE NOW HAVING WONNE YE HAVEN
  I FEARE NO STORMY SEAS
GOD IS MY HOPE, MY HOME IS HEAVEN
  MY LIFE IS HAPPY EASE
THIS HOPE THIS HOME THIS LIFE MOST SWEET
  WHO SOE WILL SEEK TO WINNE
MVST BID ADIEWE TO ALL DELIGHTS
  THE SOWER ROOTS OF SINNE

Obijt 16 Die Aprill 1617

(3)

Henry   Iohn ye
ye sone of   sonne of

Francis Bunny and
Iane his wyfe

we were and shal be

Borne Ian: xj.   Born Ivl. xj.
Ano 1585 died   Ao 1582 died
Sept. 25 Ao 1588   Oct. 14 158.

The two remaining brasses bear escutcheons of arms painted upon them. One bears the Bunny shield of nine quarters, impaling the shield of Wortley. The other bears only the Bunny shield.

Inside of the communion rails are two brass plates:—

(1)

ROBERT ALDER THORP, B.D.,
Fellow of Christ Church College, Oxford.
Died May 23rd, A.D. MDCCCXXXII.
Aged XXXIV. years.

MARY ANN THORP,
Wife of
Robert Thorp, Esq.,
of Alnwick,
Died April 1st, A.D. MDCCCXXXIX.
Aged LXX. years.

ROBERT THORP, Esq.,
of Alnwick and of Chopwell Hall,
Died April VII., A.D. MDCCCXLIII.
Aged LXXI. years.

ROBERT THORPE, D.D.,
Died April XX. A.D. MDCCCXII.
Aged LXXVI. years.

GRACE THORP,
Widow of Robert Thorp
and
Daughter of William Alder, Esq.,
of Horncliff on Tweed,
Died August III., A.D. MDCCCXIV.
Aged LXX. years.

(2)

FRANCIS WILKIE THORP,
Died April XXI., A.D. MDCCCXI.
Aged XX. years.

CHARLES THORP, D.D., F.R.S.,
Archdeacon of Durham,
55 years Rector of Ryton,
Died Oct. X., A.D. MDCCCLXII.
Aged LXXIX. years.

In the floor of the chancel, opposite to the entrance, is the vault of Robert Thorp.

Fixed in the wall of the north aisle is a monument of white marble, which bears the arms of the Tempest and Lambton families. Underneath is the following :—

Sepulturæ consecratum Nicholai Tempest de Stella, militis & baronetti (qui obijt Ano D'n MDCXXV ætatis suæ LXXIII) et Isabellæ uxoris suæ charissimæ, filiæ Gulielmi Lambton de

Lambton armigeri: quæ quatuor filios, et totidem filias, illi peperit, et obiit Ano D'n MDCXXIII ætatis suæ LXXI. Illa per tot annos præmoriens, quot illi prænatus erat. E liberis eorum sunt superstites Thomas, Henricus, Isabella, uxor Bertrami Bulmer de Tyrlesden, militis.—Jana relicta Thomæ Chaitor de Butrobee, armigeri.— Et Margareta uxor Gilberti Errington de Ponteland, armiger.—Parentibus optimis et suavissimis Thomas Tempest baronettus, eorum filius, observantiæ et amoris ergo, sibique et suis mortalitatis memor, hoc posuit. Filius extruxit tumulum, pia sacra parentum. Lambton erat matris, Stella domusque patris. Miles erat Ni'olas Tempest, pater et baronettus Isabella fuit mater; amore pares. Octo illis liberi sexu æquo: Septuaginta, Ultro viverunt, et cecidere pares.

Translation :—

Consecrated to the burial of Nicholas Tempest, of Stella, Soldier and Baronett (who died in the year of our Lord 1625, at the age of 73); and of Isabella, his very dear wife, the daughter of William Lambton, of Lambton, Knight, who bore him four sons, and just as many daughters, and died in the year of our Lord 1623, at the age of 71. In this way she died before him by as many years as he had been born before her. Of their children there survived Thomas, Henry, Isabella, wife of Bertram Bulmer, of Tyrlesden, Soldier; Jane, relict of Thomas Chaitor, of Butrobe, Knight; and Margaret, wife of Gilbert Errington, of Ponteland, Knight. To the most upright and sweetest parents their son Thomas Tempest, Baronett, out of respect and love, and mindful of mortality, placed this for himself and his. The son erected a monument, a devout offering for his parents. Lambton was the home of his mother, and Stella of his father. Nicholas Tempest was a soldier, father, and baronett, Isabella was the mother; in affection they are equal. They had eight children (four) of each sex. They lived over 70 years, and both died.

A small tablet on the west side bears the arms of the Tempests.

On a tablet of white marble on black slab is the following :—

In a vault near this church
are deposited the remains of
JOSEPH LAMB, youngest son
of Joseph and Sarah Lamb, of

Ryton House, County of Durham, Esq.,
born Dec. 11th, 1781, died Oct. 8th, 1859.
Upright, Affable, Benevolent,
esteemed alike in public and private life,
he died lamented by his family, and
regretted by all.   His trust was in the mercy
of God, through the merits of his Redeemer,
that he might live for ever in the Kingdom
of Heaven.
This tablet was erected to his memory,
by his widow and family, to whom he
was greatly endeared.

Against the west end of the south aisle is a marble slab, bearing the arms of the Humble family. Arms: a stag trippant, a chief indented. Crest: a stag's head erased. Underneath is the inscription:—

FRANCES, the Wife
of John Humble,
Obt. 3 Octr., 1754, aged 58.

A brass fixed in the floor, at the west end of the nave, is a memorial to the Lambs of Ryton House.

The achievement or hatchment at the east end of the south aisle is that of Marie Susanah (Lady Ravensworth), who died Nov. 22nd, 1845, aged 73 years; and that at the west end, of Simpson, and Anderson of Bradley, Arms: Gules, a fesse inter two lions passant Or, Simpson, impaling, Gules, three oak-trees Argent, Anderson.

RYTON RECTORY.

PATRON: the Bishop of Durham. The Rectory is valued in the King's Books at £42 10s. 10d.; Tenths, £4 5s. 1d.; Episc. pro. 18s.; Arichid. Proc., 3s.; Gross income, £1049. The tithes were commuted in 1823. The parish register commences in 1588. Rectors: Magister William de Marghe, 1254; Alan de Esyngwald, 1300; John de Botheby, 1312; Nich. Gategang, 1334; William de Olby, 1342; P. M. Gategang; John de Wyndlynburgh, 1378;

Thos. de Gretham, 1382; John de Burgh, 1402; Richard Moor, 1407; John de Nepotiis; John Wynname, 1497; Robert Davell, LL.D.; Anthony Salvayne, S.T.B., 1555; Wm. Garnet, A.B., 1558; John Bold, 1577; F. Bunny, A.M., 1578; William James, A.M., 1617; John Weld (an intruder); Ralph Blakiston, 1660; William Cave, S.T.B., 1676; Mailn Sorsby; Thos. Secker, A.M., 1727; Robert Stillingfleet, A.M., 1733; John Lloyd, A.M., 1738; John Rotheram, A.M., 1766; Hon. Richard Byron, A.M., 1769; Robert Thorp, 1795; Charles Thorp, 1807; William Webb, 1862; William C. Streatfield, 1878; Edward Prest, 1880; Thomas H. Chester, 1883; Johnson Baily, 1891.

In 1314, Bishop Kellaw pronounced a decree betwixt the Hospital of Kepyer and the rector of Ryton, viz., that Hugh de Montalt, master of Kepyer, and his successors, should continue to enjoy an annual composition of two marks, payable by the rector, in lieu of one moiety of tithe of corn of the bishop's demesne lands within the whole parish of Ryton, and should in consideration of such annual payment and perception, celebrate solemn mass with Placabo and Dirige for the soul of Bishop Anthony.

Bishop Fordham granted licence to Thomas de Gretham, rector of Ryton, to carry an aqueduct from Southwell through the bishop's ground to the rectory. Bishop Skirlaw confirmed the grant to John Burgh, Gretham's successor, in 1405.

At a general array of the clergy in Gilesgate Moor, in 1400, the rector, Thomas de Gretham, was charged with one lance and three archers, being rated in the same proportion with the rectors of Whickham and Gateshead.

Francis Bunny, third son of Richard Bunny, Esq., of Newland Hall, near Wakefield, and of Bridget his wife, was born 8th May, 1543. He became a student of the University in the latter end of the reign of Queen Mary, and Fellow of Magdalen College in 1562. He was afterwards chaplain to the Earl of Bedford, and in 1578 became rector of Ryton. He is described by Surtees as a great admirer of John Calvin, a constant preacher, charitable, and a stiff enemy to Popery. Bunny was the author of four polemical works, of "A Plain and Familiar Exposition of the Ten Commandments," and of an "Exposition on Joel," dedicated to Tobie, Bishop of Durham, in which the author saith, "he had preached sermons at Berwick twenty years ago (1595), of which the book is the summe ; which, if printed, would contain about three quire o paper."

William Cave, born in 1637, became rector of Ryton in 1676. He was a learned divine of the Church of England, and wrote several works, relating chiefly to the early times of Christianity. His best known and highly valued works are "Lives of the Apostles," "Lives of the Fathers," and "Scriptorum Ecclesiasticorum Historia Literaria."

Thomas Secker was born in 1693, and was educated for the Dissenting ministry at the Dissenting College of Tewkesbury, Butler, the future bishop of Durham, being his companion there. Scruples prevented him from prosecuting the design of his youth, and he was preparing for the medical profession when he was induced to obtain ordination in the church from Bishop Talbot, of Durham. Secker was a very popular preacher, and was quickly promoted. After being rector of Ryton, he became successively Bishop of Bristol and of Oxford, and in 1758 he became Archbishop of Canterbury.

John Rotheram was the son of the Rev. William Rotheram, head-master of the Grammar School, Haydon Bridge. John was born on June 22nd, 1725. After completing his education at the Grammar School under his father, he became, in 1745, a member of Queen's College, Oxford. He took his bachelor's degree, and was ordained deacon and priest in the year 1749. In the year 1751 he became assistant to his brother, Thomas Rotheram, at Codrington College, in the island of Barbadoes. Returning home he was, in 1760, unanimously elected Fellow of University College. In 1766 he became rector of Ryton; and in 1769 he was presented to the rectory of Houghton-le-Spring. In 1779 he obtained the vicarage of Seaham, and was made chaplain to the Bishop of Durham. Being on a visit to his friend Dr. Sharp, at Bamborough, he died there on the 16th July, 1789, in the 64th year of his age. The principal productions of his pen were "The Force of Argument for the Truth of Christianity, drawn from a Collective View of Prophecy;" "A Sketch of the One Great Argument formed from the general Concurring Evidence for the Truth of Christianity." In 1759, "An Apology for the Athanasian Creed;" 1760, a sermon on "The Origin of Faith;" 1766, an essay on "Faith and its connection with Good Works;" 1767, an essay on "Establishments of Religion, with Remarks on the Confessional;" and also three Sermons; 1780, a Sermon against Persecution; also an essay on "The Distinction between the Soul and Body of Man."

The Hon. Richard Byron, rector of Ryton in 1769, was brother to William, fifth Lord Byron, rector of Houghton-le-Skerne, who died November 5th, 1811, aged 88.

The Parish Register dates from 1581, from which the following Extracts are taken.

1600, July 30—Mr. Bartram Bulmer, Mrs. Jane Tempest (mar.).

1601, March 19—Restwold, son of Mr. Wm. Bunny, gent., soldier of Berwick (bur.).

1602, Dec. 2—Anthony, son of Bertram Bulmer (bap.).

1603—Payed to the infected of Gateside, xviis. viiid.

1605, Aug. 4—George, sone of Alex. Swinburne, of Winlawton (bap.).

1606, Aug. 26—Mary, daughter to Sir Bartram Bulmer, Knight (bap.).

Oct. 13—Isab, daughter to Tho. Chaitor of Butterby, by Durham, Esq. (bap.).

Nov. 3—Mr. Tim Drap and Mrisffra Priestley (mar.).

1607, April 9—George, sonne to John Surteise of Chopwellside (bap.).

June 14—Barbara, daughter to George Ogle of ye Whitehouse.

Aug. 23—John Noble and Charitie Bulman (mar.).

Oct. 13—Mark Errington of Holdenhead, and Katherine Tempest (mar.).

1608, April 17—Robert Gray, a workman that came from Whickham (bur.).

„ 27—Anne Silvertop, Widdow of Ryton towne (bur.).

May 1—Rafe, sonne of Rafe Gray of the Wrennes nest (bur.).

1609, March 27—William Noble, of Chopwell quarter of the Leadgate (bur.).

1610, Jan. 15—Mr. Willm. Bellassis and Miss Margaret Selby (mar.).

1612, Aug. 6—Susanna, daughter of John Lions, gentleman, of Bradley (bap.).

1613, Dec. 26—Mary, daughter to Mr. Wm. Tempest, of Winlawton (bur.).
1614, Dec. 27—Isabell, daughter of a stranger, borne at Bladon (bap.).
1616, Aug. 21—Thomas Coke and Elizabeth Selbie (mar.).
1617, April 10—Mary, bastard daughter to George Tempest of Winlinton (bap.).
 July 23—John, the sonne of Lynell Trotter of Winlington (bap.).
1617-18, Jan. 23—Henry, the sonn of Sr. Barthren Bulmer, Knight.
 Feb. 3—Mr. William Tempest of Stillaye, gentill. (bur.)
1618, July 19—William Selbye and Margaret Hollyday, wid. (mar.)
1619, Sept. 19—Jane, daughter to George Ogle of Winlawton (bap.).
 July 2—Guielmus Hancock, Elizabeth Anderson (mar.).
 Nov. 28—John Selby and Elizabeth Laborne, married at Whittonstall.
1620, March 27—John Selby, a child of Leadgate (bur).
1621, Julye —Charles, sone of George Tempest of Winlawton (bap.).
1624-5, Jan. 16—William, son of Mark Horsley of Bladon.
1625-6, Jan. 13—Henry, son of Mr. William James, Parson of Ryton (bur.).
1625, March 28—Sr. Nicholas Tempest of Stella, Knyght, Baronett.
 Aug. 21—A poore wedoe at thornellay called Alles Adams (bur.).
 Sept. 20—George, the sonn of Georg Affengton of Ryton, being slaine in a colepytt.
 Nov. 14—Robert Demster of Winlington, being slaine in a Cole pyt.
 Oct. 20—Raynold Ogill and Margaret Ridlaye (mar.).
1627, Sep. 18—William Foster of Winlinton, kilde in a Cole pyt.
 Dec.—A poore lame youth of Winlington (bur.).
1628, July 10—Dorothy, daughter of Sir Thomas Tempest of Stellay, Baronett (bap.).
 Oct. 20—Robt., the son of Robert Babbington, gentl. (bur.).
1628-9, June 24—Mr. Ambrose Dudlay, Esquire.
1629—Dorothy, daughter of Sir Thomas Tempest, Baronet (bur.).
 Aug. 12—John Taller of Colebornes, one of the poore of the pishe.

1630, May—Thomas, sonn of Sr. Thomas Tempest, Baronet (bap).
June 6—Willm. Ogill of Winlinton, kyld in Cole pyt, and Robert Allan of Winlinton, kyld in a Cole pyt, being boys (bur.).
May 10—Jane, baise daughter of William Rychard and Elizabeth Durham, boethe of Winlinton; William Robson of the said Towne bounde for to kepe the parish harmles of the said childe (bap.).
May 24—Kathren, daughter of Sr. Thomas Tempest, of Stellay.
1632, June 1—A stranger woh was smored in a Cole pyt (bur.).
1649, April 3—Sir William Selby, Knt. (bur.)
April 27—A child of Sir William Davy, Knt. (bur.)
1652, July 2—Ann Rotherforth of Crawcrook, 96 years ould (bur.).
1681-2, Jan. 23—Mr. William Bulmer of Stella (bur.).
1682—William Silvertop, and Pickering, of Bladon; Thomas Atkinson, Winlaton; and 15 women drowned.
1757, Jan. 6—Charles Halliday, of riper years, aged 41, of Woodside (bap.).
1811, Aug. 28—John Anderson of Barlow, near Ryton, died, aged 108. (He expired in the act of soling a pair of shoes. He enjoyed good health, and never wore spectacles.)

Churchwardens' Books.

The books are well kept, except during the later years of the Commonwealth.

1606, April 25—Paid for my dinner and the minister's, vid. (at the Archdeacon's Visitation.) F. Bunny.
1617, April 22—An inventory of the ornaments of the church made:—One bible, three communion bookes, one other old communion booke, the book of Canons, and Jewell and Harden.
1623—For ringing at the return of our nobil prince from Spain, 1s.
In 1627, the wages of labouring men are set down at 4d. a day.
1645—Paid for parchment for recording the Covenant, 6d.
1646—Paid 8d. for a book called the Directtorye. (This book was intended to replace the Book of Common Prayer.)

1664—Paid for book called King Charles his workes, £1 1s. 0d.
   For a Common prayer book, 10s.
   For a book of homilies, 6s.
   For a surplisse, £1 8s. 0d.
   For a book of articles, 1s.
1665—Paid for candells and drink and making fires on the gunpowder treason day, 2s.
1666—It is this day ordered that there be a sesse of 2s. per plough, and 8d. a cottage, laid on for repairs about the church. It is likewise ordered that there be 3d. per plough, and 1d. per cottage, laid on to pay for foxe heads.

      Sgn. John Clavering, Robt. Clavering, and 10 others.

1667—Ryton. 1 fox head.
  Winlington. 4 do.
  Chopwell. 36 do. and one brocke (badger) head.
  Ralph Swalwell is paid for 17 fox heads.
1669—Paid for 14 fox heads 0 14 00
    2 Catt heads 0 02 00
    2 Foumart heads 0 00 04
1689—Paid for a faste book 0 2 6
1695—Paid for a coat cloth for Newby's child ... 0 5 0
1696—Paid for a pole-cat head 0 0 4
  Paid for a table of degrees with a frame ... 0 2 1
1706—Paid for two Martin heads 0 0 4
  Paid for securing the woman that did penance 0 0 4
  Paid for a winding sheet for a cripple ... 0 4 0
  John Harrison to be paid 1s. 6d. per week for keeping the child found on Barlow Fell.
1715, Dec. 2—Robert Brown of Ryton Mill, slaine by the Mill.
1716, July 16—Cuthbert Selby drowned in Tyne.
1721, Aug. 9—Eleanor, — of Mr. James Mein, late chaplain to ye factory at Winlaton, buried.
1722, April 27—Jane, daughter to William Gilbert, roller and turner, Winlaton Mill, a spurious child, buried.
 June 22—Ralph Pearson of Winlaton Mill, killed with a waggon.

1722, Dec. 21—Barbara Smith, alias Nichols, a spurious child, baptised.

Dec. 29—Ben Nicholson drowned in a pit at Barlow.

1723, March 26—Affable Battell, chaplain to Mr. Crowley, buried.

June 25—John Wilson, a Romish Priest, Stella, buried.

Sep. 14—Nicholas Story, a dissenting teacher, buried.

Oct. 28—William Walker, clerk to Mr. Crowley, Winlaton Mill, buried.

1726, Feb. 6—Barns, a poor vagrant from High Spen, buried.

1727, May 30—Joseph, son to Thomas Andrew of Winlaton, and Elizabeth, daughter, in one coffin.

1728, Oct. 22—John Wild of Low Spen, and his horse, fell down a pit.

Dec. 5—Isabel, wife to Stephen Coulsin, sen., of Chopwell, aged 103.

Dec. 5—John Scott of Burnhill died by a fall in a coalpit.

Dec. 17—John Ramshaw killed by the waggons.

1729, May 15—James Jagues, a Presbyterian teacher, buried.

1730—A Communion Cloth was purchased at the cost of 24s.

1730—Chopwell. For exchange of 2 old flagons for basin and chambr. pot, 3s. 5d.

1741, March 31—Received from the gentlemen of the four and twenty, the contributions gathered in, rewards for taking up felons, &c., £7 3s. 10¾d., by me, J. Lloyd.

1744, July 1—Isabell Moffit did penance by order of the Court, but did not bring the order afterwards for absolution. Excommunicated a second time for the like offence.

1744—To the clark at Winlaton for giving notice to keep the Sabbath holey, 4d.

1745—To the constable of Winlaton for giving notice to people not to keep late hours, 4d.

March 29—Rachael Farrow, Blaydon Workhouse.

1749, May 3—John Fletcher, a stranger begging from Gateshead, died at Runhead.

1753, Feb. 19—William Johnson, South Biddick, died in the Lane going to Woodside, suddenly.

Aug. 29—Mr. Thomas Greenwell, a Romish Priest, Bladen —— Church.

1753, Sept. 19—Thomas, son to Jane Baulk and Joseph Blackett, excommunicated persons, Crawcrook.

1788, July 2—Number of families in the parish of Ryton, taken by J. Mirehouse, Curate :—

Winlaton Qr.	-	-	617 families.
Ryton do.	-	-	340 do.
Crawcrook do.	-	-	129 do.
Chopwell do.	-	-	124 do.
		Totus	1210

Protestant Dissenters, 63, viz.:—

56 Church of Scotland.
3 Anabaptists.
2 Seceders.
2 Independants.
63 Totus.

The number of Papists in the Parish of Ryton taken 12 September, 1780 (viz.) 324 Totus. Number taken 2nd July, 1788, 350. Jonathon Mirehouse, Curate.

July 2nd, 1788—One hundred Methodists; they do not assemble in any licened place.

One Sunday School at Winlaton, Sixty boys and Fifty girls attend it.

The Rector's house stands on the south side of the churchyard; it faces the east, and the front of the house is rendered charming by the well kept lawns and ornamental flower beds. Over the front entrance—as at Whickham—are the arms of Bishop Crewe, with the date 1709, and a motto "non nobis." On a small plate on the left side of the door is the date 1612. The arms, crest, and monogram of the Rev. James Finney, are seen at the top of the entrance hall windows. One of the spouts bears the inscription "R. T., 1795." On the west side of the house there are two old windows which look into the kitchen garden; they are about 4 feet 6 inches high, and probably of fifteenth century date. On one of the chimneys is inscribed "C. T., 1839." There is on a terrace at the front of the hall, a small conservatory to which is attached a sun-dial, bearing the motto "Pereunt et imputantur," which is the same as that above the entrance to the church. At the beginning of the present century the rectory possessed several Roman altars, found at Benwell and Jarrow, but they were afterwards removed to the old castle.

THE CHURCHYARD.

"The village churchyard : let me lightly tread among its quiet sleepers."
R. J. MILLIGAN.

THE Churchyard, which is about two-and-a-half acres in extent, is enclosed by a wall, with an entrance on the east side. Formerly there was a mound on the south side of the church, from which the beadle announced to the people leaving the service, any events of importance that were arranged to take place during the week, as a sale of furniture, a funeral, the celebration of a village festival, etc. Near to the door leading from the rectory are the remains of the village stocks, which stood at one time near the Cross.

Anyone who has spent much of his time in rural localities will have noticed the bareness of the churchyard northward of the sacred edifice. Suicides, persons of evil character, strangers, and the unbaptised were laid there :—

"On the north side were buried
The dead of a hapless fame ;
A cross, and a prayer for mercy,
But never a date or a name."

This custom prevailed at Ryton until the middle of the eighteenth century. In medieval times the north was regarded as the seat of the Evil One; hence the celebrant at mass turned towards that quarter while chanting the Gospel, because Christ came to destroy the power of the devil. Frequently, too, the garth-cross was placed to the north-east of the church as a sort of advance guard in that direction.

Lying near to the entrance of the church is a flat stone bearing the inscription :—

JOHN NEWTON of
Rickless was buried
heare the 4th of November, 1684.

The Newton family occupied Rickless-farm for nearly two centuries.

There is a flat stone lying on the south side of the chancel which possesses some antiquarian interest. Engraved on the stone are three mill-picks and a mill-rind, and around the sides is the inscription:—Heare lyeth the bodye of Jane Smith, was wife to William Smith, miller. She departed to the mercye of God the 29th of December, 1623. Near to this memorial is a stone erected

> In Memory of ANTHONY BELT
> of Winlaton,
> 54 years Agent to Mr. Crowley
> Millington and Comp.
> Died Oct. 12th, 1804, aged 68 years.

A flat stone near the footpath bears the inscription:—

> Here lyeth yᵉ body of BARBARA
> SURTEYS, daughter was to Robert
> and Katheran Surteys, of Ryton.
> She departed this life
> Jan. 25th, 1682.
> As also of the said ROBERT and KATHERAN
> SURTEES, and of MARGARET and MARY,
> two other daughters of them. Robert
> died Oct. 4th, 1710, in the 86th year of his age.
> Here lyeth also interred yᵉ body of
> ISABEL BOWRY, who departed this life
> the 10th day of June, 1723.

The above Robert Surtees was the great-great-grandfather of Robert Surtees, the historian of the County of Durham; and the arms of Surtees prefixed to the notice of Robert Surtees in "The Local Historian's Table Book," are copied from the tombstone in Ryton churchyard.

Nearly opposite to the church door is a stone to the memory of

> ROBERT LAWS of Horse-Gate,
> died Sept. 26th, 1746, aged
> 108 years and 10 months.

Another stone bears the following curious inscription :—

> So long the mason wrought on other walls,
> That his own house of clay to ruin falls;
> No wonder spiteful death brought his annoy,
> He buried to build, and death to destroy.
>
> WILLIAM WALLMASON.

The stone has sunk so far into the ground, that the year of Wallmason's death cannot be seen.

On a grave-cover, overhung with trees, near the south wall, is the following :—

> THOMAS CHANCER,
> son of Nicholas Chancer,
> died the 25th of September, 1819,
> aged 58 years.

Thomas Chancer was a well-known stonemason at Ryton one hundred years ago; he erected the Village Cross in 1795.

There is inscribed on a flat stone near the footpath, on the north side of the church :—

> Pray for the Soul of the
> Rev. WILLIAM HULL,
> who discharged the duties
> of Catholic Priest in this
> Parish for a period of
> XLII. years. He died at
> Stella Hall, the XXIII. July,
> MDCCCXL. Aged LXXXIII.

On a granite tombstone is the following inscription :—

> WILLIAM STOWELL, B.A. Lon.,
> Born at North Shields
> Oct. 30th, 1825;
> Died at the Manse, Ryton,
> Feb. 1st, 1878.
> Minister of the Gospel,
> Author, Journalist.
> "A man greatly beloved." Daniel x. xi.
> The burden of whose life and
> teaching was this:

> "Herein is love, not that we loved God, but that He loved us, and gave his Son." I. John iv. 10.

Along the side of the footpath are several tombstones erected to the memory of the Belts and the Lambs of Ryton.

On the north side of the path is a tumulus or barrow. The base of this mound is about three hundred feet in circumference, and its sloping sides twenty feet in height. It is now partly covered with trees. Undoubtedly this barrow is the burial place of one of the early inhabitants of the district. The Britons burnt their dead, and interred the charred bones in badly-baked earthen pots beneath a large mound. The Romans also incinerated some of their dead, and others they interred entire; but their cremation pottery is of better shape and texture than that used by the Britons. The Saxons, who followed the Romans, after a similar fashion practised cremation and inhumation, and used both tumuli and cemeteries. Their barrows, as in the case of those of the Britons, usually stand on elevated places, either solitary or in groups. Sometimes a large solitary Saxon barrow is found to contain the bones of a chief buried with all his personal ornaments and military trappings. A barrow similar to that at Ryton was opened near Bradley Hall, about 1792, which was found to contain a kistvaen, in which a human body had been interred. In the year 1818, a tumulus at Flodden Hill was broken into, when a large urn was found. This urn was surrounded by a number of cells formed of flat stones in the shape of graves, but too small to hold the body in its natural state. And if ever the barrow at Ryton is examined, it will probably be found to be the burial place of some British or Roman chieftain. The church was built much later than the erection of the mound; but it is thought that the early preachers of the Gospel took advantage of the reverence which was paid to these ancient tombs, and chose to build their churches near them.

On the east side of the church there is a stone coffin with the date 1610 inscribed on one end. Probably one of the early rectors was buried in it, and 1610 the date when it was disinterred.

Thirty-seven men and boys killed by the explosion at Stargate colliery, May 30th, 1830, were interred at the east side of the churchyard.

The Churchyard was enlarged in 1820, and again in 1853.

Bequests to the Poor.

By will dated 26 May, 1687, and proved 1699, Ralph Harrison of Briansleap, Gent., left £100 to the poor of the Parish of Ryton.

Sir John Clavering, of Axwell, who died ———, left £50 to the poor of Ryton Parish.

By will proved in 1708, Jane Grey left £20.

By will dated 14 Dec., 1705, and proved in 1710, Robert Surtees of Ryton, Gent., gave £20 to the poor of Ryton Quarter; the interest to be distributed by his executor during life, and afterwards by the minister and churchwardens.

By will dated 31 December, 1718, proved 4 May, 1719, Thomas Humble of Ryton Woodside, gave £20 to the poor of Ryton Parish; the interest to be distributed by the twenty-four of the Parish.

By will dated 13th July, 1717, Andrew Surtees of the Holling, in Northumberland, gave £50, to be placed at interest by the minister and twenty-four of the Parish of Ryton; and the interest to be disposed of at Christmas and Midsummer amongst poor, aged, and impotent men and women, and fatherless children, of the Chopwell Quarter of the Parish of Ryton [He also bequeathed £50 to the Parish of Ovingham, to be placed out, and the interest distributed in the same manner], proved by Anthony Surtees, son and executor, 18 May, 1725.

John Simpson of Bradley, Esq., who died 1733, left £50; the interest is distributed on the 23rd December; the principal is in the hands of Mr. Simpson's heirs.

In 1786, John Simpson, also of Bradley, Esq., bequeathed £5 per annum to the poor of Ryton Parish.

In 1795, Jane Foster bequeathed £100 to the poor of the vicinity of Ryton Woodside.

Walker Lawson, of Ryton, Esq., left £100, 3 per cents., to the poor of Ryton and Ryton Woodside; also £60 for the benefit of the parochial school.—*Surtees.*

Ryton Burnt by the Scots.

AFTER the battle of Stirling Bridge, in the year 1297, in which the English army suffered an ignominious defeat, the Scots under Sir William Wallace determined to invade England. Wallace, after making himself master of the town of Berwick, crossed the Tweed into Northumberland, where the Scots burned and plundered at their pleasure, except when in the neighbourhood of such places as Alnwick, Warkworth, Harbottle, Prudhoe, and other strongholds of the English. After having marched away westward towards Carlisle, they advanced to Hexham, where the monastery and chapel dedicated to St. Andrew, were plundered.

Retiring from Carlisle, and marching through the middle of the forest of Inglewood, Wallace carried his ravages through Cumberland and Allendale, as far as Derwentwater and Cockermouth. He was now about to enter the county of Durham, but his march was arrested by a tremendous storm. The minds of the Scots were impressed with the serious belief that the anger of St. Cuthbert was aroused by their conduct, and the idea of invading his territory was abandoned. Marching eastward, on the north side of the Tyne, the Scots destroyed a small house of Benedictine Nuns at Lambly, near Haltwhistle, and burnt the town of Corbridge. According to *Henry of Knighton's Chronicle,* "when the raiders were passing Heddon-on-the-Wall, a foraging party belonging to Wallace was seen by the inhabitants of Ryton, and no doubt considering themselves perfectly safe by the depth of the river, provoked the Scots with such opprobrious language, that they forded the stream, and burnt and plundered the town."

The inhabitants of Ryton who escaped from the vengeance of the Scots, probably fled to the woods surrounding the village when their wooden huts were burnt, and their recently erected church plundered and destroyed. We have no means of ascertaining what the population of the village was at that time. In the year 1292, the Prior and Convent of Tynemouth opened out collieries in the neighbouring Manor of Wylam; and the probability is, that coal mining also then commenced at Ryton; yet any statement in regard to the topography, or the number of the inhabitants of the village, would be mere speculation, so that we are left in a state of uncertainty as to the number of inhabitants slain by the soldiers of Wallace.

Hemingford, who was an eye-witness, gives us a striking account of the visitation of the Scots to Northumberland. He says, "At this time the Scots took up their quarters in the forest of Rothbury; nor was there anyone to make them afraid, whilst the praise of God, and the services of religion, were not heard in any church or monastery throughout the country, from Newcastle-upon-Tyne to the gates of Carlisle. All the monks, canons regular, and ministers of religion, along with the whole body of the people, had fled from the face of the Scots, who were permitted to pass their whole time in one continued scene of slaughter, burning, and rapine, from the Feast of St. Luke to St. Martin's day; nor was any one found to oppose them, except the soldiers of the garrison of Berwick, and of other castles hard by, who had ventured from their walls, and cut off a few stragglers in the rear."

THE SCOTS AGAIN AT RYTON.

IN the year 1346, David, King of Scotland, invaded England a second time. According to Froissart, his army consisted of from 40,000 to 50,000 men. The campaign commenced with the capture of the tower of Liddell, which was resolutely held for a time by Walter Selby, who was put to death after the tower was taken. After burning the Abbey of Lanercost, the Scots pursued their march through Cumberland and Tynedale. They plundered the priory of Hexham, but spared the town. Moving down to Corbridge, they assaulted Aydon Castle, which was given up on condition that the inmates were allowed to depart with their lives. Thence they proceeded in the direction of Newcastle, and crossing the Tyne at Ryton, entered the county of Durham. There is a legend that St. Cuthbert appeared to King David at Ryton, and admonished him that he should forbear to spoil or otherwise destroy his territory, otherwise his expedition should have a miserable end. The king, it seems, treated this warning with indifference, and, after probably plundering the church of any valuables it might possess, advanced westward, and crossing the Derwent, rested at Ebchester on the night of 15th of October.

Next morning his army passed through the village to Beaurepaire (Bearpark), was defeated at Neville's Cross, on Oct. 17th, by the army of Queen Phillipa, the consort of Edward III., after a three hours fight, and David made a prisoner.

THE MARKET CROSS.

THE cross stands on the village green, a short distance east of the rectory. The column, which is composed of four shafts, with the pedestal is about eighteen feet high, surmounted with a cross. It bears the date 1795. Thomas Chancer, a well-known mason in Ryton one hundred years ago, was the sculptor.

In olden times the village fair was held in the churchyard, on the anniversary of the founding or dedication of the parish church, and thus became at the same time a church festival and a general holiday, which brought together the parishioners and people from the surrounding locality, who availed themselves of the opportunity of buying and selling, or bartering and exchanging, or otherwise disposing of things that were marketable. Afterwards, the scene of the fair was changed from the churchyard to the open space in the town, or to a convenient place near the churchyard.

At the hirings for farm servants, which took place at Ryton annually, on the Fridays before May 12th and November 22nd, the scene was gay, lively, and interesting. Multitudes of people of both sexes from all parts of the neighbouring country, flocked to the fair to witness the sports and other attractions provided for the visitors. The public-houses were whitewashed; the doors and windows of cottages were painted; in fact, everything was done by the villagers to render the hirings attractive and successful. The servants who offered their services stood around the Cross, each sex forming a distinct company; and in order to distinguish themselves from the ordinary visitors, the young men fixed a green sprig in their hats, and the young women held a similar sprig in their hands, or had it fixed on the breast. At the time of hiring the servants received their "arles" (to bind the contract), which usually amounted to 2s. 6d., and occasionally to 5s., after which they either repaired to the public-house, or enjoyed themselves in other ways.

The stalls containing articles for sale lined both sides of the street, while the caravans, with their usual accompaniments, stood opposite to the rectory cottages. The scene was often enlivened by itinerant minstrels, who endeavoured to "make a penny" by offering their songs for sale; and a juggler would astonish the servant lads by his feats of legerdemain. It is needless to mention that extraordinary sights were sometimes witnessed at the fair or hirings. On one occasion a well-known Ryton "character," named Ben Renwick, drove into the village on the back of a bull, and galloped several times around the Cross, making the sight-seers run in all directions. Dancings were held at night in the public-houses, which were frequented by the youth of both sexes, and which were carried on until the following morning.

Ryton Hirings and Swalwell Hopping were times when many a hard fought pugilistic encounter took place between those who had old scores to pay off, or old disputes to settle; the village constable being powerless to maintain law and order.

Mr. Housman, who gives us so lively and accurate a description of the fairs in Cumberland at the beginning of the present century, thus describes their dancings, which were similar to those held at Ryton Hirings. He says:—"In their dances, which are jigs and reels, they attend to exertion and agility, more than ease and grace; minuets and country dances constitute no part of the amusements of these rural assemblies. Indeed, these dancing parties often exhibit scenes very indelicate and unpleasant to the peaceful spectator. No order is observed, and the anxiety for dancing is great; one couple can only dance their jig at the same time; and perhaps half-a-dozen couples stand on the floor waiting for their turns: the young men busied in paying addresses to their partners, and probably half-intoxicated, forget who ought to dance next; a dispute arises; the fiddler offers his mediation in vain; nay, the interference of an angel would have been spurned at: blood and fury! it must be decided by a fight, which immediately ensues. During these combats the whole assembly is in an uproar; the weaker part of the company, as well as the minstrels, get upon the benches, or stand up in corners, while the rest support the combatants, and deal blows freely among each other; even the ladies will not unfrequently fight like Amazons in support of their brothers, sweethearts, or friends. At length the fight is over, and the bloody-nosed pugilists, and unfeathered nymphs, retire to wash, and readjust their tattered garments; fresh company comes in—all is again quiet, and the dance goes on as before; while the former guests disperse into different public-houses, and the encounter—which generally commences without any previous malice—is rarely again remembered." After 1866, Ryton Hirings became an institution of the past.

RYTON IN 1895.

The winding lane, the mossy well,
  And name-carved oaken tree,
Weave round my heart a potent spell—
  Old Ryton's banks for me.

AFTER leaving Ryton Station, you pass the house on your right hand belonging to the Ryton Golf Club, and another on your left used by the Curling Club. Scores of golfers play on the Willows whenever the weather will permit. A few minutes' walk up the steep hill, formed into an avenue by overhanging trees, and you enter the village. At the top of the lane stands the Parish Hall, which is a neat building in the Domestic Gothic style. It consists of large hall or assembly room, and other rooms intended to contain library, reading apartments, and to be used for meetings, lectures, etc. The cost of the building, which was opened December 14th, 1893, was £1600, raised by voluntary subscription.

Proceeding eastward past the Post Office and Elvaston Cottages, you reach the entrance to The Grove, the residence of Thomas Spencer, Esq. The house is a brick building, two storeys high, and facing the south. From the north side of the house there is a commanding view of the Tyne for several miles. Opposite to The Grove stands Elvaston Hall, a large modern stone mansion. A high wall encloses the grounds and gardens, which are tastefully laid out.

At the east side of Elvaston Hall is Whitewell Lane, which runs to the Hexham turnpike; and which received its name from a well on the west side, which was usually whitewashed on the outside.

The well is now closed. At the foot of the lane, on the east side, there is an old mansion, which is now divided into tenements, the lower part being a butcher's shop, and that adjoining, the residence of Miss Hindhaugh. The mansion was occupied by Robert Surtees more than two hundred years ago. Like a great many of the houses built at that time, the rooms are low, and panelled with oak; the stairs are also of oak, having the balusters beautifully carved. There is inscribed on a mantel in one of the rooms R. S K. 1682 (Robert and Katherine Surtees), and on a stone in the front wall of the house R. S K. 1669. The following is scratched on a pane in one of the windows:—" Peggy Weatherly, 1772, aged 5 years 16 weeks & 5 days." The principal entrance seems at one time to have been at the east side of the house, as the pillars of the old gateway are still standing.

Robert Surtees of Ryton was the second son of Edward Surties or Surtees of Broad Oak, in the parish of Ovingham (who died in 1655), by Margaret Coulsin, niece and heiress of Robert Surtees, alderman of Durham. Robert Surtees of Ryton, who married Catherine, daughter of John Hauxley of Crawcrook, died October 4th, 1710. He left several daughters and two sons. Hauxley Surtees married Ann Watson of Silksworth, and died 1719, without issue. Edward Surtees of Mainsworth died 1744, aged eighty-four years. Robert Surtees of Redworth, eldest son of Edward, by Jane Crozier, married Dorothy, daughter and co-heir of Thomas Lambton, Esq., of Hardwicke, and had two daughters, one of whom, Jane, married her cousin, Crozier Surtees of Redworth. George Surtees of Mainsworth, second son of Edward, died unmarried, 1769. Crozier Surtees of Merrysheels, in the county of Northumberland, married Jane, daughter of Ralph Hodgson, Esq., of Alwent, and was father of Crozier Surtees, Esq., who married his cousin, Jane Surtees of Redworth. Hauxley Surtees of Newcastle married Elizabeth Steele, and was father of Robert Surtees, who had Mainsforth by gift of his uncle, George Surtees, Esq. James Surtees was the youngest son of Edward Surtees.

Robert Surtees of Ryton was the great great-grandfather of Robert Surtees of Mainsforth, the historian of Durham, born 1st April, 1779, at Durham, in the parish of St. Mary, in the South Bailey. In his will, dated 10th June, 1700, Robert Surtees devised to his nephew, Ralph Ord, the house at Ryton Loaning Head.

Robert Surtees was an extensive landowner in Ryton, Crawcrook, Hedgefield, and Whickham.

Wallace Terrace, which comprises a number of substantial houses, with gardens back and front, runs up the east side of Whitewell Lane. At the top of the terrace is the residence of Dr. Smith. The Tower, built about thirty years ago by Mr. Gustav Schmalz, stands in well-sheltered grounds on the east side of Whitewell Lane. The grounds are laid out with great taste, and are attractive in appearance. The house is occupied by John Mc.Intyre, Esq. At the top of the lane, on the west side, is the residence of James Hindmarsh, Esq., after leaving which the lane meets the Hexham turnpike. On the north side of the turnpike stands the Ryton Hotel, and on the south side the Wesleyan Chapel, which is the cathedral of Methodism in the villages on the south side of the Tyne.

Charles Wesley preached at Ryton in 1742, his subject being "The Great Supper," which made a powerful impression on the minds of his hearers. Tradition has not handed down to us the exact spot on which Wesley preached, but it was probably on the village green, where the Cross now stands. In the religious census of the parish of Ryton, taken in 1788, by Jonathan Mirehouse, curate, it is stated that there are "one hundred Methodists: they do not assemble in any licensed place." John Wesley preached several times in Mr. Newton's house in Dene Head; and for several years prior to 1835, the Wesleyans conducted their services in this house; but from 1835 till 1881 they were without a place in which to worship. The present chapel is a structure of attractive appearance, in the Early English style, consisting of nave, aisles, north and south transepts, and a handsome square tower, containing a clock with two dials at the north-west angle of the building. The interior contains a gallery, and there are sittings for three hundred and twenty persons. The basement is used as a lecture hall, the Sunday school being placed at the east end, and can be used when required as a transept. The Chapel was opened in 1881, the cost being £4,107, half of which was contributed by Mr. I. O. Game, who also presented the organ, which is a powerful and fine instrument, at a further cost of £474.

A road on the east side of the chapel leads southward to Stargate and Stephen's Hall; and a few minutes' walk from the chapel brings the visitor to Ryton Cemetery, five acres in extent It has a neat mortuary chapel, and was opened in 1884.

Dene Terrace, which runs along the south side of the Hexham road, on the east side of the chapel, is formed by a row of substantial and attractive-looking houses with small flower gardens in front. Following the Hexham road eastward for a quarter of a mile, the Runhead farm is reached. This spot receives its name from its being the site of one of the old coal-ways down which the waggons ran on their way to Stella. At the Runhead a road branches from the Hexham turnpike, and leads to the old part of Ryton. The road is extremely pleasant, especially when you approach Holburn Dene, where there is a deep ravine which terminates on the north side of the hill. Tradition says that a flour mill formerly stood on the side of the ravine, driven by the water which ran down the dene. At present all traces of the mill have disappeared. On the east side of Holburn Dene is Ryton Park, until recently the residence of the late Richard Morce Weeks, who fifty years ago kept a private school for gentlemen's sons. It will undoubtedly interest visitors to Ryton to know that it was in Mr. Weeks' house that Mr. Joseph Cowen, late M.P. for Newcastle, was educated before he went to Edinburgh University. At the bottom of the dene, the road makes a bend westward to the Cross. At the north side of the road are a number of the oldest houses in Ryton, one of which bears the date 1672. In a house near to Mr. Josh. Tate's blacksmith's shop, lived Mr. Robert L. Galloway, at the time he wrote his admirable book, "A History of Coal Mining in Great Britain," published in 1852. He was also author of "The Steam Engine, and its Inventors." Mr. Galloway was mining engineer at the Stargate Colliery, and only lived a short time at Ryton. At the opposite side of the road is Ryton Lawn, the residence of C. M. Ormston, Esq.

Passing the north end of Whitewell Lane, a few minutes' walk brings the visitor to "The White House," standing on the south side of the Cross. Eighty years ago, this interesting building was the Savings Bank. Soon after the Rev. Charles Thorp became rector of Ryton (1807), he founded the bank to encourage thrift among his parishioners; it was open on Saturdays from six o'clock till eight, to receive deposits. During its existence it was of great benefit to the numerous body of smiths, colliers, and other industrious workmen of the neighbourhood. This Savings Bank was the first established in England. The Independents afterwards conducted religious services in the White House, having for their minister the Rev. D. Wilson.

Ryton House, the residence of Joseph Lamb, Esq., stands on the west side of the White House. It is a large modern brick building, well sheltered, and adorned with well-kept lawns. The "Court Room," in which Petty Sessions were formerly held at Ryton on the first Monday in every month, was in Ryton House, at that time the residence of Humble Lamb, Esq. The following were the acting magistrates :—C. J. Clavering, Esq.; Humble Lamb, Esq.; and the Rev. Charles Thorp; to whom Mr. John Dobson of Gateshead, officiated as clerk. The Lambs belong to one of the old Ryton families.. Joseph Lamb, who died December 21st, 1800, married Ann, daughter of Ralph Humble of Ryton House. Humble, the son of Joseph Lamb, was widely known and highly respected. He was a magistrate for Durham and Northumberland. He died suddenly on April 13th, 1844, and was succeeded by Joseph Chatto Lamb, Esq., who died November 6th, 1884, aged eighty-one. He was the father of the present owner of Ryton House.

Opposite to Ryton House is Dene Head, where stands the fine residence of Mrs. Thorp, with its handsome doors and windows, after the Norman and Decorated styles. The stones of which they are built were brought from the Market-House, Durham, by the Rev. Charles Thorp. Near to Mrs. Thorp's house once stood the Subscription School, built in 1791, and endowed with five pounds per annum by Lord Crewe's trustees. On the erection of the present school at Barmoor, the old school was demolished. At the top of the Dene is the old Pinfold, in which stray cattle were formerly impounded till claimed by the owners; the bailiff exacting a sum of money for their liberation.

In a house at the west end of Dene Head, was born, on the 5th August, 1858, Mr. Herbert Schmalz, a distinguished living artist. His father, the late Gustav Schmalz, was for many years German Consul at Newcastle, and lived for the greater part of that time at Ryton. After the birth of Herbert, his father built the mansion known as The Tower, in Whitewell Lane, into which he removed and lived for about ten years. Herbert's mother was the daughter of the late J. W. Carmichael, the marine painter. When seventeen years of age, Herbert was considered to have completed his general education, and was sent to London to study at the Kensington Art Schools, and a year later became a student at the Royal Academy Schools. Subsequently he spent some months at Antwerp. His first picture, "I cannot Mind my Wheel, Mother," was hung in the Academy of 1879. In that year Mr. Schmalz removed from Newman Street to Holland Park Road, afterwards making Addison Road his residence. Among the productions of this clever artist are "Christianæ ad Leones," "Zenobia's Last Look on Palmyra," "The King's Daughter," "The Daughters of Judah in Babylon," "The Return from Calvary," and "The Resurrection Morn."

Turning to the right, a short walk through the Dene brings you to Ryton Ferry, which is one of the fairest spots around the old village. The place is remarkable for its stillness, which is only broken by the shriek of the whistle of a passing train, or the chiming of the hour by the church clock. The scenery is exceptionally picturesque. On the south side of the river are the banks of Ryton, richly wooded, and teeming with bird life; on the north side is the old-fashioned house of the boatman, protected from the north winds by a belt of trees running east and west along the bank of the stream. Rising gracefully from the low lying ground, the southern hills, with their hamlets and woods, and pretty cottages, form a splendid background. Half a mile westward the river makes a graceful bend to the north, and eastward in the same direction till it reaches Newburn. Altogether the Ryton Ferry is one of the most delightful pieces of scenery on the Tyne. Although the boatman's house is at the north side of the river, it is in the parish of Ryton, the boundary line being immediately behind the house. The river has evidently changed its course at a time not very remote. Old inhabitants of the villages in the neighbourhood affirm that sixty years ago traces of the former course of the stream were plainly discernible. Sykes informs us that formerly tremendous floods frequently caused the river to overflow its banks, the waters bearing destruction to the low lying grounds adjoining the river. In the great flood of 1771, Jos. Foster, the ferryman at Ryton, had to escape from a window in the second storey of the old house, to a boat sent to his rescue. Sir John Lubbock tells us how easy it is for a river to change its course under the

conditions already mentioned. He says:—"If the country is flat, a river gradually raises the level on each side; the water which overflows during floods being retarded by trees, bushes, sedges, and a thousand other obstacles, gradually deposits the solid matter which it contains, and, then raising the surface, becomes at length suspended, as it were, above the central level. When this elevation has reached a certain point, the river, during some flood, overflows and cuts through its banks, and deserting its old bed, takes a new course along the lowest accessible level." The object of the ferry in olden times would be to put the Cistercians of Newminster, near Morpeth, in direct communication with their land in Chopwell. At that time the ferry would be higher up the river, near to Wylam. The following interesting reference to Ryton Island, and Haughs, appeared in the *Newcastle Journal*, March 2nd, 9th, 1766 —"To let, a parcel of land on Ryton Haugh, Fog-gates for four Beasts; a Horse-gate once in five years in Ryton Island; and a Fishing-Side." *Fog* is the second crop, that follows a hay crop. *Gate* is a stint, or right of pasture.

In 1872 the owners of stints on Ryton Willows were: Owners of Townley Estate, 17½; Joseph Cowen, Esq., 5; G. Silvertop, Esq., 4½; Mr. R. M. Weeks, 4; Mr. Joseph Lamb, 3; Lady Kinlock, 2½; Messrs. Tweedy and Hindmarch, 3; Mrs. Matthewson, 2; Rev. C. Thorp, 2; Rector of Ryton, 1⅔; The Greve, 1; Mr. Bates, 1. The stints are still held by the representatives of the above families.

Returned to the top of the Dene, and advancing to the Bar Moor, the attention of the visitor is arrested by what appears to be the remains of two drinking fountains, built into the wall, which possess some curiously carved heads of stone. These stones were brought from the Market-House, Durham, by the Rev. C. Thorp, and erected in their present shape as ornaments to the village. Passing the East Grange Farm, and St. Mary's Terrace, you reach the Bar Moor. Before arriving at the Hexham turnpike, a lane branches from the Ryton road to the Grange farm. This farm belongs to Mr. Jos. Cowen; it was purchased by the late Sir Joseph Cowen from the Saunders of Ryton, at that time the representative of the oldest family in the parish. Mr. Jos. Cowen has in his possession several relics of the Saunders, amongst them a curious wood sugar basin, bearing the inscription, "G. and I. Saunders, Ryton Grange,

1792." This George Saunders was a direct descendant of John Saunders, who, in 1498, granted lands in Ryton "to William Clark, and his successors, Chaplain of St. Mary's Altar, for the perpetual maintenance of a light before the image of the Virgin."

In 1863, Ryton was formed into a Local Board district of nine members, comprising the townships of Crawcrook, Ryton, and Ryton Woodside. It contained an area of 5149 acres, and had a population of 5553, in 1891. Its rateable value at that time was £27,474. In 1894, an Urban District Council of nine members was formed.

Bar (Bare) Moor.

At the beginning of the present century, the Bar Moor was a tract of waste ground, which in 1825, was enclosed by Act of Parliament.

At the juncture of the road from Ryton with the Hexham turnpike, stand the Thorp Memorial Schools, which are fine stone buildings, erected to the memory of the Ven. Archdeacon Thorp in 1861, by public subscription. In 1886, they were enlarged and improved, consisting now of mixed and infants' schools, with accommodation in the former for 130, and in the latter for 90.

A little farther westward, on the same side of the Hexham turnpike, is the Congregational Church. Before the erection of this church, the members of this body in the neighbourhood travelled to Horsley to worship, where there had been a "meeting house" for two hundred years. It was started by the Rev. Thomas Trewren, or Trurant, who was ejected from his church at Ovingham, upon the passing of the celebrated Act of Uniformity in 1662.

The Church at Barmoor is a neat stone building in the Early English Style, erected in 1861, at a cost of £400, and was afterwards enlarged at a further cost of £500. It consists of a well fitted nave, with seatings for 260. A Sunday School was built at a cost of £200, which was enlarged in 1878, the extra cost being £700. Adjoining is the Manse, the residence of the minister, the Rev. Hugh Rose Rae. The Rev. William Stowell, B.A., was the minister of the church till his death in 1878. There is a tradition in the neighbourhood, that a great number of the keelmen, and the drivers of horses on the old waggon ways, came from the borders, and were Presbyterians. They held religious services in a house at Woodside, early in the eighteenth century. The following entries are in the Ryton Register:—"1723, Sept. 14th, Nicholas Story, a dissenting teacher (bur.). 1729, May 15th, James Jagues, a Presbyterian teacher, buried." The society at Woodside seems to have been for a short time without a house to hold their services in, when they attended different churches in Newcastle. In 1732 they again secured a dwelling house at Woodside, and were placed under the care of the Rev. John Crossland. In 1750, the society was removed to Swalwell, where a chapel was built, in which services have been conducted for one hundred and forty-five years. When the "religious census" was taken, in 1788, there were fifty-six members of the Church of Scotland.

On the south side of the Hexham turnpike is the Emma Pit, belonging to the Stella Coal Company, sunk in 1845. It has two shafts; the Emma being eighty-three fathoms deep. The houses of the workmen are built in rows at the north side of the pit.

The Blaydon Co-operative Society have a large branch store on the north side of the turnpike, built in 1893; which comprises grocery, drapery, butchering, hardware, and boot and shoe departments.

On the same side of the road is Moor House, which was purchased from Lord Ravensworth by Messrs. Potter, Hall, Budle, and Dunn, for the use of the engineer at the Emma Pit.

CRAWCROOK,

Crawrok, Craucrue, Crawcrok, Crowcrok.

CRAWCROOK—from *crau*, the crow, and *cruik*, a corner. This village may be said to be a continuation of Ryton Barmoor, and consists of houses built on the north and south side of the Hexham turnpike. With the exception of a few old-fashioned thatched cottages, the houses are mostly modern. Population: 1801, 325; 1811, 268; 1821, 308; 1831, 340; 1841, 290; 1851, 320; 1861, 319; 1871, 346; 1881, 450; 1891, 1054. Rateable value in 1821, £1,614; and in 1894, £7,365.

Crawcrook, according to Boldon Buke (1183), was on lease with the villein service; but before Hatfield's Survey it had become a free manor, and it is stated, "Robert Horsley holds half the vill. of Crawcrook, by Knight service and ten shillings (and a toft and forty acres, called Bradley, by one penny rent, on St. Cuthbert's Day, in September)." In 1544, Margery, sister and heir of Roger Horsley, married Cuthbert Carnaby, of Haydon Bridge, Co. of Northumberland. After the lapse of a few generations, the Carnabys sold this estate in small parcels.

The other moiety of Crawcrook was the property of the Hospital of St. Giles of Kepyer, and after the dissolution, was distinguished by the name of Little Kepyer, which John Watson of Newcastle, acquired in 1587 by purchase, of John Heath, Esq. It consisted of four messuages, a water mill, four gardens, two hundred acres of arable, as many of pasture, a hundred and forty of meadow, forty acres of woodland, two hundred of furze and heath, three hundred of moor, thirty of marsh, a free fishery in the Tyne, and 27s. rent in Little Kepyeare, near Crawcrook. This John Watson, and his son Thomas, granted parcels of land in Crawcrook to Delaval, Sander, Jollie, Hauxley, and French. Catherine Hauxley intermarried with Robert Surtees, of Ryton, whose descendants continued for some time to occupy lands in Crawcrook. At the present time the principal owners are Messrs. Thornton and Croft, Joseph Cowen, Esq., J. B. Simpson, Esq., A. M. Dunn, Esq., and the Stella Coal Company.

Crawcrook, at the present time, may be said to be an entirely modern village. The houses which compose the principal thoroughfare, especially on the north side, are chiefly built of stone, and respectable in appearance.

At the entrance of the village, and on the south side, are the school connected with the Colliery, and the Wesleyan Methodist Chapel. The latter is a handsome building of stone, erected in 1875, as a memorial to Robert Young, missionary and preacher.

This distinguished man was born at Crawcrook, Nov. 14th, 1796. His parents were devout Methodists; his mother having been converted under the ministry of the Rev. John Wesley. From his childhood he was a subject of deep religious influence, and his religious life may be said to have commenced in 1814, when only eighteen years of age. Early in the year 1820, under a strong conviction of duty, he offered himself as a missionary, and having been accepted, was ordained on Nov. 9th, 1820, and immediately sailed for the West Indies. His labours were eminently successful; and in 1830 he returned to England, where his labours in all the circuits to which he was appointed were rewarded with success. As a pulpit orator his powers were of a high order. Some of the best gifts of a public speaker were found in him in happy combination, and these were diligently cultivated. His labours and counsels in connection with the formation of the Australasian Conference were highly valued, both in the colony and at home. Two years after his return from this mission, his brethren shewed their appreciation of his character, by electing him to the office of President of the Conference. After a life of unintermitting but joyous labour, he was obliged, in consequence of paralysis, to become a Supernumerary at the Conference of 1860. Full of peace and hope he died at Truro, on November 16th, 1865, in the seventieth year of his age.

The Primitive Methodists have a small chapel on the same side of the turnpike, a little farther westward, which was erected in 1848.

Crawcrook farm lies on the south side of the village.

A lane known as Kepyer Chare branches off the Hexham turnpike, past the Fox and Hounds public-house, to the farm. Kepyer, in Crawcrook, obtained its name from Kepyer Hospital, on the banks of the Wear, to which certain lands in Crawcrook belonged at the time of the Reformation. The name is derived from *Kep* = to catch (the fish), and *yare* = a dam thrown across a river, to impede the free run of salmon, and to force them through the lock or trap, in which they were taken. *Chare* means a narrow lane, but the word is seldom found on the south banks of the Tyne. Having passed the "Fox and Hounds," a road branches from the north side of the Hexham turnpike, to Claraville colliery and Castle Hill.

Where the road leaves the turnpike, there is a neat school-chapel. Mr. Archibald Dunn of Castle Hill, gave the site, and built the school, which was opened in February, 1886; in 1889, an infant school was added. In 1892, Mr. Dunn added a sanctuary to the little school. The chapel is dedicated to St. Agnes, virgin and martyr. In the same year a priest was appointed, the Rev. Philip Fitzgerald. He was succeeded by the Rev. Edward Beech, who had been curate at New Tunstall. The Claraville Pit belongs to the Stella Coal Company, and was opened in 1893. The seams worked are the Five Quarter and the Towneley, the latter seam at a depth of seventy fathoms. About one hundred and forty men and boys are employed, and excellent houses have been built for the workmen.

On the west side of Claraville stands Castle Hill. A large and handsome mansion has been built on the hill at the north side of Castle Hill farm, by Archibald Dunn, Esq. There is a charming drive from the main road to the house, through the beautiful grounds on the south side of the park. The scenery which the residence commands on every side, is wild and romantic in the highest degree. Mrs. Sarah H. Dunn, the wife of Mr. Dunn, is the writer of an interesting book, "The World's Highway, with some First Impressions while Journeying along it," which contains an account of her travels in the east. It was published in 1894.

Returned to Crawcrook by the road which leads to Castle Hill, the Hexham turnpike forms a bend southward, towards the "Lamb Arms" public-house. This modern house is erected on the site of an old house which had stood for two centuries alongside of one of the old waggon-ways. A road here branches to Greenside, and on the hill-side there is an old-fashioned public-house, the "Rising Sun," which also existed for the convenience of the men employed in the early coal trade of the district. After passing the "Lamb Arms," the road strikes westward towards Bradley. About fifty yards west of the "Lamb Arms," two houses occupy the site of Crawcrook school, at which the most of the gentlemen's sons in the neighbourhood were educated. It was endowed at the beginning of the present century with £25 a year, by Miss Simpson of Bradley Hall; and Lady Ravensworth, for a number of years, contributed £20 a year for the education of poor girls. The school was conducted by two well-known schoolmasters, Mr. John Craiggy, and afterwards his son, Mr. John Alexander Craiggy. Some of the boys who attended "Craiggy's school," including George (afterwards Sir George) Elliot, Nicholas Wood, Thomas Y. Hall, and J. B. Simpson, Esq., the present owner of Bradley, have attained to a foremost rank as mining engineers. Other gentlemen who fill high positions as mining engineers on the continent of Europe, and in America, attended the Crawcrook school; and it is a question whether any other village school in England has turned out so many distinguished men who have been connected with the coal trade. The endowment to the school was withdrawn soon after the Bradley estate was sold by Lord Ravensworth, and this well-known seminary was abandoned. At the west end of Crawcrook may be seen, on the hill-side, a long line of one of the old waggon-ways, which extended from Hedley Fell to Ryton, after which it passed down Holburn Dene, and across Ryton Haughs to the Tyne, near to the old Alnwick House—standing on the south side of the river—nearly opposite to Newburn church, where the coals were emptied into keels and conveyed down the river to their destination.

At the extreme west point of Crawcrook, there is a road known as the Sledd Lane, which leads to Wylam Station. On the west side of the lane is the Daniel farm, which is one of the oldest in the old Ryton parish. About three-quarters of a mile west of Crawcrook, are the delightful woods of Bradley.

Bradley Hall is a modern mansion, after the design of Payne, built of stone, and two storeys high. It is sheltered by fine woods, which extend to the Tyne, and impart a rich and warm aspect to the place. The gardens and pleasure grounds, which lie on the north side of the hall, are laid out with great skill and good taste. The estate surrounding the hall—which comprises about 1140 acres—is entered by two carriage roads: one from the Hexham turnpike on the south side, the other from the road which leads to Wylam Station. The latter road passes through some most charming scenery.

Bradley Corn Mill, with its water-wheel driven by the Stanley Burn, is one of those old-fashioned places seldom seen in our generation. It is pleasantly situated at the north side of the Bradley estate, near to where the burn empties itself into the Tyne. Mr. Robert Marshall has been the miller for thirty years.

According to Mackenzie, the Horsleys held Bradley with Crawcrook. Before the year 1610, it was held by John Lyon; and Bradley Hall, and lands in Crawcrook, seem to have been in possession of his son in 1626. Shortly after, the Andersons of Newcastle acquired the whole of Bradley.

The Andersons of Newcastle and Jesmond were a wealthy mercantile family. Francis Anderson was sheriff of Newcastle in 1595, and mayor in 1601 and 1612. He married Barbara Nicholson in 1581; and his eldest son, Roger Anderson of Jesmond, was sheriff of Newcastle in 1612; in which year he married Anne, daughter of William Jackson of Newcastle. His only son, Sir Francis Anderson of Jesmond and Bradley, Knight, married Jane, daughter and heir of John Dent. He was a devoted loyalist, and, on the ruin of the royal cause, became an object of peculiar persecution to the successful party. He was fined £1200, sequestered, imprisoned, and stripped of his title of knighthood, which fell within the list of proscribed honours, conferred after the 4th of January, 1641, when Charles separated himself from his parliament. He was sheriff of Newcastle in 1641, mayor in 1662 and 1675, and M.P. for the town in 1660-61, and 1678-9, in which last year he died. His son and successor, Henry Anderson of Bradley, Esq., in 1681 married Dorcas Matfen. Their daughter Jane, married John Simpson of Newcastle, and in their right of Bradley, John Simpson, their second son, married Anne, daughter of Richard Clutterbuck of Warkworth. He was succeeded by his only son, John Simpson of Bradley, Esq., who married 12th July, 1768, Anne, daughter of Thomas, Earl of Strathmore. John Simpson was a benefactor to the Keelmen's Hospital, Newcastle-upon-Tyne, and on the south front of the Hospital is the following inscription :—

In the year 1786,
The interest of 100£ at 5 per cent. for ever,
to be annually distributed
on the twenty-third of December,
among the ten oldest Keelmen
resident in the Hospital,
was left by
John Simpson, Esq., of Bradley,
Alderman of the town,
and forty years Governor of the Hoastmen's Company.
The grateful objects of his remembrance
have caused this stone to be erected,
that posterity may know
the donor's worth,
and be stimulated to follow
an example so benevolent.

This John Simpson left three daughters—Anne, Marie Susannah, and Frances Eleanor. Marie Susannah became the wife of Thomas Henry, Lord Ravensworth, who inherited through her the Bradley, Tanfield, and Sleekburn estates. In 1851, Bradley was purchased from Lord Ravensworth, by John Walker, Esq., for £40,000.

The estate was afterwards purchased by Owen Wallace, Esq., who in 1894 sold it to John Bell Simpson, Esq., who makes it his residence.

After leaving Bradley Hall, and advancing westward for half a mile, a road on the north side of the Hexham turnpike leads to Sourmires, where there is a splendid old mansion, with farm buildings attached, and known as Bradley Hall Farm.

It was in this house, on April 24th, 1795, that Nicholas Wood, the celebrated mining engineer, was born. At the time of his birth his father was mining engineer for Crawcrook Colliery, and at a famous old school at Crawcrook, Nicholas Wood received his education. He was afterwards sent to Killingworth Colliery to learn the profession of mining engineer, and subsequently became viewer of the colliery. It was at Killingworth that he formed the friendship of George Stephenson, and the active genius of the young engineer was of the highest service to the inventor of the "Geordy" Lamp. It was Nicholas Wood who executed the drawings of the lamp according to the inventor's explanation; and on the 21st of October, 1815, accompanied by Nicholas Wood and John Moodie, George Stephenson descended the shaft of Killingworth pit, to test the lamp in a part of the mine that was highly explosive. Having been urged to bring his invention under the notice of the Literary and Philosophical Society of Newcastle-upon-Tyne, Stephenson consented, but on the understanding that Nicholas Wood was to act in the capacity of spokesman upon the occasion; and on the 5th of December, 1815, at a meeting of upwards of eighty gentlemen, the interesting lecture was delivered. When Edward Pease wished to consult George Stephenson in reference to the formation of the Stockton and Darlington Railway, Mr. Nicholas Wood accompanied Stephenson on the occasion. This interview, which took place on the 19th of April, 1821, had the effect of Stephenson being ultimately appointed engineer to the Stockton and Darlington Railway. In 1825, Mr. Wood published a treatise on Railroads, to remove some of the objections to them advanced by civil engineers at the time. When we consider that at this date Mr. Wood was only thirty years of age, his attainments must have been of a high order. In the year 1838, he read a paper before the Geological Section of the British Association, at Newcastle-upon-Tyne, on "The Geology of the County of Northumberland." In 1862 the Association of Mining Engineers was established, when Mr. Wood was appointed President; and the handsome building in Newcastle, belonging to the Northern Institute of Mining Engineers, possesses an apartment known as "The Wood Memorial Hall." Robert Stephenson, the famous son of a famous father, was apprenticed to Mr. Wood, to learn the duties of a viewer. Nicholas Wood died in London on the 19th of December, 1865.

From Sourmires there is a pleasant footpath, leading through fields and plantations to Wylam Railway Station.

Following the Hexham turnpike, on the south side you pass West Wood Farm; the rising ground between this farm and Kyo Hall is known as Hagg Hill.

Half a mile west of West Wood farmhouse are Stanley Burn Cottages. At this spot the burn passes through a bridge fifty feet high, and takes a north-easterly direction to the Tyne. The burn is the western boundary of the parish of Ryton.

PETH-HEAD.

Returned to Stella, after leaving Stella House, and proceeding in a south-westerly direction for about half a mile, you reach Peth or Path-head, which is a delightful hamlet lying mostly on the west side of the turnpike. Several of the houses are old, thatched, and picturesque; and for centuries have been connected with the Nunnery and the Hall at Stella. Tradition states that there has been a village here since the times of the Saxons, and that a peth or path led through the forest in olden times to Hexham—hence Peth-head.

On the west side of the cottages are the pretty and well-trimmed gardens of the workmen. A small burn, fed by the neighbouring hills, runs past the gardens, and drives a flour-mill. As you walk to Stella there are cool and pleasant retreats in the wood, and lately, Mr. Joseph Cowen, by repairing the roads and planting trees, has done much to beautify the place and make it attractive.

A road from Peth-head, past the old Bog Pit, leads to Stargate Colliery, opened in 1800. A serious explosion occurred at this pit on May 30th, 1830, when thirty-seven men and boys were killed. Messrs. Dunn were at that time owners, but in 1833 the lease expired, and the colliery having been laid in soon after the accident, was not used until 1840, when it was attached to the Rector's Glebe and Stella Freehold Collieries, by the present firm. The workmen live in houses near the colliery. At the end of one of the rows is a neat Wesleyan Methodist Chapel, erected in 1877, at a cost of £500.

Returned to Peth-head, and advancing westward by the turnpike, you have a commanding view of the Bues Hills range, the practice ground of the Tyne and Derwent Rifle Club.

About a mile from Peth-head, and before you reach Greenside, there is a house standing on the north side of the road, which is known as Stephen's Hall. The front of the house has been altered; but the old chimney, which is very wide, is against the west gable. On the north side interesting portions of the old Hall remain. There is an arch thirteen feet at the base, and nine feet high. On a stone over the arch is the inscription:—

DUM SPIRO SPERO,
Whilst I breathe I hope.

On two stones at the top of a low wall, resting on the arch, are the words—LAUS DEO. There is under the arch a square-headed doorway, six feet high and three feet wide. On the head is the inscription:—

NON NOBIS DOMINE   S.C.   SED NOMINITVO
NON NOBIS   1635. DA GLORIAM.

Translation—Not to us, O Lord, but to thy name; not to us, give glory.

This door leads into a small yard, on the left of which is another doorway, now built up. The door-head bears the inscription:—

OMNIA BONA DOMIN—.

The letters S.C., in the centre of the inscription over the arch, are the initals of Stephen Coulsin, who lived in the Hall in 1635. The Coulsin family were closely related to the Surtees family of Ryton; in fact, Robert Surtees was the son of Edward Surtees of Broad Oak, in the parish of Ovingham, by Margaret Coulsin, niece and heiress of Robert Surtees, Alderman of Durham. Edward Surtees died in 1655, so that he would be living about the same time as Stephen Coulsin. Stephen Coulsin had a son named Stephen, whose wife lived to an extraordinary age. There is in the Ryton parish registers the following entry:—"1728, Dec. 5th, Isabel, wife to Stephen Coulsin, of Chopwell, aged 103." The old Hall is one of the most interesting houses in the old parish of Ryton, and no visitor to the neighbourhood should leave without seeing it.

GREENSIDE.

GREENSIDE became a separate parish by an order in council, dated May 6th, 1886, and comprises the townships of Crawcrook and Ryton Woodside, with a small portion of Ryton. It embraces the villages of Greenside, Crawcrook, Emma Colliery, and (Ryton) Woodside, having a population of 3000.

The village of Greenside is two miles from Stella, and one mile and a half south of Ryton. It is chiefly composed of houses built on the north side of the turnpike. Several of the cottages at the west end of the village are thatched, and picturesque in appearance.

Greenside was included in the forfeiture of John Swinburne, Esq., of Chopwell, in 1570; and was granted by Bishop Barnes to Cuthbert Carnaby, Esq., by copy of Court-roll. The same bishop granted other lands between Rickley-forde and Abbotford, near Rickley Hill, to Robert Dodd. Formerly, coals were extensively worked in the neighbourhood, and several of the old waggon-ways are still to be seen.

The site of one—of the "Folly Pit,"—may be seen at the east end of the village; and another at the south side, near to the "big" pond. With this pit were connected several eminent mining engineers. John Buddle, senr., served in the capacity of manager at this colliery during the closing years of the last century, and was succeeded by James Hall, Esq. Mr. Hall was for about half a century mining engineer under Messrs. G. Dunn and Sons, G. Silvertop, Esq., &c.; and for many years during the latter portion of that period mining agent for Capt. Blackett, M.P., W. P. Wrightson, Esq., M.P., P. E. Townley, Esq., and other gentlemen. He served as engineer under John Buddle, at Wallsend Colliery; and acquired his position as mining engineer by going down the A Pit, Greenside, and bringing to bank the bodies of several men who had been killed by an explosion, after Mr. Newton, viewer, had declined to do so. The father of John Buddle, then chief manager for J. Silvertop, Esq., resigned in favour of Mr. Hall, who continued to reside in the house of his predecessor until his death, which took place in 1841.

Mr. Thomas Young Hall, son of James Hall, was born at Greenside, October 25th, 1802. Mr. Hall, after being a pit boy, served an apprenticeship under his father and the eminent John Buddle, at the Townley, Whitefield, and Crawcrook collieries. He then acted as mining engineer, under an agreement for four years, at North Hetton Colliery; afterwards for a similar period as engineer and manager of Black Boy, or Tees Wallsend Colliery, belonging to Jonathan Backhouse, and which, in 1852, was sold to Nicholas Wood, Esq., of Hetton Hall; and next in the same † HETT capacity at South Hetton Colliery. Subsequently he became a coal-owner, by entering into partnership with his former employer, Mr. Buddle, and Alderman Potter of Heaton Hall, as lessees of the rector of Ryton's Glebe, and of Stella Freehold Collieries, to which was afterwards added (after a cessation of six years' working) Stella Grand Lease, comprising Townley Main and Whitefield Collieries, and in conjunction with Mr. Buddle and others, of the royalties in Crawcrook, thus including the whole extent of Ryton Parish.

In 1839, upon the recommendation of Robert Stephenson, the celebrated engineer, Mr. Hall was induced to go out to Virginia, in the United States, to look after the collieries belonging to the Blackheath Company, which on account of the prevalence of gas, were considered too dangerous to work. All the difficulties connected with the mines were surmounted by Mr. Hall, and the collieries were afterwards purchased by a wealthy English company, known as "The Chesterfield Coal and Iron Mining Company." Mr. Hall became one of the principal partners, and his services were retained at a salary of £2000 a year, as resident superintendent and manager.

Previous to Mr. Hall's engagement in America, and whilst sojourning there, he sent various plans and documents to eminent Russian engineers on mining matters, and, in 1840, addressed a letter to the editor of the *New York Herald*, in which he pointed out the advantages that would result to Russia by the formation of a line of railway between St. Petersburg and Moscow. Mr. John S. Carr, the Russian Consul at Newcastle, forwarded a copy of the paper, and some other of Mr. Hall's documents, to Russia; and the subject having afterwards attracted the attention of the Czar; and the Russian nobility, General Tcheffkine and other engineers were sent to England to obtain the best information respecting the formation of a line of railroads, and the working of coal and iron mines. General Tcheffkine afterwards visited Stella, and spent several days with Mr. Hall. Mr. Hall was afterwards presented with several valuable medals, and a letter of thanks from the Emperor of Russia.

Several improvements in colliery engineering were introduced by Mr. Hall. Formerly the men and boys were drawn up the pit by being slung to a loop at the end of a rope or chain; and the coals were sent up in baskets, or corves. Mr. Hall originated the improved method of drawing coals at great speed by means of guards and cages in the pit shaft, and introduced tub carriages with bogey and edge-rails, into the pit workings underground. Mr. Hall was also the inventor of a patent Safety Lamp. The closing years of his life were spent in cultivating the Wylam Hill Farm. He died on the 3rd February, 1870.

The house in which Mr. Buddle and Mr. James Hall lived, and in which Mr. Thomas Young Hall was born, is still standing, and although old—with its pretty flower garden, and waving trees in front, is one of the pleasantest in Greenside.

At the west end of the village is the School, built by subscription in 1813. It has lately been enlarged, to accommodate an increasing population.

John Wesley visited Greenside in 1751, where he had the largest congregation he ever saw in the north. In 1781 a large house was converted into a place of worship for the Methodists. Formerly the chapel possessed a gallery, but it has now been removed. A chapel-keeper's house has been erected at the north end of the building. The chapel, although old, has a substantial appearance; and its services are well attended. It has been for many years in the hands of the Free Methodists.

A Mechanics' Institute was erected in 1848, at the expense of Alderman Potter, John Buddle, M. W. Dunn, and T. Y. Hall, lessees of the Townley, Whitefield, and Stella Freehold Collieries. The site was presented by G. Silvertop, Esq., Minsteracres.

The Church (St. John the Evangelist)

Is pleasantly situated on the north side of the village, and is approached by the road which leads to Ryton Woodside. It was designed by Mr. John Henry, of Bamborough. It is in the Decorated style; and consists of nave and chancel, a south porch, and western turret. The east window is in three compartments, and filled with stained glass; it bears the inscription:—" Grace Aider, of blessed memory, wife of Robert Thorp, D.D., died August 2nd, 1814. The tribute of her surviving children, Jane and Charles Thorp, A.D. 1857."

The west window is in four compartments, and filled with stained glass; it is also a memorial to a member of the Thorp family. There are two bells in the turret at the west end of the church. The larger one was formerly the workmen's bell, at Crowley's ironworks, at Swalwell; it was afterwards taken to Ryton church, and was used in connection with the clock, to strike the hours; subsequently it was placed in the turret at Greenside church. A graveyard surrounds the church. At the entrance of the churchyard, on the east side, there is a lich-gate, or corpse-gate, where the body may rest while the funeral procession is formed. Lych is the Saxon word for a dead body.

The vicar's house, which stands at the south side of the church, is a neat and substantial residence.

The church was consecrated September 18th, 1857, by the Bishop of Durham. The Rev. R. M. Nason is vicar.

A road at the south side of the village leads to the Spen.

A pleasant road westward for a mile and a half conducts the pedestrian to

COALBURNS.

This little hamlet, which contains about a dozen houses, including Coalburns Hall, and a public house ("Fox and Hounds"), is pleasantly situated in a valley, and surrounded with rich and varied scenery. It is a favourite "meet" for "the Braes of Derwent" foxhounds. A road which passes Coalburns Hall leads to Kyo, Bucks Nook, and French's Close.

Kyo has been extensively worked for coal; and a number of old pits, and the remains of several old waggon-ways, may still be seen in the neighbourhood.

Bucks Nook Farm is an old-fashioned residence standing on a hill, facing the south. Ralph Lambton, Esq., of Murton House, so celebrated as a huntsman in the neighbourhood, and who kept a pack of hounds at his own expense, was in the habit of visiting Bucks Nook on the last day of the season, for the purpose of killing his May fox.

Leaving Coalburns by the Leadgate road, and advancing westward, a branch road is reached which leads to Coalburns Farm, the birth-place of Christopher Hopper.

Christopher Hopper was born on the 25th December, 1722. When five years old he was sent to a school kept by one Mr. Alderson, who taught not only the branches of learning he professed, but the fear of God, and the first principles of religion. When about eight years of age his father died, and young Hopper was placed in a shop under one Mr. Armstrong, with whom he was afterwards bound by indenture for seven years. Tiring of the drudgery of standing behind the counter, he returned home. His father being dead, his eldest brother occupied the farm, and kept waggon horses. Christopher was engaged at the age of sixteen to go with horses on the waggon ways, at which employment he remained until he was twenty-one. About the year 1742, he heard Charles Wesley preach at Tanfield Cross; and in 1743, John Brown, a farmer, who had been converted under a sermon of John Wesley's at Tanfield, removed to the Low Spen, and opened his house for preaching. It was at this time, and in John Brown's house, that the religious life of Christopher Hopper commenced. He afterwards became a class leader and a local preacher. When preaching in the neighbouring villages he sometimes was roughly treated. Once in particular, when preaching at Whickham, the constable came with his attendants to apprehend him; they guarded the door, and waited until the conclusion of the service to seize him. When he had finished, he escaped through a window, after which an encounter took place between the constable and his men, and some of those who had formed the congregation, which ended in "hard blows and bloody faces." In the year 1744, he taught a school at Barlow, and while there married Jane Richardson, a farmer's daughter, at Ryton, on May 28th, 1745. In 1746 he removed from Barlow to the preaching-house at Sheephill; and in the year 1748 he removed to Hindley Hill, in Allendale, where he began his arduous and faithful work among the people in the dales. He went about "from town to town, and from house to house, singing, praying, and preaching the word." In the year 1749 he was wholly separated to the work of the ministry. On March 20th, 1750, he visited Ireland along with John Wesley; returning on July 22nd of the same year. In 1756 he paid a second visit to Ireland, and returned in 1758. In 1760 he visited Scotland for the second time, remaining until 1765. In 1776 he again visited Ireland, returning 1777. After being stationed at Bradford, Colne, Leeds, Newcastle-upon-Tyne, Liverpool, and other places, he went to his rest on Friday, March 5th, 1802, in his eightieth year. Thus passed away the Apostle of the Dales; the companion of Wesley, and the friend of George Whitfield.

Returning to the Leadgate road, in a few minutes you reach Penny Hill, where an old pit is to be seen. At the close of the last century, this pit and the Stella Grand Lease A Pit, were worked by steam engines put up by Mr. T. Y. Hall, which pumped water from large ponds constructed for the purpose, and which water being conveyed into a cistern fifty-two feet high, was made to turn a wheel, constructed with a brake, whereby the men and boys, as well as the coal, were drawn up the shaft. These two engines—the last employed in this manner in the north of England—were abandoned in 1800 and 1808.

Mr. Robert Edington, in writing of the coal trade in the north of England in 1813, says:—"Before I quit the Parish of Ryton, I must not omit the colliery of Chopwell (Penny Hill), belonging to Lord Cowper, and which had been wrought by Mr. Silvertop. This was called the famous White Field Colliery, which was so highly esteemed at all foreign markets, but not working at present.

Leadgate is one mile and a half west of Penny Hill. It consists of a farmhouse, a cottage, and an old-fashioned public-house ("Three Horse Shoes"). A few years ago, a woman, Mrs. Hunter, ninety-three years old, lived in the public-house with an unmarried daughter about seventy years of age. When asking for the daughter, the mother invariably called her the "bairn." From this circumstance, the public-house is frequently called "The Bairns." The west side of the "Three Horse Shoes" is the western boundary of the old Parish of Ryton.

RYTON WOODSIDE TOWNSHIP.

This straggling hamlet, which is in the parish of Greenside, lies on the south side of Ryton. The population in 1801, was 885; 1811, 838; 1821, 1057; 1831, 951; 1841, 1059; 1851, 1133; 1861, 1051; 1871, 1066; 1881, 1082; 1891, 1106. Area, 2813 acres. Rateable Value in 1821, £3169; 1895, £5775.

In 1592 Robert Hedworth died, seized of his messuage of Ryton Woodside; but in 1691 it passed to Henry Jenison of Newcastle, Esq., and in 1697 became the property of Robert Surtees, Esq., of Ryton.

In 1825, in pursuance of Act of Parliament, a tract of waste ground in Ryton Woodside was enclosed; and four acres, two roods, ten perches of Woodside Green was allotted to the churchwardens and overseers of the township of Ryton Woodside, to be by them employed and cultivated for the use of the poor of the said township, and in relief of the inhabitants rateable for their support.

Ryton Woodside is reached by a road which branches from the Hexham turnpike on the south side of Ryton. A pleasant walk of half a mile brings you to the Glebe Farm on your right hand. Running along the south side of the farm is a road which leads to what remains of the old Glebe Pit, with which Mr. John Buddle and Mr. T. Y. Hall were connected. Stretching away in the distance westward are the Kyo, Rockwood Hill, and Westwood Farms. In a field on the north side of the Glebe Farm, may be seen about one hundred yards of the old waggon-way, by which the coals were led from Glebe Pit. At a short distance from the Glebe is the Maiden Hill Farm. From this part of Woodside there is a pleasant walk—having the church on the right hand—to the village of Greenside. On the south side of Greenside are the Rickless, Realy-Mires, and Burn Hill Farms. In the year 1713, a Mr. Henry Marmion held a copyhold estate, part lying in the lordship of Winlington, near Ryton Woodside, known by the name of Realy-Mires, alias Benson's Farm. This farm, comprising one hundred and seventy acres, was purchased on the 2nd July, 1895, by Mr. Joseph Cowen of Stella Hall.

Returned to Ryton, after leaving the Runhead Farm, and passing "River View"—a row of neat modern houses on the south side of the Hexham turnpike—a few minutes' walk brings the visitor to High Hedgefield.

In the year 1828, High Hedgefield House was the residence of Mr. Edward Martinson, parish clerk, schoolmaster, and overseer for the parish of Stella. In the year 1880, the Right Rev. Monsignor Canon Thompson removed from Esh to High Hedgefield, and occupied the house till his death in 1893. At the time of his death, Canon Thompson was the patriarch of the Hexham Clergy. He was born at Stella, on the 17th May, 1811. His early youth was spent at Darlington. He was sent to a junior school at Scorton, in Yorkshire. At the age of fourteen he went to Ampleworth College, where he completed his classical education. Subsequently he went to Rome, where he lived until 1841. In the year 1839 he was ordained priest. While at college, a life-long intimacy sprung up between him and the distinguished Dr. Wiseman. After his ordination, the young priest became the colleague of Monsignor Witham, incumbent of Esh; and after Mr. Witham's removal to Berwick, Mr. Thompson was placed in charge of the mission, remaining there without change for forty years; it was his first and his last mission. On the 23rd Nov., 1880, he sent his resignation to the Bishop. From this time until his death he resided at High Hedgefield, where he died on the 17th August, 1893. Tradition states that a public-house once stood on the site of the present residence, and that the road to the ford at Newburn passed through the grounds attached to the house.

A little eastward, on the south side of the road, is Hedgefield Church (St. Hilda), which is a chapel of ease to Ryton. It is a stone edifice of somewhat quaint appearance, in the Perpendicular Gothic style, consisting of nave, south aisle, north transept, and a short embattled tower with strong buttresses. At the east end is a fine Perpendicular window; and in the west wall of the tower is the principal entrance doorway. The nave and aisle are divided by an arcade of pointed arches, springing from cylindrical pillars. It contains three hundred sittings. The church was opened in 1892, at a cost of £2800.

At the north side of the Hexham turnpike is the Addison Colliery, the property of the Stella Coal Company. It was sunk in 1864, and the depth is sixty-four fathoms. This pit, as well as the "Emma" and "Stargate" pits, is drained by a pumping engine at the Addison, of one hundred horse power. About eight thousand tons of water are drawn daily, and taking the year through, about twelve tons of water are drawn to one ton of coal. The ventilation of the shafts is accomplished by two Guibal ventilating fans, one sixteen feet in diameter, the other thirty feet in diameter, and producing together a ventilation equal to a hundred thousand cubic feet of air per minute. The Addison pit is situated on the line of railways to which all the coal from the other pits, except that sent to the Stella Staith, is conveyed by means of a three mile line of private railway belonging to the company. There are one hundred and eighty coke ovens.

The miners live in rows of well-built houses, many of them with gardens in front, and altogether the little village has a thriving and prosperous appearance.

There is a Primitive Methodist Chapel at the end of one of the rows of houses, provided by the colliery proprietors, and fitted by the members, with accommodation for two hundred people.

Hedgefield House, which stands on rising ground on the south side of the turnpike, is a handsome villa, possessing a commanding view of the Tyne. On a plan of Stella, dated 1767, the site of the villa is occupied by "Ralph Shipley's House and Stack Garth." About the beginning of the present century the old house was removed, and the present house built by William Matthias Dunn, Esq., who made it his residence. Until his removal to Bradley Hall, in 1894, the villa was occupied for many years by John B. Simpson, Esq.

On the east side of Hedgefield House is the burn which divides the modern parish of Stella from the old parish of Ryton.

...Robert Simpson's son, for ... this week, Ald Dr John Bell ... sense of the term a worthy ... For many years his name ... high honour by those who know ... As a pioneer in scientific ... he has furthered both by ... suasive pen and a generous ... mist whose essays on the sub... labour have aroused widespread ... g engineer whose knowledge ... once profound and extensive ... perienced public servant; as a ... benefactions have been of ... to all sections of the com... the tried and trusted f... has for its object the ... nkind generally, Dr Sim... ice to the north of quite ... ety, and generosity.

BELL SIMPSON.

Bacon.

... was born in 1837 at the ... of Ryton Woodside, and ... the village school of Craw... rds under the celebrated Dr ... Adopting the mining pro... is articles of apprenticeship ... d also with the late Mr T. ... Mr G. C. Greenwell, and ... these skilled engineers was ...

... of a million tons of coal. For many years Dr Simpson has been the managing owner, and under his expert advice and guidance the collieries have developed and prospered.

ENGINEERING SKILL.

For many years he has been extensively associated with the chief enterprises in the northern coalfield. As mining engineer to the Duke of Northumberland and other royalty owners, as an expert valuer and arbitrator, and in many other directions his services have been frequently in request, while what may be termed the more practical and active side of his busy life has been marked by many feats of engineering skill and foresight. For many years, the Wallsend and Hebburn Collieries were directly under his charge, and he was responsible for the erection of extensive pumping machinery. The drainage of Hebburn Colliery, after being inundated for a lengthy period, was one of his most successful undertakings. But his business activities are not exclusively confined to the coalfield; he is a director of several well-known public companies, while many of the highest honours in the mining engineers' world have been bestowed upon him. A member of the Institutions of Civil Engineers, an ex-President of the North of England Institute of Mining Engineers, and a Fellow of the Geological Society, in these and other capacities he has rendered eminent service along lines of research to the profession of which he is so distinguished a member.

BENEFACTOR TO ARMSTRONG COLLEGE.

The affairs of local administration, too, have claimed a large share of his talents and attention. To the Durham County Council, the Local Board at Ryton, as a churchwarden, overseer of the poor and member of the Board of Guardians, and last but not least, as a member of the council of Armstrong College, he has rendered conspicuous service. By reason of his lengthy association with the latter institution, not less than by his munificent donation of £10,000 towards the cost of the handsome School of Art which has been opened during the past year, his name will ever be identified with this Newcastle College. Indeed, it might not be too much to claim that the College itself was founded chiefly through the instrumentality of Dr Simpson. At all events, more than half a century ago he gave a course of lectures in Newcastle on geology, and it was from these and others which followed them that the movement was inaugurated which culminated in the establishment of Armstrong College. And he has been one of its staunchest and most generous friends ever since.

THE FRIEND OF ALL CLASSES.

But Armstrong College is only one of many northern institutions which owes a deep debt of gratitude to Dr Simpson. To the movement for the establishment of homes for aged miners he has also been a warm friend and generous supporter as the groups of cottages at Throckley tangibly testify; while ve... stance of the generous sentiments by contributed £500 towards the erection of a new church for the United Methodists of Greenside. We need not stop to insist that his generosity is accompanied by no show of ostentati... or he is not only a gentleman of sterling cha... er but of rare modesty and reticence as well. ...is notable services to the community, which might be multiplied ad lib. did space permit, have been ren... ed ungrudgingly and with great good grace. ...he outstanding features of his character have been industry, forebearance, integrity and generosity As an employer he has ever been anxious to promote the welfare of his workmen, and by none is he ... e highly esteemed. The proper complement to the quotation with which we opened this article is one from the same source. Sir Benjamin Browne once said of the subject of our sketch "No honour that can be conferred upon him is more than he deserves." And this opinion will be ...dorsed by every section of the northern community.

STELLA.

STELLINGLEY, Stelley, Stella—from *Stell* = a patronymic or family name, *ley* = uncultivated land. The parish of Stella was formed in August, 1844, and comprises the township of Stella, formerly in Ryton parish, and the town of Blaydon, and the district of Derwenthaugh, formerly part of Winlaton parish.

Stella township comprises an area of two hundred and eighty-six acres, which forms part of the Townley estate. Population: 1801, 314; 1811, 385; 1821, 421; 1831, 482; 1841, 563; 1851, 565; 1861, 542; 1871, 592; 1881, 743; 1891, 788. Its rateable value in 1821 was £1031, and in 1894, £2955.

Stella village stands on the south side of the Tyne, and west of Blaydon burn. It is straggling in appearance, and several of the houses are old and thatched. Nearly the whole of the land is in the possession of the Townley family.

About the year 1149 William de St. Barbara, Bishop of Durham, granted Stellingley, "with all its appurtenances in woodland, champian, roads, ways, metes, boundaries, mills, and meadows, waters, fish-dams, and fisheries, free of forest-right and pasturage of the Bishop's hogs, to St. Bartholomew and the Nuns of Newcastle." According to Boldon Buke (1183), "The son of William the Moneyer holds Stellingleye by the correct boundaries which the bishop caused to be perambulated for him, and pays one mark."

"There can be little doubt," says Surtees, "that this Monetaims, whose fame was so permanent, that his son needed no other description than to be of such a son the child, was the master worker of Bishop Pudsey's mint. It is not easy to understand how, only forty years after Stella was granted to the nuns, it was held by the Bishop's moneyer. It is conjectured," says Surtees, "that Pudsey had merely taken, by virtue of his power and dignity, a life interest of his office out of a portion of an estate which did not belong to him, as he subsequently confirmed the former grant of Stellinglei to the nuns, giving them by the same charter, in pure and perpetual alms 'Twille,' in exchange for 'Olworthe.'"

According to a manuscript in the Bodleian library, this Nunnery owed its origin to an ancient baron of the name of Hilton. Numerous and valuable donations and grants poured into this receptacle of fair devotees. Notwithstanding these advantages, the convent fell into a state of miserable poverty, accompanied by a relaxation of discipline; for in 1363 Bishop Hatfield appointed a commission to visit the convent, in order to punish crimes and reform abuses. In 1513 the Mayor and Corporation of Newcastle-upon-Tyne obtained a lease of the Nun's Moor for one hundred years, at the annual rent of 3s. 4d. This was one of the religious houses which Henry VIII. re-founded and preserved from the general dissolution in 1537; but it was suppressed on the 3rd January, 1540, at which time the establishment consisted of a prioress and nine nuns. The house was granted to William Barantyne Kenelme Throgmorton and Henry Annetson; it became afterwards the property of Lady Gavecre, from whom it passed by purchase to Robert Anderson, who levelled the fabric with the ground. Stella seems to have been one of their wealthiest possessions, and just as Benwell Tower was the summer residence of the Priors of Tynemouth, Stella probably would be a similar residence for the Nuns of Newcastle. At the time of the Dissolution, among the estates of the Nunnery within the Bishopric of Duresme, occurs Stellingley, by yer £3 13s. 4d.

Shortly after the Suppression, Stella became the property and residence of the Tempests of Newcastle, a mercantile branch of the ancient house of Holmeside. Nicholas Tempest of Stella, born 1553, was created a baronet the 23rd December, 1622. He married Isabel, daughter of Robert Lampton of Lampton, Esq. Sir Nicholas is described on the monument to his memory in Ryton Church, as "Soldier and Baronet." He died March 28th, 1625. Stella seems to have been the home of other members of the family, for the following entry occurs in the parish register:—"1617-18, Feb. 3rd, Mr. William Tempest of Stillaye, gentill' [bur.]. As Sir Nicholas had no son of that name, probably William was his brother.

Sir Nicholas Tempest was succeeded by his eldest son, Sir

Thomas Tempest of Stella, Bart., who married Troth, daughter of Sir Richard Tempest of Bracewell, Co. York, Knt. He was succeeded in 1641 by his son, Sir Richard Tempest, Baronet, colonel of a regiment of foot in the service of Charles I., styled of Stanley. He married Sarah, daughter of Sir Thomas Campbell, Lord Mayor of London, and dying in 1662, was succeeded by his only surviving son, Sir Thomas Tempest, Bart., who was baptised 6th September, 1642. He married Alice, daughter and co-heir of William Hodgson, of Hebburn and Winlaton. By this marriage the Tempests became owners of three-eighths of the manor of Winlaton. Sir Thomas Tempest died in 1692, leaving Jane, an only surviving daughter and heir to her brother Sir Francis Tempest, who married, in 1700, William, the fourth Lord Widdrington. This lady died in 1714, up to which period, and during the reign of the four Stuart kings, the Tempest family had resided at Stella "in Catholic splendour and loyalty." The Tempests were largely interested in coal-mining at Stella and the neighbourhood.

The Widdringtons received their surname from a fine old castle at Widdrington, which stood in a large beautiful park of six hundred acres, eight miles north-east of Morpeth. Widdrington was long the seat of a family of that name, who had often signalised themselves by their valour in the wars against the Scots. Sir William Widdrington was expelled from the House of Commons in 1642, for refusing to attend it, and for raising forces for the defence of Charles I., who created him Baron Widdrington of Blankney in 1643. After the Battle of Marston Moor, he fled beyond the seas, and his estates were sequestered by Parliament. Lord Widdrington returned to Britain along with Prince Charles in 1650, and accompanied him on his march from Edinburgh to Carlisle, where he was proclaimed King of England. At Wigan, in Lancashire, he was left behind with the Earl of Derby and several other gentlemen, with about two hundred horse. But Lord Derby was surprised next day by a superior force under Major General Lilbourne, and after a short encounter, they were all either slain or taken prisoners. Among the killed was Lord Widdrington, who had so loyally and gallantly fought for the two Stuart kings. Lord Widdrington was succeeded by William, Lord Widdrington, who was one of the Council of State entrusted with the executive power by the "Rump Parliament," previous to its dissolution by General Monk in 1660. This nobleman was succeeded by his son William, Lord Widdrington, who, as we have seen, married in 1700 Jane, the daughter of Sir Thomas Tempest of Stella, at which place he resided for sixteen years.

In the year 1715, Lord Widdrington joined the Earl of Derwentwater and Mr. Forster in the first Jacobite Rebellion, which had for its object the restoration of the family of Stuart to the throne. Those who favoured the rising were principally old families of rank in the north and west of England, and in Scotland. It was only in the north of England that the English Jacobites presented in any degree a formidable appearance. Attended by a number of retainers, the Earl of Derwentwater met Mr. Forster, with a few followers, at a place called Green Rig, on the top of a hill in the parish of Birtley, North Tyne. Next morning they proceeded to Warkworth, where they were joined by Lord Widdrington. Forster was now made commander-in-chief, not for any military skill that he possessed, but because he was a Protestant, it being considered unwise to select a Catholic to fill that position. From Warkworth the insurgents marched to Alnwick, where they proclaimed James III. Proceeding to Morpeth, they were joined at Felton Bridge by seventy horse from the Scottish border, so that they now amounted to three hundred, the highest number which they ever attained. At this critical juncture the Corporation of Newcastle evinced their loyalty and attachment to the House of Hanover by embodying the militia and train bands, and placing the town in a state of defence. This action on the part of the Corporation was a severe disappointment to the insurgents. Sir William Blackett at that time represented Newcastle in Parliament; he was extensively engaged in the coal trade, was a large employer of labour, and one of the best known men in the north of England. The Jacobites regarded Sir William as being favourable to their project, and on this account expected an easy capture of the town. And to add to the disappointment of the insurgents, the Earl of Scarborough, lord lieutenant of the county of Northumberland, entered Newcastle, accompanied by his friends and the neighbouring gentry, with their tenantry, all mounted and well armed. A body of seven hundred volunteers were raised for the immediate protection of the town; and the keelmen, who, with the rest of the loyal inhabitants, had signed an article of association for mutual defence, offered an additional guard of seven hundred men, to be ready at half an hour's notice. A battalion of foot, and part of a regiment of dragoons who arrived during these military preparations, completed the garrison. Not only were the inhabitants of Newcastle loyal to the House of Hanover, but the owners of Ravensworth, Gibside and Axwell espoused the same cause, which compelled the insurgents to retire to Hexham, where they proclaimed King James, nailing the proclamation to the market-cross, where it was allowed to remain several days after they had left the town.

In the meantime the Jacobites in the south-west of Scotland had also risen in insurrection, and placing Viscount Kenmure, a Protestant nobleman, at their head, proposed by a sudden effort to possess themselves of the town of Dumfries; but finding that he could not with a handful of cavalry obtain possession of the town, he resolved to unite his forces with those of his Northumberland allies, and with that object he proceeded through Hawick and Jedburgh, over the border to Rothbury, where the junction was effected.

Intelligence of this rising in the south of Scotland and in the north of England, having reached the Earl of Mar, he was urged to quit Perth, for the purpose of effecting a junction with the forces of the south; it being considered essential to the success of the insurrection, that considerable detachments of Mar's army should be sent to strengthen the cause in the south; and it was arranged that two thousand five hundred men under Brigadier Mackintosh of Borlum, should attempt the exploit of eluding the English squadron of observation in the Forth, and march southward.

The main body of the insurgents entered England on the 1st of November, and passed the night at the small town of Brampton, about nine miles east of Carlisle, where they proclaimed the Chevalier with the usual ceremonies. Here also Mr. Forster opened his commission as their general, which had been sent to him by the Earl of Mar. The force under Mr. Forster at this period consisted of only nine hundred Highlanders, and about six hundred Northumbrian and Dumfriesshire horsemen. Mr. Forster pushed through Appleby and Kendal, to Kirkby Lonsdale, and afterwards to Lancaster and Preston. · Here he was joined by several Roman Catholic gentlemen, who brought with them their servants and tenantry, to the number of twelve hundred men.

In the meantime, General Willis had collected the royal forces which were quartered at Manchester and Wigan, and advanced to Preston, to give the insurgents battle. For some reason, which it is impossible to reconcile either with common sense or military experience, Forster had neglected to defend a most important post, the bridge over the Ribble, by which road alone the enemy could have reached him; and drawing his men into the centre of the town, contented himself with causing barricades to be formed in the principal streets. General Willis attacked the insurgents at two different points of their temporary defences. The attack is described as a highly spirited one; but they were received with at least equal gallantry; and night shortly afterwards setting in, the royalists were compelled to withdraw, after having suffered considerable loss. The slight success, however, obtained by the insurgents, proved but of little service to them. Early the following morning General Carpenter, who had followed them by forced marches from the south of Scotland, made his appearance with a reinforcement of three regiments of dragoons: immediately the town was invested on all sides; and it became evident to the besieged that further opposition was out of the question. The Highlanders expressed their determination to sally out, sword in hand, and cut their way through the King's troops; but with some difficulty they were prevailed upon to listen to the arguments of their leaders; and accordingly, the whole of the insurgent force laid down their arms and surrendered themselves at discretion. Among the persons of note who fell into the hands of the government, in consequence of the surrender at Preston, were Lords Derwentwater, Widdrington, Nithisdale, Wintoun, Carnwath, Kenmure, and Nairn, besides several members of the first families in the north of England. The noblemen and principal leaders of the insurrection were sent prisoners to London, and after having been led through the streets pinioned as malefactors, were committed either to the Tower or to Newgate. The common men were imprisoned chiefly in the gaols of Liverpool or Manchester. About a month after their arrival, they were severally impeached of high treason.

On Lord Widdrington being asked what he had to say, why

judgment should not be passed upon him according to law, he replied:—"My lords, I have abandoned all manner of defence ever since I first surrendered myself to his Majesty's royal clemency, and only now beg leave to repeat to your lordships some circumstances of my unhappy case. You see before you an unfortunate man, who after leading a private and retired life for many years, has by one rash and inconsiderate action, exposed himself and his family to the greatest calamity and misery, and is now upon the point of receiving the severest sentence directed by any of our English laws. I do protest to your lordships that I was never privy to any concerted measures against his Majesty's royal person or the established government. As to the insurrection in Northumberland, I only heard of it accidentally the night before it happened; and being soon after informed that all my neighbours and acquaintances had met in arms, a crowd of confused and mistaken notions hurried me at once into a precipitate resolution of joining them—a resolution which I must own, I could never since calmly reflect upon, without part of that confusion I find myself under in the public acknowledgment of so much rashness and folly. After thus plunging out of my depth, as unprepared for such an enterprise as the action was unpremeditated, I cannot for my own particular, upon the strictest recollection, charge myself with any violation of the principles of my fellow-subjects; but on the contrary, I always endeavoured to encourage humanity and moderation during the whole course of our miserable expedition; and in order to make the best atonement in my power for the great fault I have been guilty of, I can justly say that I was in no small degree instrumental in procuring a general submission to his Majesty. . . . . I have only to add my most solemn assurance before this august assembly, that no future time will ever find me wanting in the most inviolable duty and gratitude to that merciful prince who gives me my life, and restores a father to five miserable and distressed orphans; and I shall always retain the highest esteem and veneration for your lordships and the honourable House of Commons."

Lord Widdrington was correct when in his statement of defence he declared that he was "in no small degree instrumental in procuring a general submission to his Majesty," for it was at the instigation of Lord Widdrington and a few others, that Colonel Oxburgh went to the English general to ask terms of surrender.

On the 9th February, 1716, Earl Cowper sentenced the prisoners in the old fashion, namely:—"That you, James, Earl of Derwentwater; William, Lord Widdrington; William, Earl of Nithisdale; Robert, Earl of Carnwath; William, Viscount Kenmure; William, Lord Nairn; and every one of you, return to the prison of the Tower from which you came; thence you must be drawn to the place of execution, when there you must be hanged by the neck—not till you be dead; for you must be cut down alive, then your bowels taken out and burned before your faces. Your heads must be severed from your bodies, and your bodies divided into four quarters, to be at the king's disposal. And God Almighty be merciful to your souls." After the sentence was passed, the prisoners were removed to the Tower. Lord Derwentwater and Lord Kenmure were executed on the 24th of February, 1716. Lord Nithisdale and Lord Wintoun escaped, and Lord Widdrington was reprieved. The estates of Lord Widdrington, worth about £12,000 per annum, were confiscated; but the estates of Stella and Stanley were restored to him in the year 1733. After living many years in retirement, he died at Bath in 1745. According to all accounts, Lord Derwentwater held Lord Widdrington in high esteem, declaring "my Lord Widdrington was a man of greater experience than himself, and thought a wise man by most people, therefore could serve his king and country better than he (Lord Derwentwater) could." Patten, the historian of the Rebellion, says of Widdrington, "I never could discover anything like boldness or bravery in him;" but the writer of the Jacobite melody, "Lord Derwentwater's Good Night," describes Derwentwater as saying:—

"Then fare thee well, brave Widdrington."

Unlike his great grand-father—Lord Widdrington, who gallantly fell in the cause of Charles I. at Wigan Lane—the owner of Stella was no soldier; but the little that is known of him marks him as pious, charitable, and honourable.

The eldest son of the attainted Lord Widdrington, Henry Francis Widdrington, succeeded to the estates of Stella and Stanley, which were his mother's inheritance. Deprived of his paternal estate and his hereditary honours, but commonly known as Lord Widdrington, he led a long life of peace in obscurity, and dying at Turnham Green in the year 1772, was buried in St. Pancras, London. By his will he left the Stella estate first to Thomas Eyre, of Hassop, Esq., and his heirs male. Thomas Eyre died without heirs male on March 26th, 1792, and the estate became the property of Edward T. S. Standish of Standish, Esq., who also died without heirs, on March 27th, 1807, when Stella fell to John Towneley of Towneley, who died on May 14th, 1813, and was succeeded by his son, Peregrine Towneley, who died on December 31st, 1846. Charles Towneley, the eldest son of Peregrine, held the estate till his death on November 14th, 1876, leaving three daughters. Charles was succeeded by his brother John Towneley, who died on February 21st, 1878. John Towneley had a son Richard, who did not live to enjoy the estates, and for some time they were held by the widow of John Towneley. Afterwards a private Act of Parliament, called the "Towneley Estate Act," was passed, which apportioned the Lancashire estates to the daughters of Charles Towneley; and those in Yorkshire and Durham to the daughters of John Towneley.

Theresa Harriet Mary, daughter of John Towneley, is the wife of John Delacour, of Thorneyholme, county of York; Lucy Evelyn, the wife of Lieut.-Colonel John Murray of Polmaise, in the county of Stirling; Mary Elizabeth Towneley, of Namur, in the kingdom of Belgium, unmarried; and Mabel Anne, the wife of the right honourable Lewis Henry Hugh, Baron Clifford, of Chudleigh, in the county of Devon.

STELLA HALL.

This fine old mansion, the residence of Joseph Cowen, Esq., is pleasantly situated at the east end of Stella village. It occupies the site of the old Nunnery, which fell into disuse at the Suppression of the Monasteries. Erected by the Tempests of Newcastle—a mercantile branch of the ancient house of Holmeside—the Hall is built in that style of architecture which prevailed in the reign of Queen Elizabeth. It is in the form of a cross, and consists of centre, east and west wings, and a range of rooms on the north side. The house was considerably altered at the end of the last century, the alterations including the removal

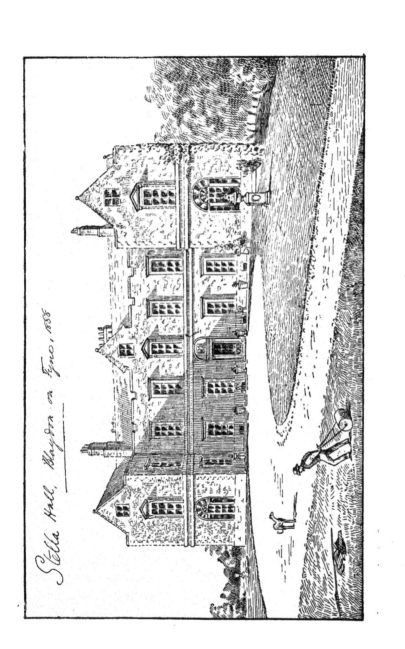
Stella Hall, Blaydon on Tyne, 1885.

of several of the Elizabethan windows, and the insertion of the present ones. Payne, who designed Axwell Hall, Bradley Hall, and Gibside Chapel, superintended the alteration of the structure Other alterations were made in 1840, under the direction of Mr. John Dobson, architect. Over the principal entrance, on the south side, are the arms of the Tempests. Argent: a bend engrailed between six martlets, sable; Crest: on a wreath, a martlet, sable. Under the arms is the following Latin inscription: CONIVIGIO INSIGNI MANIBVS, COGNOMINE, CORDE, VT LAPIDI LAPIS, EST FEMINA IVNCTA VIRO. Translation: By a noteworthy union—a union of hand, name, and heart—a woman is as closely united to her husband as is a stone set to a stone.

The Entrance Hall extends the whole length of the building between the east and west wings. It was in this spacious apartment that Lord Widrington entertained his friends and servants to breakfast on the morning of their departure to join the Earl of Derwentwater and General Forster, in the ill-fated Rebellion of 1715. The Library is on the ground-floor of the east wing, and contains many rare and costly volumes. The walls are adorned with portraits of a number of remarkable men, including Cromwell and Milton, Mazzini, Orsini, Garibaldi, and Lincoln. There is in one of the windows of the Library, a portrait in stained glass, of the late Dr. Rutherford. The west wing contains a handsome Drawing Room, from the windows of which a beautiful view of the Park may be obtained.

One of the original features of the Hall is the old domestic chapel, which was used for public worship until the erection of the present Catholic chapel at Stella, in 1831.

The Dining Room contains several fine portraits of the Cowen family, including a painting of the late Sir Joseph Cowen by Mr. H. H. Emmerson, presented to Sir Joseph by the inhabitants of Blaydon, and portraits of the late Mrs. Cowen, Mr. Joseph Cowen, Mr. Joseph Cowen, junr., and Miss Jane Cowen. An old painting of Lord Widdrington, as well as a great number of valuable and interesting pictures, adorn the walls of the Hall. There are on the Stair-walls pieces of old tapestry; one of which represents "Hero and Leander," and another, "The Voyage of the Argosy in search of the Golden Fleece." The latter is considered to be one of the finest pieces of tapestry in England.

The Hall fronts a park comprising about twenty-one acres, which is pleasantly diversified with rising grounds and clumps of trees.

Formerly the park wall enclosed Image Hill, five acres; and Summer-house Hill, thirty-three acres. The principal entrance was at Peth-head. Two images, representing Apollo and Æsculapius, once stood on Image Hill; these interesting relics of a bygone time are now preserved near the hall. The old summer-house of the Widdringtons still stands on the hill which bears its name; but for many years it has ceased to answer its original purpose. A figure of Garibaldi, placed there by the late Mr. Robert Eadie of Blaydon, stands on the north side of the summer-house. Part of Summer-house Hill has, for a number of years, been used by the people of Blaydon and Stella, as a recreation ground.

The gardens connected with Stella Hall, which are large and well sheltered, are on the west side; and the stables are on the north side of the house.

There is in the park an old oak, said to be a remnant of the forest which formerly extended from Newcastle to Hexham.

The Battle of Stella Haughs.

In 1637, King Charles I. and Archbishop Laud endeavoured to force on Scotland the religious service of the Church of England. A riot took place in St. Giles's Church, Edinburgh, when the minister began to read the printed service, and all Scotland was in a state of excitement.

In 1638, Scottish nobles, gentry, ministers and citizens joined in signing the Covenant, in which they agreed to help each other in preventing religious changes in Scotland. At the end of the same year, a General Assembly at Glasgow declared that there must be no bishops in Scotland, no High Commission Court, and no liturgy, or printed form of service.

War then arose between England and Scotland, and Charles went to Berwick; but want of money soon forced him to disband his army. At last, in April, 1640, Charles was obliged to call a new Parliament. The Commons would grant him no money in taxes, until his evil rule was amended. Thereupon the King dissolved the Parliament in anger; and a riot arose in London, the people attacking Laud's palace at Lambeth. Soon after this, a mob forced its way into St. Paul's Cathedral, and drove off in terror the High Commission Court, which never sat again.

On the 21st August, 1640, the Scots crossed the river Tweed, in order, as they said, "to lay their most humble and loving petition, for the redress of grievances, at the royal feet of their most sacred sovereign," Charles I. Upon the arrival of the Scots on the English border, the soldiers were commended by their ministers in prayer to the care of the Lord of Hosts; and then—for the purpose of obtaining forage for their horses, and the droves of cattle and sheep which they carried along with them out of Scotland—they divided the army into three bodies, one under the command of L. Almond, the Lieutenant-General; another was led by Major-General Baillie; and General Leslie brought up the rear. They kept all within sight, or ten miles from one another; and, after a slow march through Northumberland, they met by appointment on Newcastle Moor, on the 26th of August. From thence the committee wrote two letters, one to the commander-in-chief of the army at Newcastle, and another to the mayor and aldermen. These letters they sent by the drum-major of Lord Montgomery's brigade, but they were sent back unopened. Whereupon the army turned to the right, and encamped beside Newburn, on the north side of the Tyne, on August 27th. Rushworth, in his "Historical Collections," states that, "On the 27th of August (1640), in the forenoon, his majesty received intelligence from the Lord Conway, that the Scots would that night be near Newcastle with their army, craving his majesty's pleasure and directions about the disposing of his army to the interruption of the march of the Scots.

"The king immediately called the gentry of Yorkshire, then at York, together, to wait upon his majesty, to whom the Earl of Strafford made a speech; presently after he prepared a packet to be sent post to the Lord Conway, then understanding the Scots were come near Newcastle; and the author of these 'Collections' being newly come post from London to York, and hearing a packet was about to be sent to Newcastle, took the opportunity to bear the messenger company therewith; but when the author and the messenger with the packet came to Newcastle, upon the 28th of August, in the morning, they were informed that the Lord

Conway was gone to the main army, near Newburn, whither we went immediately, and found the Lord Conway and the field-officers at a council of war at Stella, half a mile distant from the army, and delivered the Lord Conway the packet, which, being opened, it contained special orders to prepare the army for an engagement with the Scots."

The council of war would probably be held in Stella Hall. A few years ago, a thatched cottage stood nearly opposite to the Catholic chapel, in which tradition states that the officers of the royalist army under Conway stopped the night before the battle. The dwelling was a public house, containing three rooms—one large room and two smaller ones. It would be in the large room that the gallant cavaliers spent the night in riot and drinking. The estimated number of the Scots army was 20,000 foot and 2,500 horse. According to Rushworth, the number of the English was 3,000 foot, and 1,500 horse. Baillie fixes the number of the English at 4,000 or 5,000 foot, and 2,500 horse.

Stella Haughs, the scene of the battle, is about a mile long from east to west, and four hundred yards from the river to the hill-side at Hedgefield, where the English cannon were placed. Formerly the Haughs, on account of the Tyne frequently overflowing its banks, consisted almost entirely of marshy or boggy land. In a plan of Stella, dated 1779, about ten acres at the east end of the Haughs are named "The Hassocks," from the ground producing nothing but rushes. The river was crossed by four fords: the Cromwell, at the northern bend of the river, at the east end of the Haughs, received its name from the Protector crossing the river at this point when marching to Dunbar in 1650. About four hundred yards west of the Cromwell ford was the Kelso ford, which was seldom used, on account of the depth of the river even at low tide.

There were two other fords at the west end of Stella Haughs, one about forty yards on the west of the old "Alnwick House"—which is still standing; and the other where the Newburn Bridge crosses the river. These were undoubtedly the two fords by which the Scots crossed the river to attack the English. In the field on the south side of the "Alnwick House," are the remains of an old waggon way, which have been regarded by some people as erections to protect the English soldiers from the Scots cannon. In the plan of Stella (1779), the rising ground at Hedgefield, on the west side of Addison colliery, is named "The Forts," where in all probability the English placed their cannon. The "Forts" are directly opposite to the two fords at the west end of the Haughs, and at a distance of four hundred yards from the river. Here the English raised two batteries, one opposite to each ford, and set about five hundred musketeers, with four pieces of cannon, to defend each battery, and thereby stop the passage of the Scots, if they should attempt to cross the river; and the rest of their forces were drawn up in a meadow, at the foot of a hill, nearly a mile behind them, probably on the rising ground behind Hedgefield church. On the north side of the river lay the Scots army, and the ground on that side being higher than on the south, they had the advantage of seeing the exact position of the English trenches, and by the help of the houses in Newburn, and of the trees and shrubs, to plant their cannon directly opposite to them without being discovered. While the two parties were thus stationed, the Earl of Strafford sent an express to Lord Conway, acquainting him of his near approach with the rear of the king's army, and ordering him to gather the rest of the army together, and to prepare for an engagement. But before this order could be put in execution, a change of affairs was occasioned by a slight incident. A Scottish officer watering his horse in the river, an English soldier seeing him fix his eyes on their trenches, shot him; and he falling from his horse, the Scots musketeers fired upon the English, and their cannon— especially some which they had placed upon the steeple of Newburn church, fired with so much success upon the English trenches, that, immediately, the soldiers placed in them were greatly disordered: about twenty of them were killed, and notwithstanding the bravery of Colonel Lunsford, who commanded there, the rest could hardly be restrained from flying. Burnett says that the cannon were made of bar-iron, hooped like a barrel with cords and wet raw hides. They were carried on horse-back, and bore several discharges. Several cannon balls have been found at Newburn; one found about two years ago, imbedded in a beam of timber, is three inches in diameter, and weighs three pounds. By this time it was low water, and Sir Thomas Hope the younger, of Craighill, having the van of the horse, was ordered to march through the river with his troop, consisting all of gentlemen, members of the College of Justice, commonly called "the General's life-guards;" and, to support these, passed also Colonel David Leslie, with four troops of his own and a troop of Sir Patrick Mc.Ghie's, who pursued the English with great success, and made every man prisoner who had the courage to abide by the batteries. The rest fled towards their main body, till they came to a narrow pass, where they rallied. The narrow pass was probably the bridle path which at that time led from Ryton to Blaydon, and which afterwards became the present Hexham turnpike. Sir Thomas Hope's troop being still in the van, encountered the English with great bravery, and, being well supported by Colonel Leslie, bore down all before them; but, pursuing their advantage too far, they were in hazard of being cut off: for no less than twelve troops of the best horse the English had, were by this time come up to support their foot, and the rest of the forces were fast advancing (probably by the old Blaydon road), which, General Leslie perceiving, he sent up Colonels Ramsay and Blair with six troops of horse and one thousand musketeers to their relief, with orders to retire, if forced to it, under the protection of the Scots cannon, till a sufficient number of foot were got up to support them. The English horse, not attending sufficiently to the Scots cannon, ventured too far, and received two or three smart fires, which threw them into great disorder, and obliged them to retire in the utmost confusion, for the assistance of the main body. The whole of the Scots army now marched to the scene of the battle; but by the time the brigades commanded by Lords Lowdoun, Lindsay, Queensberry and Montgomery, who were in the van of the foot, had joined the horse, the battle was ended, and the English had thrown down their arms and retired in great disorder. The foot retreated up Ryton and Stella banks, to a wood not far off, and their horse, covering the retreat, were considerably worsted, a number of them being killed, and many taken prisoners. The wood was probably near to Stargate. Tradition states that when the Scots reached this place, that on account of the steepness of the hill which they had to climb in pursuing the English, they were "staw'd" of the engagement; hence "Stawgate," *staw* in the north country signifying more than enough of anything.

"In this engagement," says Rushworth, "Cornet Potter, son of

Endymion Potter of the bed-chamber, was slain, and during the whole fight about sixty men more, as the Scots told us after the cessation of arms was agreed unto, for the Scots buried the dead; and afterwards they further told us that most of them that were killed lay about the works; how many of the Scots were slain we know not." After the retreat of the English, Lord Conway called a council of war at Newcastle, and it was there resolved at twelve at night, that the whole army should retreat to Durham, horse, and foot, and train of artillery, and to quit Newcastle. Tradition has it that part of the English army rested in the church lands at Whickham, and in the fields adjoining, and that before leaving they fired their tents; this fire communicated with a small seam of coal, which burned for several years, and at night flames issued from different parts of the village and grounds adjoining. This tradition is supported by the fact that a stratum of calcined stones and earth extends from the east end of Whickham to the west end, and for about one hundred yards on the north side of the village.

The day after the English army left Newcastle, the Scots entered the town by the bridge, where the General with his life-guards, the Lieutenant-General, and a considerable number of the committee, and several other nobles and barons, with Sir William Douglas and his troop were heartily received by the mayor and aldermen, after which they went to St. Nicholas' church and heard a sermon by Mr. Alexander Henderson.

This defeat of the English army produced the greatest consternation on the south side of the Tyne. "The parsons of Rye (Ryton) and of Whickham, first rifled their own houses and then fled, leaving nothing but a few play books and pamphlets, and one old cloake, with an old woman, being the only living Christian in the towne; the rest being fled."

The Bishopric was ordered to pay a fine of £350 a day so long as the Scots remained. Before this heavy exaction the people fled in dismay, so that not one house in ten was occupied. The county suffered equally from the ravages of the troops, and from the attempts of the Royalists to prevent them from obtaining food. An order was made that the upper millstones were to be taken away, and buried, so that the Scots might not be able to grind their corn. When the Scots withdrew their forces, the Bishopric was saddled with a payment of £25,000.

Blaydon Races, which commenced in 1861, and which were held for a few years on the Island, have, since 1864, been held on Stella Haughs.

CROMWELL AT STELLA.

On June 29th, 1650, Oliver Cromwell left London to march into Scotland, where he was to meet General Leslie, who defeated the English under Lord Conway on Stella Haughs, in 1640.

On July 15th, the main army of Cromwell was at Newcastle. For two days the army had rested at Whickham. The cannon and heavy baggage had been sent round by Clockburn Lane, and after fording the Derwent at Winlaton Mill, and advancing by the Birk Gate to Winlaton and Stella, crossed the Tyne at the bend of the river at the east end of Stella Haughs, and met the Protector with his main army on the north side of the Tyne. The ford by which part of the army crossed the river is still called "the Cromwell." On July 22nd, Cromwell crossed the Tweed, and on September 3rd he met the veteran Leslie at Dunbar, where the Scotch were defeated, 4,000 being killed, and above 10,000 taken prisoners.

Meldon old water corn-mill stood at the foot of the Temple Bank, a little within the west wall of the park, and about one hundred yards below the dam or weir-head of the present mill. Here, according to the statement of Mr. Ralph Nixon, a respectable and intelligent man, whose ancestors for several generations resided in the vicinity of Meldon, Oliver Cromwell tarried and fed his troops of horse, on his return from Scotland in 1651. If we suppose the tradition to be founded on truth, this occurrence must have taken place on the 11th of August, the day on which the lord-general left the manor house of Netherwitton; for on the 12th he crossed the Tyne at Newburn, and proceeded forthwith to encamp his forces on the haugh below Ryton, himself withdrawing to Stella Hall, where he resided previous to his departure southward for Worcester.—*Richardson.* Among the accounts of the Corporation of Newcastle there is the following entry:—" 1651, Paid for a present to the Lord-General Cromwell when he was at Stella, £50."

STELLA HOUSE.

This house stands at the east end of Stella, and at the bottom of what is known as the old Leadgate. It is two storeys high, with projecting attic windows. It was built about the beginning of the eighteenth century, and was evidently smaller at one time than it is now, as the ends of the house appear to be of a more modern date than the centre. It was probably erected for the accommodation of one of the managers at the staiths. At one time it was the residence of the Silvertop family. Robert Edington, who wrote in 1813, "A Treatise on the Coal Trade, with Strictures on its Abuses, and Hints for Amelioration," says:—
" On the east side of Stella, close adjoining to the river, facing the rising sun, is the seat of the late George Silvertop, Esq. From its beautiful situation the keelmen call it by the name of the 'Rising Sun.' He was one of the leading coal owners of his day, was of extensive knowledge and of strict honour and integrity; he had travelled and had been introduced to all the foreign courts of Europe, was so much respected that his famous Whitefield coals had the preference of all other collieries on the continent. By his industry he had accumulated an ample fortune honourably got." The Silvertops lived at Ryton in the sixteenth century. There is the following entry in the parish register :— "1608, April 17th. Anne Silvertop, widdow, of Ryton towne [bur.]." The family seems to have left the village of Ryton about that time, and removed to Stella.

William Silvertop of Stella, married Ann Galley. They had a son, Albert Silvertop, born February 16th, 1667. The Ryton parish register contains the following entry :—"William Silvertop of Bladen, and 17 more, buried 28th May, 1682. These 18 were drowned 28th May, 1682." This William Silvertop, who may have removed to Blaydon after his marriage, was probably the father of Albert. Albert Silvertop married Mary, the daughter of Joseph Dunn of Blaydon. He died in 1738, and left a son, George Silvertop, born 22nd February, 1705, who married Bridget, daughter of Henry Whittingham of Whittingham Hall, Lancashire. He purchased the estate of Minsteracres, built the Hall, and founded a mission on the estate in 1766, for the use of the family. He was succeeded by his only son, John Silvertop, who married in 1777, Catherine, second daughter of Sir Henry Lawson of Brough Hall, Yorkshire, by whom he had issue—first, George Silvertop, born January 6th, 1775; second, John, who died young; third, Henry, born 28th May, 1779, married Elizabeth, daughter of Thomas Witham, Esq., niece and heiress of William Witham of Cliffe, Ebor, Esq., on which he assumed the name of Witham, and had a numerous offspring; fourth, Charles, born 16th January, 1781, colonel in the Spanish service; fifth, Mary, died young.

George Silvertop visited Napoleon at Elba, and it was partly on account of a conversation that Silvertop had with Napoleon that the latter was induced to quit the place of his imprisonment. O'Meara, in his "Voice from St. Helena," says, " He (Silvertop) visited Napoleon at Elba, and in the course of conversation related that he had dined a few weeks before with the Duke de Fleury, with whom he had a conversation relative to the sum of money to be allowed the exile annually by France, according to the agreement that had been signed by the ministers of the allied powers. The Duke laughed at him for supposing for a moment that it would be complied with, and said they were not such fools. 'This,' said that extraordinary man, Napoleon, 'was one of the reasons which induced me to quit Elba.'" George Silvertop thus was an indirect factor in bringing about the Battle of Waterloo, for had Napoleon not been induced to quit Elba, the famous struggle at Waterloo would not have taken place. It was George Silvertop who invited John Graham Lough to his beautiful mansion at Minsteracres, and showed him several works of art by Michael Angelo and Canova. Those art treasures were probably the first that Lough saw, and no doubt would produce a powerful impression on the mind of the young sculptor. George Silvertop died on the 20th February, 1849, and was buried at Ryton. No member of the Silvertop family resides at present in the township of Ryton.

Stella House, in the year 1828, was the residence of Edward Emerson, iron founder. Afterwards it was occupied by Thomas Young Hall, mining engineer, and subsequently by Mr. Joseph Cowen, late M.P. for Newcastle-on-Tyne. At present it is the residence of Mr. Joseph Roberts.

The Coal Trade.

Coals were extensively worked at Stella and the neighbourhood, at an early period in the history of coal-mining. Stella, lying alongside of the river, was suitable for the erection of staiths, to which the coals were carried from Winlaton, Ryton, Kyo, Crawcrook, &c., which has made the village for centuries an active hive of industry. Taylor, in his "Archæology of the Coal Trade," says:—"Among the documents in my possession, on the subject of the coal trade, I find a lease from (2 Eliz.) to Nicholas Tempest, of coal mines in Stella, which is called Stelley of Stellington. In this deed, sufficient way-leave and stay-leave are granted, with power to lead away the coals by all kinds of carriages. In the year 1622, the four principal coal owners have the following output:—Sir Nicholas Tempest, 600 tens; Mr. Charles Tempest, 140 tens; Mr. Thomas Tempest, 900 tens; Sir George Selby, 750 tens." To ascertain the value of a ten, we will again have recourse to Taylor. He says:—"I find in a lease, Tempest to Emerson, 1684, a ten specified to be 'forty fothers,' each fother a wainload containing seven bolls and one bushel of coals, at the pit, Newcastle usual coal measure." A ten was equivalent to about twenty-two chaldrons. The price of a chaldron in 1622 was seven shillings, so that the price received by Sir Nicholas Tempest of Stella Hall, for his 600 tens, was £4,620. We find from the "Compleat Collier," a clear account of the state of coal-mining in the latter part of the 17th century. There were then no underground railways or horses, the coals being dragged to the bottom of the pit by one or two persons, in corves placed on sledges. The coals were drawn up the pits by horses in a whin-gin, and in a pit of forty fathoms deep, eight horses were required every day to draw twenty-one scores of coal (about ninety tons), in corves made of hazel-rods with wooden bolts, carrying fourteen or fifteen pecks each. From a pay-bill in the possession of the writer, the wages received by the workmen at Stella Grand Lease Colliery, in the year 1740, are stated.

Sir Henry Liddell, Bart., and Partners.
Charge of Working, August, 1740.

Hewing 30 scores at 6d. per score	£0 15	0
Putting ditto at 6d. per ditto ...	0 15	0

		£	s	d
Bearing 30 scores at 12d. per hund	...	0	6	0
Drawing ditto at 10d. per ditto	...	0	5	0
Horsedriver at 4d. per day	...	0	2	0
Shoveller per week	...	0	1	6
Smith per day	...	0	1	0
Under Overman per ditto	...	0	1	0
Corver, for making 3 corfs and mending ...	...	0	2	2
To burning 6 sacks cinders at 1½d.	...	0	0	9
To ½ lb. soap for Ginn ...	...	0	0	3
		£2	9	8
Paid G. Russell for bringing 10,000 corf rods from Teasbank and getting them out of ye wood, last year		0	13	0
		£3	2	8

In 1582, Queen Elizabeth obtained a ninety-nine years' lease of the manors and royalties of Gateshead, Whickham, Winlaton, Ryton, and Stella, at the yearly rent of ninety pounds, from the Bishop of Durham. The Queen, however, soon after, transferred it to the Earl of Leicester, who afterwards assigned it to his secretary, Thomas Sutton, the founder of the Charter House. Sutton again, in consideration of £12,000, transferred it to Henry Anderson and William Selby. This lease, known as the Grand Lease, was apportioned among the Society of Hostmen, for the benefit of the town, and was the fruitful source of contention in after years. While Sutton held it, the price of coal in London was six shillings a chaldron; on its assignment to the Corporation, they ran the price to eight shillings. In 1590, the current price in London was advanced to nine shillings, upon which the Lord Mayor complained to the treasurer, Burleigh, against the town of Newcastle; setting forth that the Society of Free Hosts consisted of about sixty persons, who had consigned their right of the Grand Lease to about eighteen or twenty, who engrossed the collieries at Stella, Ravensworth, Newburn, &c., and therefore requested that the whole of these might be opened and the price fixed at a maximum of seven shillings a chaldron. Such is the early history of the Grand Lease. The name is still retained by the Stella Coal Company, and is now applied to about five thousand acres of royalty, which they hold from the sub-lessees of the Bishop of Durham and the Ecclesiastical Commissioners. There are now five collieries belonging to the Stella Coal Company: the Emma Pit, sunk in 1845; the Stargate Pit, sunk in 1800; the Addison, sunk in 1864; the Blaydon Main, purchased in 1884; and the Clara Ville, sunk in 1893. The seams at present worked are the Towneley, Stone Coal, Five Quarter, and Brockwell. The Stella Coal Company became proprietors of the Stella and Towneley Collieries in 1837, when they succeeded the previous proprietors, Messrs. Dunn, John Buddle, and T. Y. Hall, Alderman Addison Potter, Humble Lamb, R. T. Atkinson, and others.

STAITHS.

In the account of the purchase of coals at Winlaton by the King, in 1367, the coals were conveyed in keels and boats from Winlaton to Newcastle. The coals would, in all probability, be carried in wains, or in panniers, over the backs of horses to Stella, and there transferred to the "boats and keels," which had to convey them to Newcastle.

John Buddle, Esq., the father of the late John Buddle, had in his possession a manuscript containing the following passage :— "It also appears that from the year 1409, demises by copy of Court Roll remaining in the Exchequer of Durham, have been, from time to time, made by the Bishop of Durham, as lord of the Manor of Chester, to different persons, of the coal mines and coal pits in Ryton and Kyo Field, which is part of Ryton, for the working of sea-coal, or coal to be vended and exported by sea, with sufficient way leading from the pit to a staith granted to be made upon the River Tyne, within the lord's forest, by the view of the forester." This document does not mention the situation of the staith, but there is every reason for believing it would be at Stella. We may infer from this interesting document, that in the early part of the 15th century, the south side of the higher reaches of the Tyne was chiefly forest.

In a poem, "News from Newcastle," printed in 1651, celebrating the coal mines of Northumberland and Durham, there is the following couplet :—

STELLA CHAPEL.

> " Our staiths their mortgaged streets will soon divide
> Blathon own Cornewall, Stella share Cheapside."

Blaydon own *Cornhill* is probably intended by the writer. During the 17th and 18th centuries, several staiths were erected at Blaydon, but in the coal trade it never possessed the commercial importance that Stella did, and at the beginning of the present century the staiths at Blaydon fell into disuse. In the year 1749, there stood between Stella Burn mouth and the "Bogle Hole," a distance of only three hundred and thirty yards, the staiths belonging to Lord Widdrington, Mr. Morton and partners, Sir T. Clavering, Mrs. Newton, Sir W. Blackett, Mr. Jennison, Lionel Vane, Esq., Mr. Davison, Mr. Rodger, Mr. Snow, Mr. Emerson, and Miss Jenny Hunter. In the year 1784, a number of the staiths had disappeared. On the west side of the southern bend of the river, near to the present saw mills, was the Grand Moor staith, and eastward was the Whitefield staith. The west staiths have not only been abandoned, but even the water-course by which the keels were taken for coals, has been filled up. An old warehouse still marks the situation of the west staiths. There were three principal waggon ways by which the coals were taken to Stella. The Coalburns way brought the coals from Hedley Fell, Chopwell, and Coalburns. The Grand Lease, or Moor way, brought them from Ryton, Woodside, and the Bare (Bar) Moor. The Cowclose way brought them from the Strothers, Greenside and Cowclose. Another waggon way carried the coals from French's Close, Kyo, Bradley Moor, and Crawcrook, to the staiths on the side of the river opposite to Newburn. Another waggon way was that afterwards used in carrying the coals from the A, B, and C Pits to the Towneley staith. These coals bore the Whitefield "brand." All the coals of the Stella Coal Company are now sent by a private line of railway to the Addison Colliery, except those sent to the Stella staith. At the beginning of the present century, the river side from Dunston to Stella was lined with staiths, all of which have been abandoned, except one at Derwenthaugh and one at Stella.

Roman Catholic Chapel.

At the Dissolution of the Monasteries in 1540, the nunnery at Stella passed into the hands of the Tempests, who, however, appropriated a portion of Stella Hall to a Catholic church, and worship was uninterruptedly conducted there until the year 1831. A religious census of the inhabitants of Ryton parish was taken by the Rev. Jonathon Mirehouse, curate, on the 12th of September, 1780, when the number of " Papists " was 324. At another census, taken on the 2nd of July, 1788, the number had increased to 350.

In the year 1794, a number of the members of the English Catholic Secular College at Douay, who had been taken and imprisoned by the Republican army in the citadel of Dourlens, in Picardy, managed to effect their escape to England. Some of them took up their residence at Crook Hall, and others at Stella. They subsequently settled and founded a college at Crook Hall; Dr. Lingard, the historian, being the first professor of divinity, and vice-president. Crook Hall, in the course of a few years, was found too restricted for the increased establishment, and on the 19th July, 1808, Ushaw College, one of the most important of the Roman Catholic collegiate establishments in the county, was opened for their use.

The Rev. John Wilson was priest at Stella in the year 1715—the year of the first Rebellion; he was, along with many others, thrust into prison for being a Roman Catholic priest; but he was afterwards set at liberty, and returned to Stella, where he died. There is the following entry in the Ryton register :—"1725, June 25th. John Wilson, a Romish priest, Stella [bur.]." The Rev. N. Witham was the next priest, but in 1726 he resigned, and his place was filled by the Rev. N. Rogers, who also resigned in 1730. The Rev. N. Hutton was the next priest, but he remained only a few months.

For about two years the chapel at Stella was supplied by neighbouring pastors, when the Rev. Luke Wilson was appointed to this station in 1732. After staying a few years at Stella, he removed; and in 1737 the Rev. Thomas Greenwell, from the College of SS. Peter and Paul, Lisbon, took the superintendence of the worshippers at Stella; but in 1750 the Rev. J. Turner was invited by Lord Widdrington to Stella. At this time Mr. Greenwell seems to have formed a church at Blaydon, where he remained until his death. There is the following entry in the Ryton register :—"1753, August 26th. Mr. Thomas Greenwell, a Romish priest, Blaydon ——— Church [bur.]." Whoever inserted the entries in the registers at Ryton, seems to have looked upon the word

"Catholic" with horror, for we never at this time find it entered in the books. We find the words "Romish" and "Papist," but never the word "Catholic."

The Rev. J. Turner remained at Stella for about twenty-five years, when he was succeeded in 1775 by the Rev. Thomas Eyre, who remained at Stella until 1792. The Right Rev. Dr. Matthew Gibson, Bishop of Comana, and Vicar Apostolic of the Northern District, also officiated at Stella about this time. The local papers of the time report his death as taking place on the 17th May, 1790.

George Silvertop, Esq., died at Stella Hall, on March 11th, 1789, aged eighty-five years; and Edward Horsley Widdrington Riddell, on the 26th June, 1793.

The Rev. Thomas Eyre was succeeded, in 1793, by the Rev. William Hull, who continued missionary here till 1830, when being incapacitated to do the duty, was succeeded by the Rev. Thomas S. Witham, January 11th, 1830.

The Rev. Thomas Eyre, D.D., when chaplain at Stella, began to make arrangements for building a chapel, for which purpose he obtained a grant of £500 from Lady Mary Eyre, fifth daughter of Charlotte, Countess of Newborough, who died at Warkworth Castle, county of Northumberland, 27th August, 1798. The interest of this sum subsequently swelled the amount to £900. George Silvertop of Minsteracres, also subscribed £100 towards the building of the chapel; George Dunn of Newcastle, Esq., and his family, £230; Mrs. Dunn of Stella Hall, £100; Mr. William Dunn of Hedgefield House, Esq., £50, and Mrs. Dunn, £10; the Rev. William Hull, £50; besides a number of smaller subscriptions from Protestant gentlemen in the neighbourhood.

The chapel, which is dedicated to St. Mary and St. Thomas Aquinas, was opened on the 12th day of October, 1831, by Bishop Penswick. The chapel is built of stone, in the Early English and Later Gothic styles, consisting of nave, chancel, and a lady chapel. The chancel opens to the nave by a handsome decorated pointed arch, and is lighted above the altar by three lancets filled with stained glass; and the nave by single lancets, four of which on the west side, and two on the east side, are filled with stained glass. There is a gallery at the north end. Sittings are provided for about four hundred and fifty people. The entrance to the chapel is by a Decorated doorway on the west side. The Presbytery, which is at the north end, is fifty feet high, and embattled; it is lighted by a handsome window, mullioned and transomed, and forms a pleasant and convenient residence for the chaplain.

The old burial ground is on the east side of the chapel. A cross at the east end bears the date 1836. The present graveyard is on the west side, in the centre of which stands a handsome carved stone cross. On the south side of the church grounds is the school, which accommodates about one hundred and twenty.

The priests since 1840 have been the Rev. Vincent Joseph Eyre; 1845, Rev. Thomas Parker; 1847, Rev. Ralph Platt; 1857, Rev. Aisenius Watson; 1865, Rev. H. Wrenall.

THE COWENS.

The Cowens came from Lindisfarne, or Holy Island, to Stella. At what time they removed to the "Catholic" village on the Tyne, is uncertain, but it is supposed it was after the dissolution of the Monasteries that they took shelter under the wing of the Tempests at Stella Hall, where they were employed about the brewery connected with the house. Some time after Sir Ambrose Crowley established his ironworks at Winlaton, members of the Cowen family became workmen under the famous firm. John Cowen, born in 1774, and Mary, his wife, born in 1777, may be said to have lived for the greater part of their lives at Winlaton.

Joseph Cowen, afterwards Sir Joseph, was the son of John and Mary Cowen, and was born at Greenside, on the 10th of February, 1800. He served his apprenticeship to the trade of a chain maker, at Winlaton, where he continued to work until the period of middle life. He married Mary, the daughter of Anthony Newton of Winlaton, who was connected with one of the oldest families in the neighbourhood. While still a young man, Mr. Cowen took an active interest in all movements for the social improvement of his fellow workmen. On the formation of the Blacksmith's Friendly Society, in 1826, he was chosen secretary, a position which he held for many years, discharging its duties gratuitously. On January 1st, 1834, he was elected president of the society. The library established at Winlaton in 1819, also received Mr. Cowen's warm support. The books kept by Mr. Cowen while secretary of the Blacksmith's Friendly Society, are still preserved by the members.

Mr. Cowen was one of those stalwart reformers known in the North of England as "Crowley's Crew." At the great meeting held on the Newcastle Town Moor on October 11th, 1819, to condemn the Manchester Massacre, "Crowley's Crew" were there in strong force.

> As with hop, step, and jump,
> Through the town they did troop,

led on by the Winlaton Female Reformers. On that occasion the contingent from Winlaton was led by Mr. Joseph Cowen and Mr. Thomas Hodgson, the latter being one of the speakers at the meeting. In 1828, we find Mr. Cowen, along with his brother-in-law Mr. Anthony Forster, a manufacturer of fire bricks at Blaydon Burn, under the firm of Mr. Joseph Cowen and Company. He soon developed the resources of his business, while the superior quality of his clay secured for him an increased patronage. Gas retorts also became a speciality in the business, and at the International Exhibitions of 1851 and 1862, he was awarded prizes for the superiority of his bricks and other fire-clay goods. Gasworks were erected by the firm, who originally intended them for lighting their own manufactory alone, but at the request of the inhabitants of Blaydon, the firm extended their establishment, and on November 26th, 1853, the village was lighted with gas. Mr. Cowen was held in such high esteem by the people of Blaydon, that they presented him with a large portrait of himself, which now adorns the Dining Room at Stella Hall. In the year 1853, he was elected to the Municipal Council of Newcastle-upon-Tyne, and was afterwards invested with the civic honour of an alderman. In 1836, he was elected a Guardian for Winlaton, and for thirteen years he was Chairman of the Gateshead Board of Guardians. He was also a Justice of the Peace for the County of Durham. On the formation of the River Tyne Improvement Commission, in 1850, Mr. Cowen was appointed one of its life members, and for a period of twenty years, the Chairman of the Commission. The Commissioners have made the river the wonder and admiration of all beholders rom all quarters of the globe. They have straightened, widened, and deepened the river from Tynemouth to Hedwin Streams, a distance of nineteen miles, and the unsightly old bridges they have replaced by the present handsome structures. For the willing and valuable services rendered by Mr. Cowen in promoting the interests and developing the resources of Tyneside, he received the honour of knighthood, on March 14th, 1872. The following is a copy of the official notification of Her Majesty's intention :—

"10 Downing Street,
"Whitehall, Nov. 21st, 1871.

"Dear Mr. Cowen,—Allow me to tender you, with Her Majesty's approval, the honour of knighthood, in acknowledgment of the public service you have rendered, for so long a time, and with so much ability, as Chairman of the River Tyne Improvement Commission.

"If it be agreeable to you to accept this proposal, it will be very gratifying to me to have tendered it.—I remain, with sincere respect, faithfully yours,

"W. E. GLADSTONE.

"Jos. Cowen, Esq., M.P."

In the year 1865, Sir Joseph, then Mr. Cowen, at the request of above two thousand of the Burgesses of Newcastle, came forward as a candidate for Parliamentary honour and usefulness. At the poll, Mr. Cowen stood first, with 2941 votes recorded in his favour; Mr. Headlam was second, with 2477; the Whig candidate, Mr. S. A. Beaumont, being defeated. Sir Joseph Cowen was by birth and education a Radical. During his Parliamentary career he seldom addressed the House of Commons, yet he seldom, if ever, absented himself from his Parliamentary duties. This close attention to duty in itself is sometimes more effective for good than the most closely studied and eloquently delivered speeches. Sir Joseph remained M.P. for Newcastle until his death, which took place at Stella Hall, December 19th, 1873.

Sir Joseph was succeeded by his eldest son, Joseph, who was born at Blaydon Burn, July 9th, 1831. He attended a private school at Winlaton, first under the Rev. Mr. Kitchen, and afterwards under Mr. Lee. Mr. Kitchen was a man of great and varied ability, and his school was attended by nearly all the gentlemen's sons in the neighbourhood. Mr. Cowen subsequently attended Mr. Richard M. Weeks' private school at Ryton Park. The school at Winlaton having been given up, the Ryton school became the centre of a large district, from which young gentlemen came to receive their education. Mr. Weeks died at Ryton, on February 14th, 1894. After attending Mr. Weeks' school for a few years, Mr. Cowen proceeded to the University of Edinburgh, which then, by reason of the renown of its professors, enjoyed something like European fame. Russell, Palmerston, Landsdowne, had been there before him. His chief extramural instructor was the Rev. Dr. John Ritchie, who, although a Scottish preacher, was a fearless Radical, and a popular platform speaker. After his return to Blaydon Burn, Mr. Cowen engaged actively in his father's business of fire-proof brick and retort manufacturer. The time he could spare from business was devoted to improving the social condition and elevating the moral tone of all classes of workmen in the neighbourhood. The Mechanics' Institute of Winlaton and Blaydon received no small share of his attention, and for a number of years he personally discharged the duties of a teacher at the latter institute. But his labours extended far beyond the neighbourhood of his birth.

In January, 1854, we find Mr. Cowen, along with Mr. Ingham, M.P., Mr. J. C. Grant, and the Rev. James Carr, addressing the members of the South Shields Working Men's Institute; and in the same month, along with Lord Seaham and Lord Adolphus Vane, speaking at the Stockton Mechanics' Institution. During this year, Dr. John Ritchie, Mr. Cowen's former instructor at Edinburgh, was in the North assisting his former pupil in promoting the social welfare of the workmen on Tyneside. In 1854 appeared the first number of the "Northern Tribune," with Mr. Cowen as editor. The interesting sketches of the villages of Winlaton, Stella, and Blaydon, are from the pen of the editor. In the account of "Crowley's Crew," which he gives in his sketch of Winlaton, Mr. Cowen rescued the history of that remarkable colony of workmen from oblivion. Mr. Cowen about that time wrote a pamphlet on Education, which provoked a reply from the then Earl of Ravensworth. The correspondence ultimately found its way into the "Times" newspaper, and produced no small amount of excitement at the time. As a friend of temperance, Mr. Cowen always found time—forty years ago—to address the working men, usually at open-air meetings in the villages on Tyneside, at which meetings he was generally associated with George Charlton, George Dodds, and W. Peel, names well known in the North of England at that time. In 1858, Mr. Cowen formed the Northern Reform League, and in company with Mr. R. B. Reed, its secretary, he is said to have visited every colliery village in Northumberland and Durham, teaching the principles of "Christian Democracy." In the Reform Demonstration of 1857, the League played an important part, bringing out to a "Demonstration" in Newcastle-upon-Tyne, an army of supporters which London itself could scarcely equal. On the formation of the Northumbrian Education League, Mr. Cowen was appointed chairman, and secured for Board Schools the votes of the Northern Counties.

By this time Mr. Cowen possessed a European reputation. In 1854, on Garibaldi visiting Tyneside, he formed one of a deputation who waited on the General at Shields, to present to him a sword and telescope, purchased by a penny subscription. Mr. Cowen, in presenting the sword and telescope, made one of those appropriate speeches for the delivery of which he has become so famous. Garibaldi afterwards visited Tyneside, and was the guest of Mr. Cowen. In 1856, the illustrious exile, Louis Kossuth, visited Newcastle, and delivered a number of lectures and speeches. Mr. Cowen was closely associated with Kossuth during his stay on Tyneside. At the first lecture, held in the Music Hall, Mr. Cowen was on the platform; at the second lecture he was chairman; and during Kossuth's stay at Blaydon, he delivered an address in the Mechanics' Institute, when Mr. Cowen again took the chair. The great Hungarian paid other visits to Tyneside, and on each occasion he was the guest of Mr. Cowen. Louis Blanc also, was often under Mr. Cowen's roof. Mr. Cowen was an intimate friend of Mazzini, whom he declares to be the greatest man he has known. Mr. Cowen was also a close friend of Orsini, and of Ledru Rollin; and of the Polish revolutionary leaders, Worcell, Darasz, Mieroslawski, Dombrowski, and Langiewiez. For years his house had been an asylum for the victims of Russian tyranny, and a considerable part of an ample income had been spent by him in keeping alive the patriotism of the Polish insurgents and other enemies of Russia. On the 22nd September, 1862, Mr. Cowen was elected a member of the Newcastle Town Council, and on the 9th of November, 1877, he was invested with the honour of an alderman. On the 11th August, 1886, he resigned, after having sat in the Council for twenty-four years. In 1859, Mr. Cowen became proprietor of the "Newcastle Daily Chronicle," and in a short time largely increased its circulation. During the agitation in the North of England, in 1873, known as the "Nine Hours' Movement," Mr. Cowen, both by his purse and his paper, rendered invaluable service to the workmen, which resulted in the concession of the "Nine Hours'" day to workmen in all parts of the country.

On January 14th, 1874, Mr. Cowen was elected to fill the Parliamentary seat vacant by the death of his father. At the poll the numbers were:—Cowen, 7,356; Hammond, 6,353. Mr. Gladstone, however, dissolved Parliament before Mr. Cowen had taken his seat, and in the following month another election took place, when he was again returned. He entered Parliament with a brilliant reputation. A Radical by birth, education, and tradition, he had been for years the champion of the weak against the strong; in social, educational, and philanthrophic matters, and in the extension and broadening of christian effort, he had become an acknowledged authority. He was in 1874, what Charles Attwood of Whickham had been in 1831—the political guide and adviser of the working classes on Tyneside. His platform training, which was of the most complete description, had been received in the open fields and on village greens, while addressing multitudes of his fellow men. With these considerations in view, it is not surprising that great things were expected of Mr. Cowen in Parliament; and his parliamentary achievements in no way belied the high hopes that his friends reposed in his great abilities and immense experience. His speeches on the Friendly Societies' Bill, on the County Suffrage Bill, on Mr. Plimsoll's Bill, on the County Courts Bill, and the Licensing Boards Bill, which were made early in his parliamentary career, gave proof of a varied capacity for legislative work of a very high order; but it was his speech delivered in opposition to the bill introduced by Mr. Disraeli, then prime minister, conferring the title of Empress of India on the Queen of England, which stamped him an orator ranking with Gladstone and Bright.

Mr. Cowen was returned for Newcastle-upon-Tyne in 1880, and in 1885. At the end of the last mentioned Parliament, which lasted till 1886, he retired from political life. Since that time Mr. Cowen has only appeared on two occasions before Newcastle audiences, namely, on October 5th, 1892, when he laid the foundation stone of the Rutherford College; and on September 12th, 1894, when he delivered an address at the unveiling ceremony of the Memorial Fountain to the late Dr. Rutherford.

The following speeches delivered by Mr. Cowen deserve careful reading and attentive study:—

"America and England;" speech at a banquet given by the Corporation of Newcastle-upon-Tyne to Ex-President Grant, Sept. 22nd, 1877. "The Spirit of our Time;" address delivered at the opening of the Winter Session of the College of Physical Science, October 1st, 1877. "Art in Trade;" delivered at the presentation by Mrs. Lough of the models executed by her husband, the late Mr. Lough, to the town of Newcastle, October 24th, 1877. "Art and Education;" delivered on the occasion of laying the foundation stone of the Science and Art School, Newcastle, November 21st, 1877. "Eulogy on a Local Orator;" delivered on the occasion of unveiling a memorial to the late Mr. Charles Larkin at Newcastle-upon-Tyne, September 30th, 1880. "Art: its History and Future;" delivered at the annual distribution of prizes in connection with the Bath Lane Science and Art School, October 12th, 1880. "Mechanics' Institutions and Oratory;" delivered to the members of the Working Men's Club, September 18th, 1882. "Modern Preaching and Preachers;" delivered at a public breakfast given in honour of the jubilee of the Rev. George Bell, May 26th, 1884. "Religious Liberty and Tolerance;" delivered when presiding at a lecture by the Rev. Mr. Macrae, in the Congregational Church, Gateshead, October 13th, 1884. "Education;" delivered on the occasion of the laying of the foundation stone of the Rutherford College, October 5th, 1892. "Dr. Rutherford;" delivered at the unveiling ceremony of the Memorial Fountain to the late Dr. Rutherford, at Newcastle-on-Tyne, September 12th, 1894.

Although Mr. Cowen has retired from active public life, he still takes a keen interest in political and social questions. Privately he is sociable and pleasant, and when conversing on topics in which he is interested, talks with all the animation and eloquence of former days.

Miss Jane Cowen, Mr. Cowen's only daughter, is the authoress of "Tales of Revolution and of Patriotism," published in 1884. She has' also contributed to the "Weekly Chronicle," "Colburn's Monthly," and other magazines.

One hundred years ago, there stood at the west end of Stella, on the south side of the present Newcastle and Carlisle Railway, a forge belonging to Peter Hutchinson of Ryton, which afterwards passed to his son, James Hutchinson. The forge was driven by a water-wheel, and stood in a secluded spot, excellently adapted for the purpose. This establishment was afterwards enlarged by the addition of an iron foundry, which, in 1828, belonged to Mr. Edward Emerson. It subsequently passed into the hands of Messrs. R. J. and R. Laycock, who manufactured waggons for railways, and under whose direction the little factory flourished for many years. At present, not a vestige remains to apprise the visitor to Stella of this industry.

On the south side of the Hexham turnpike, there is a lane which winds past a number of pretty cottages, and which at one time terminated at the old turnpike at the top of the hill. This lane was formerly "The Lover's Walk," but unfortunately for the young men and maidens of the neighbourhood, the road was closed a number of years since, and has not been re-opened. At the east side of the road, which leads on to Stella Haughs, is "High Stella House." This old house, which has a pleasant outlook on the north side, has evidently seen better days. On a plan of Stella (1767), it is marked the residence of Thos. Foster. In 1828, it was the residence of Mr. Thomas Emerson, ironfounder. At present it is occupied by Mr. William Douglas.

About the middle of the village is the old Stella brewery. The brewery is not marked on the above mentioned plan of Stella, and was probably erected at the date inscribed on the weather-cock, "I. H. & Com. 1778." I. H. are the initials of James Hutchinson, the owner of the forge. The brewery subsequently passed into the hands of Mr. J. C. Thompson. In 1854 it belonged to Messrs. Parker & Co., and was last used for manufacturing purposes by Mr. John P. Dalton.

Considering the number of keelmen that lived at Stella and Blaydon, it is not surprising that some of them should be first-class oarsmen. William Galley of Stella, in the early years of the present century, was champion oarsman of the Tyne. At the celebration of the coronation of His Majesty George IV., July 19th, 1821, a great boat race took place from Walker Quay to the Tyne Bridge. Thirteen boats started, including the "Laurel Leaf" (William Galley), Stella. The "Laurel Leaf" arrived seventh in order, but a dispute having arisen, the race was deferred till August 1st (the anniversary of the Battle of the Nile), when the competitors pulled from Hebburn Quay to the Tyne Bridge, in the following order: 1st, "Laurel Leaf" (William Galley), 6 sovs.; 2nd, "The Swallow" 3 sovs.; 3rd, "Lord Ravensworth," 2 sovs.; six boats competed. William Galley belonged to one of the old Stella families, William Silvertop having married a Galley of Stella in the 18th century. There were also a four-oared and a six-oared crew, formed by the keelmen of Stella and Blaydon. The village has remained stationary for many years; the only industries at present are the staiths, and the brick manufactory belonging to Messrs. Joseph Cowen & Co.

BLAYDON.

This village, in the township of Winlaton, lies immediately on the south side of the Tyne, and east of Blaydon Burn. The name is probably derived from *blac* = bleak, and *dun* = a hill. The population in 1891 was : males, 2570; females, 2291 ; total, 4861.

Blaydon has no historical record of any importance. It belongs exclusively to the modern days of material development. Few villages on Tyneside have risen so rapidly in commercial importance during the last fifty years; and with a growing population, and a yearly increasing trade, it will undoubtedly play an important part in the great volume of Tyneside industry. In a plan of Blaydon dated 1775, the village was composed of a number of houses bordering the Hexham turnpike, on the east side of the Blaydon Burn. The present road from Winlaton to Blaydon was Sir Edward Blackett's "lead-way," by which the lead was carried from the mines at Allenheads to the smelt mill at Blaydon. At the east end of the village, where the bridge crosses the railway near to Blaydon Haughs, there was a windmill. On the site of the present railway station was the smelt mill belonging to Sir Edward Blackett. Between the smelt mill and the west end of Tyne-street was the village Green, extending southward to the present turnpike. Alongside of the Green, at the river side, was Lord Strathmore's quay. On the south side of the turnpike was the Dockendale estate, the property of George Silvertop, Esq.; and on the north side of Dockendale stands the house at present occupied by Mr. Michael Hawdon, which, prior to 1775, was the residence of the Silvertop family before their removal to Stella House. Mr. Hawdon's house is still designated the Manor House. On the west side of Mr. Silvertop's mansion were the Horse-crofts, and on the north side of the turnpike, and opposite Mr. Silvertop's house, was a number of small houses, probably the residence of keelmen. Such is the picture of Blaydon one hundred and twenty years ago. The old houses on the east side of the Horse-crofts, which form Fountain-lane, are among the oldest in Blaydon. The word "croft" is Saxon, and signifies a little close or piece of ground adjoining a house for pasture, probably used for the horses working at that time on the lead-gate.

By following a road commencing at Fountain-lane, for about half a mile southward, the site of Dockendale Hall may be seen in a field on the east side of Blaydon Burn. As already stated, Dockendale formed part of the estate of G. Silvertop, Esq. The Hall was probably only a large farm house, as many of such houses are still called halls. In the year 1810, the house was made into tenements and occupied by Mr. Dunn's keelmen. Sixty years ago, only a few out-houses were standing, and to-day only the foundations indicate its former existence. It may interest the people of Winlaton and Blaydon to know that the following curious history, taken from "Richardson's Table Book," is connected with Dockendale. At a sale in the beginning of 1760, a woman bought a very old bureau for 4s. 6d., being considered nothing better than lumber. After the sale, she with difficulty prevailed on a nailer, a neighbour, to assist her in removing it; he, in forcing it open by the middle, discovered some papers and loose gold, told her about it, and made it fast again; got more help, and took it away whole. In getting it out, one of the papers fell, and the gold jingling was taken notice of by one of the assistants, but the nailer saying it was only a bag with a few nails he had put out of his pocket, he was believed. After getting it home and dismissing the assistants, the purchaser and her friend, the nailer, went to work and took it to pieces, and were paid for their trouble with several purses and papers of gold to a considerable amount. She gave the nailer five papers untold, which enabled him to pay his debts and purchase a house and shop to work in, which amounted to upwards of £200; and was told by the woman to apply to her if he wanted more; but he was satisfied, and looked upon it as a particular case of Providence, being deep in debt and out of work, with a sick wife and a small family. It was remarkable that this old piece of furniture was recollected to have passed through several sales during the preceding forty years; that none of the gold was of a later coinage than James II.; and that it was in the possession of an opulent family in the neighbourhood of Newcastle in the year 1715. This piece of furniture was bought by a woman living at Dockendale Hall (1760), the sale being at the "Blacksmiths' Arms," Winlaton.

Hutchinson says :—" The wharfs at Stella and Blaydon receive the greatest part of the lead which comes down the Tyne. The proprietors are the London Company, the heirs of Sir Thomas Blackett, Bart., and Henry Errington, Esq., and Company. The smelt mills are chiefly on the Derwent river, at Whitefield, Jeffreys, and Acton, belonging to the London Company; Dukesfield, Allenheads, and Rookhope, belonging to the heirs of Sir Thomas Blackett; and Feldon, near Edmundbyers, belonging to Mr. Errington. Sir Thomas's heirs have a refinery at Blaydon. The yearly receipt of lead at the above wharfs is 60,000 pieces of twelve stone each. There are ninety-three carriages constantly employed to bring down the lead, each carrying ten pieces at a time. The average number of pieces of lead sent to Blaydon from the western mines, in the county of Durham, is about 100,000."

Before the introduction of carriages or wains, the lead was conveyed from the mines by small Scotch galloways. A wood frame was fixed over the backs of the galloways, containing a piece of lead on each side. The leading pony had a bell attached to his head, in order to guide those behind. It would be an interesting sight to see forty or fifty galloways coming across the fells and moors all under the direction of two men—from Allenheads in Cumberland, to Blaydon. It was after the roads were improved that wains were used,

The London Lead Company's wharf was at Stella, and the road by which the lead was conveyed to the wharf was called Lead Gate. The route from the mines was over Hedley Fell to Lead Gate, where the ponies were changed; they then proceeded by the road past Coalburns, Greenside, and Path-head to Stella. The lead belonging to the heirs of Sir Thomas Blackett, was refined at Blaydon, and afterwards shipped to its destination. Every ton of lead-ore produced nine or ten ounces of silver, and from this fact, the road from Blaydon church to Winlaton was called "Silver Hill." The lead mines in Allendale afterwards became the property of Colonel and Mrs. Beaumont, who also came into possession of the refinery at Blaydon. It was while Hugh L. Pattinson, Esq., was manager of the establishment, that he made many of those discoveries which raised him to a high place in his profession. Since the construction of the Newcastle and Carlisle Railway, in 1835, both the staiths and the smelt mills have disappeared.

In the year 1828, Blaydon was still one of the smallest villages on Tyneside, although a few manufactories had commenced. William G. Hawdon had an iron foundry; Emerson and Milner, iron and steel foundries, and a fire-brick manufactory; and the Beaumonts, the lead-yard. Blaydon House had been built, and was occupied by Mr. John Mulcaster, agent to Thomas Richard Beaumont, Esq. The village possessed eight public-houses. The dwellings of the keelmen, who comprised the most numerous class of workmen in Blaydon and Stella, occupied nearly the whole of the houses in the village. In the year 1850, the village possessed a thriving and important trade, and manufactories lined the side of the river. Industries of nearly every description were commenced. The following works were in active operation:—North Durham Bottle Works; W. C. Carr, clay-retort manufacturer; W. Harriman, fire-brick manufacturer; A. Thatcher, glass manufacturer; R. Hall & Co., chain manufacturers; Blaydon Chemical Company; W. G. Hawdon, engine builder and founder; R. Lynn, lamp-black manufacturer; and B. Stokoe, fell-monger.

It was not until the opening of the Blaydon Main Colliery, in 1853, that the village assumed its present shape. At that time Cuthbert-street and Robinson-street were built for the workmen at the colliery; and since that time Blaydon has greatly enlarged in size and in population.

Upon the 5th November, 1865, Mr. John Nicholson, timber merchant, died. He built three or four small vessels; but this industry has not been pursued.

The opening of the Newcastle and Carlisle Railway, in 1835, gave a great impetus to the trade of Blaydon, but it also sounded the death-knell to the vocation of the keelman. On the 9th March of that year two trains, drawn by the "Rapid" and the "Comet," started from Blaydon for Hexham amidst tremendous cheering and the booming of cannon. The trains brought back the passengers to Blaydon in an hour and a quarter—quite a marvellous feat in those days. On March 1st, 1837, the line between Redheugh and Blaydon was opened; on May 31st, 1839, the line from Newcastle to Blaydon for minerals, and on October 21st, Newcastle to Blaydon for passengers.

The keelmen were not the only class of men whose trade suffered by the introduction of the railroad system: the "British Queen" coach, which started from Hexham, and called at "The Beehive," Blaydon, at half-past ten in the morning and at half-past four in the afternoon, to take up passengers, was compelled by the cheapness of railway travelling to retire from the road, and the jolly coachman of sixty years ago has disappeared for ever.

On November 26th, 1853, Blaydon was first lighted with gas, the supply being obtained from the works of Messrs. Joseph Cowen & Co., who originally intended them for lighting their own manufactory alone; but who, at the request of the inhabitants, extended their establishment, so as to light not only Blaydon, but the other villages in the neighbourhood as well. The gas was made from cannel coal, and gave every satisfaction, both as regards its purity and brilliancy. On December 6th a large and influential meeting of the inhabitants was held in the lecture hall of the Mechanics' Institution, with Dr. Brown in the chair, at which resolutions were passed thanking Messrs. Cowen for having offered their gas to the public, and for agreeing to light the streets; the meeting pledging themselves to raise the requisite funds to pay for the same.

THE CHURCH.

The Church, dedicated to St. Cuthbert, occupies a commanding position at the head of the street to which it gives name, and faces the Hexham turnpike. The site was given by T. W. Beaumont, Esq. It is a stone structure in the Early English style, comprising nave, chancel, north aisle, and handsome pinnacled tower. The aisle is under a separate roof, and divided from the nave by four pointed arches springing from round pillars. The nave and south porch were erected in 1844, at a cost of about £800, and the aisle, chancel, and tower were afterwards added.

In 1876 a peal of six bells and a clock of three dials were placed in the tower by subscription, at a cost of about £600; the tenor being given by the late Sir Henry A. Clavering, Bart., and the clock by John B. Simpson, Esq. In 1882 the church was partially restored, when the south porch was removed, the nave re-pewed, the organ removed from the gallery into a chamber in the chancel, and the chancel and choir screens were erected. The cost of the restoration was about £500. The present number of sittings is six hundred and fifty, all of which are free.

The east window is in four compartments, and filled with stained glass. In each of the lights there is represented a scene in the life of our Saviour.

Against the north wall of the chancel there is a tablet with the inscription :—

> In loving memory of
> The Rev. WILLIAM BROWN, M.A.,
> Rector and first Incumbent of
> this parish for 32 years,
> who died November 15th, 1877, aged 59 years.
> Thanks be to God, which giveth us the
> victory through our Lord Jesus Christ.
> Therefore, my beloved brethren, be ye
> steadfast, unmoveable, always
> abounding in the work of the Lord,
> forasmuch as ye know that your
> labour is not in vain.   1. Cor. xv. 57-58.

In the nave, at the east end, there is a window of two lights, filled with stained glass, representing—first, Job; second, St. Paul. On a brass plate underneath the window is the inscription :—

> The above window, erected by his widow and
> children in affectionate remembrance of.
> CHARLES ARMSTRONG, Esq., of Newcastle-on-Tyne,
> who died Oct. 22nd, 1868, aged 69 years. Also JAMES ARMSTRONG,
> son of the above, who died January 19th, 1858, aged 19.
> Also ANN ELIZABETH ARMSTRONG, daughter of the above,
> who died January 27th, 1864, aged 26.

A window at the east end of the north aisle bears the following :—

> In affectionate Memory of HENRY POOLE,
> first warden of this Church. By A.A. and J.B.A., of
> London, 186—.

In the west wall of the north aisle another window has the inscription:—

> Erected in Memory of JAMES MITFORD, who died Nov. 14th, 1865, aged 74 years; and left £100 towards the completion of this church, by his executors, P. Brown, M.D., and J. Parker.

The handsome cover on the altar-table was the gift of Mrs. Greene, wife of the rector. The brass reading desk, chastely designed, and surmounted by an eagle, took the first prize at the Newcastle Exhibition.

The living is valued at £300, and the patronage is vested in the Crown and the Bishop of Durham. The tithes were commuted in 1855 for £27. The Rev. Matthew Greene is rector.

The rector's house stands at the east side of the church. There is a small graveyard at the north side of the church.

Prior to the erection of the church, religious services were conducted in a chapel of ease at the west end of Blaydon, near to the Burn Side; the building is now used as a joiner's shop, and has the following inscription above the door:—"Cura Caroli Thorp, A.D. 1832."

The Wesleyan Methodists have a handsome chapel, which is situated on the north side of the Shibdon-road, at the east end of the village. The Methodists had a preaching house at an early period of their history. The house in which services were first conducted belonged to William Hawdon. Mr. Michael Hawdon has in his possession a mantel bearing the inscription, "W. H. M. (William and Mary Hawdon), 1737;" this stone belonged to the house in which the early Methodists worshipped, and which stood on the site of a house now in Bridge Street (No. 11). The house comprised a kitchen and a room above. The upper room was entered from the kitchen by a trap-door. Mr. Hawdon also possesses a stool on which the preacher stood to address the congregation. The stool was placed immediately under the trap-door. It sometimes happened that the congregation was too large for the kitchen, on which the upper room was also used; the preacher by standing on the stool, and raising his head above the door, could then see the congregations in both rooms. The Methodists afterwards removed to a more commodious room in the "Horse-crofts," in which they worshipped until 1856, when they took possession of their new chapel in Wesley-place. After conducting services there for nearly forty years, they built their present chapel, which was opened in 1893. It is built in the Early English style, and serves at present as a school-chapel. The seating at present provided is for four hundred; and the cost was £2,600.

THE BLAYDON AND DISTRICT CO-OPERATIVE LITERARY INSTITUTE.

Since 1847 there has been a Mechanics' Institution in the village. In the year 1852, a large and handsome building was erected by subscription. The foundation stone was laid in May of that year, by Mr. Blackett, M.P., and it was opened in September. The cost of the erection was £600. In the early days of the Institution, the late Mr. Thomas Vallance, keelman, was president, and Mr. James Eadie, secretary. In 1875 it became the property of the Blaydon and District Co-operative Society, at a cost of about £1300, and the Institute became free to all members of the society, at present numbering 4114. It is a commodious structure, comprising library, reading-room, and lecture-hall. The news-room is well supplied with the various metropolitan and provincial journals and magazines, and the library contains upwards of 2200 volumes. There are also science and art classes, which are fairly well attended during the winter months.

BLAYDON DISTRICT CO-OPERATIVE SOCIETY.

The Blaydon Society is one of the oldest in the Co-operative Union. Mr. Holyoake, in his "History of Co-operation," declares that, next to Rochdale, it is the most remarkable store in England. It has grown from a house to a street. Perhaps no man had more to do with the formation of the store than Mr. Joseph Cowen. A number of shrewd and intelligent men met weekly in the Mechanics' Institute of the village, when Mr. Cowen read portions of Mr. Holyoake's "History of the Rochdale Pioneers," and impressed them with the wisdom of the Co-operative movement, and the utility of the "store." The Blaydon Society was commenced in the year 1858, in a cottage situated in Cuthbert-street. Thirty-eight members were enrolled at the first public meeting. In a short time the rooms in Cuthbert-street were too small for the amount of business to be transacted by the members, and the present large and handsome premises in Church-street were commenced. Additions have several times been made to the original building. At present the Society's business is carried on in grocery, butchering, tailoring, drapery, shoemaking, green-grocery, and hardware departments. In 1894, there were one hundred and thirty-five employees in the service of the society.

The following figures will show the doings of the Society since its commencement:—Sales, £3,338,027; capital subscribed by members, £120,646; capital withdrawn, £469,996; members' dividends, £382,845; interest on members' capital, £57,994; depreciation of property, fixed and rolling stock, £27,497; capital invested in other societies, £10,445; investments withdrawn, £14,748; present amount of investments, £19,486; present members' claims, £80,054; present nominal value of fixed and rolling stock, £24,430; present number of members, 4,000; sales for the year 1893, £130,450. The Blaydon Society has also branch stores at Prudhoe, Lemington, Spen, Winlaton, Westwood, and Barmoor. The Burnopfield and Throckley stores were formerly branches of Blaydon, but are now independent societies.

The Blaydon society has built at Blaydon sixty-seven houses; at Lemington, twenty-seven; at Prudhoe, twenty; at Spen, sixteen; and at Barmoor, eighteen—which are occupied by members of the stores.

In 1875 the Blaydon Society commenced to apportion $2\frac{1}{2}$ per cent. of the profits per annum towards education: and up to the present time £8,000 has been devoted to that purpose.

The Catholic School (St. Joseph's) stands on the south side of the Hexham turnpike, and opposite to the church (St. Cuthbert's). It was opened in 1870, to accommodate 230 children.

A little west of St. Cuthbert's Church is the Primitive Methodist Chapel. It is a good stone building, and was erected in 1854, with sittings for 300 persons. The Primitive Methodists have a smaller chapel at Blaydon Haughs, erected in 1881, to seat about 200.

The United Free Methodists have a small chapel in Tyne-street, built in 1859, at a cost of £300, having seats for 150.

There are on the river side the following industries, which give employment to several hundreds of workmen:—Blaydon Iron Works; Blaydon Manure and Alkali Company; Blaydon Bottle Works; Messrs. Douglass Brothers, Engineers; Messrs. Smith, Patterson & Co., Ironfounders and Sanitary Engineers; Messrs. William Harriman & Co., Brick Manufacturers; Messrs. Hoyle, Robson, Barnett & Co., Paint, Colour, and Varnish Manufacturers; Cinder Ovens (Stella Coal Company).

At a short distance from the Wesleyan Chapel, at the east end of Blaydon, is the Cemetery (St. Cuthbert's, Stella), which occupies an elevated position on the south side of the Hexham turnpike. It was opened in March 1873, the first interment taking place on the 17th of that month. It covers an area of three and a quarter acres, and contains two mortuary chapels, in the Early English style, which are divided by an archway in the usual manner, as also a house for the curator. The total cost was £2,600.

In the Cemetery, on a handsome granite vault cover, which marks the resting place of the last of the long line of Claverings, there is the following inscription :—

>   SIR HENRY AUGUSTUS CLAVERING,
> Of Axwell Park, Tenth and last Baronet,
>   Born 30th August, 1824,
>   Died 9th November, 1893;
>   Aged 69 Years.

There is also in the Cemetery a neat monument erected to the memory of James Ramsay. The base of the structure supports the figure of that well-known and highly-respected man, holding in his hand a "rattle," used in calling the pitmen to their work. On the base of the monument is inscribed :—

>   Sacred
>   To the Memory of
>   JAMES RAMSAY,
>   Aged 61 Years.
> Erected by the Miners of Durham,
> As a Tribute to his long and Self-sacrificing
> Labours in the Cause of Human Progress.
> He was a Zealous Worker, a Faithful Friend,
>   a Christian Patriot.

A little further eastward, and at the foot of Winlaton Bank, is the Board School, built in 1889 for the accommodation of the children living at Blaydon. It is a magnificent structure, occupying a commanding position on the south side of the turnpike. It was built from a design by Thomas C. Nicholson, Esq., of Blaydon, and comprises departments for boys, girls, and infants, with a total accommodation for over 700 children. The cost of the building was £8,700.

On the north side of the Hexham turnpike is situated the Blaydon Main Colliery, worked by the Stella Coal Company. This colliery was opened in 1853, and at present the Brockwell seam, 2 feet 10 inches at a distance of 46 fathoms, is being worked. There are about four hundred men and boys employed, including the coke-ovens at Derwenthaugh. The miners live at Winlaton and Blaydon.

Returned to Blaydon, a road opposite to the church, known as Blaydon Bank, leads to Winlaton. At the bottom of the road, and on the west side, is Blaydon House—already mentioned—the residence of Dr. Brown; whose father Dr. Brown, is well-known and highly respected in the neighbourhood. For many years he has been identified with all movements for the elevation of the working classes.

It was nearly at the top of Blaydon Bank, on October 5th, 1860, that John Baty was murdered by Thomas Smith, who was afterwards hanged at Durham.

The Blaydon Local Board was first formed in 1861, at which time it comprised Blaydon village only. The district was twice extended: in 1875 Winlaton and Stella townships were taken in, and in 1877 Chopwell township was added—which altogether embraced an area of 9,348 acres.

In December 1894, the Blaydon Urban District Council was formed. The district is divided into two wards, Blaydon with twelve, and Chopwell with three members.

A Burial Board, numbering six members, was formed in 1873.

Old House in Back St., Winlaton.

WINLATON.

THE parish of Winlaton was constituted November 6th, 1832, and includes the whole of the townships of Winlaton and Chopwell previously forming the eastern, southern, and western boundaries of the parish of Ryton. It is bounded on the north by the Tyne, from Blaydon Burn foot to the confluence of the Tyne and Derwent, a distance of about a mile. The boundary on the east is still the Derwent, extending for about two miles between Axwell Park and Swalwell, to Gibside Hall, where it takes a westerly direction past Rowlands Gill, the western part of the Crown Lands in Chopwell, and Milkwell Burn, and divides Winlaton from Northumberland. The line proceeds in a northerly direction past Hedley Fell—dividing that place from the townships of Ryton and Chopwell—to Bucks Nook. On the south this is the boundary line which separates the parish of Winlaton from that of Ryton. On the formation of the Chapelry of Stella, August 8th, 1845, the northern portion of the township of Winlaton was added to it (Stella).

The village of Winlaton, which is about two miles south-east of Ryton, stands on a high exposed ridge, sloping on the south and the east to the Derwent, and on the north to the Hexham turnpike. The houses are generally irregularly built, and apparently without any plan.

Winloctun, Winlaghton, Winlauton, Winlawton, Wynlaton, Winlaton is probably derived from *Win* or *Whin*—formerly many parts of the township were covered with whins, and bore the name of Whiney Close, Whiney Common, &c.; *law*, from the Anglo-Saxon word *hleaw* = rising ground; and *ton* = town or village.

Population of the township, 1801, 3021; 1811, 3063; 1821, 3532; 1831, 3951; 1841, 5006; 1851, 5627; 1861, 6809; 1871, 7494; 1881, 8330; 1891, 10,390. Rateable Value in 1821, £5,576; in 1894, £34,713. Area, 5,217 acres.

There are strong grounds for supposing that a branch of the Roman highway (Watling-Street) passed through the vicinity of Winlaton. At a small distance from Binchester, a military way has been observed to leave the Watling-Street, supposed to go to Chester-le-Street. Again, the remains of such a way have been found on Gateshead Fell, pointing to Newcastle. Having passed the Derwent at Ebchester, this old road proceeds towards Corbridge. About half a mile north of Whittonstall there is a remarkable turn in it, and at this turn an exploratory fort of about thirty yards square. There was most likely an easterly continuation of the (Maiden) way through Hedley, Coalburns, Winlaton, etc., connecting it with the Reken Dyke, which ran to Jarrow and South Shields. Several querns have been found in the neighbourhood. In taking down some old houses at Swalwell, a few years since, four querns were discovered in the foundations; and in 1889, a quern was found in the old foundation of the National School at Whickham.

In Boldon Book, 1183, Wynlaton and Berley are on lease with the demesne and the villein service, and with the farm stock, under £15 rent. Besides, the tenants in villenage mow the lord's meadows (each two days' work with one man), and then receive their corrody—whence our northern word "crowdy;" and win and lead the hay, one day's work. The marsh, the meadow, and the wood (nemus) are reserved to the lord. The mill pays five marks and a half.

Coals were obtained at Winlaton at an early period of the history of this industry. From the Pipe Rolls, 40 Ed. III., 1367, we have the particulars of the account of Henry de Strother, sheriff of Northumberland, of monies by him paid for the provision and purchase of sea-coals, for the use of "our lord ye king," the same being purchased by virtue of the letters of our lord the king under his privy seal, addressed to the said sheriff under date 19th day of February, in the 40th year of our said lord, the King of of England. "Purchase of Coals—The same accounteth for 676 chaldrons of coals, counting by the long hundred of sea coals, purchased at Wynlaton at 17 pence per chaldron, £47 17s. 8d.; and for 33 keels and one boat, with men labouring in the same, namely in each keel five men, and in the boat four men, each of the said keels containing 20 chaldrons, and the aforesaid boat containing 16 chaldrons; conveying and carrying the said coals from Wynlaton to the port of Newcastle-upon-Tyne, and there putting the same on board ship; each of the said men having for his wages 6 pence, and for the hire of each keel and boat 12 pence, 118s. 6d.; and for the wages of one John Tavener, superintending the loading and conveyance of the said coals, and the procuring and freighting of divers ships for taking the said coals on board, and bringing the same to London, namely, from the 14th day of April, in the 40th year (of our lord the king) to the 6th day of June next following, being 54 days, reckoning each day, he receiving 12d. per day by agreement, 54 shillings; and to one Hugh Hankyn, for his labour and expenses in travelling to London and there abiding to receive the said coals from the masters of the ships, and delivering the said coals by indenture to Adam de Hertyngdone, clerk of our lord the King, and thence returning to his own home, viz: 74 days, he receiving 18 pence per day by agreement.

"And to the divers masters of the ships for the freight of $589\tfrac{3}{4}$ chaldrons of coals from the aforesaid port to London, and there delivered as appears by the indentures of delivery of the said coals, indentured between the said Henry Strother and the aforesaid masters testifying of the said delivery, namely for every chaldron 3s. 6d.—£103 4s. Total sum, £165 5s. 2d."— *T. J. Taylor*, "Archæology of the Coal Trade."

From this account we can ascertain the price of coals at Winlaton in the 14th century. It is rather uncertain what the chaldron was rated at in 1367. In the year 1530, the Priory of Tynemouth let a colliery called Heygrove, at Elswick; another in the East-field there; besides one in the West-field, and one near Gallow-flat, for £20 a year, on condition that more than twenty chaldrons, of six bolls each, should not be drawn in a day. Six bolls were equal to about 1600 lbs., or $14\tfrac{1}{4}$ cwts. "17d." was paid for a chaldron equal to about $14\tfrac{1}{2}$ cwts.; so that the price paid at the Winlaton pits for the king's coals was a fraction more than one penny per cwt. The carrying capacity of the keels was twenty chaldrons, and the sum paid to the keelmen for carrying the coals, probably from Stella to Newcastle, was sixpence per man. Since that time (14th century), every available part of Winlaton and its vicinity has been worked for coal. One part of the village—The

Groves—has taken its name from the coal-mining carried on at the north side.

In 1368, Ralph Nevill, Chivaler, died seized of the manor, held by twenty marks exchequer rent. "Hatfield's Survey," 1345—1381, states only that Lord Nevill held the village of Winlaton by knight's service and £20 rent; and in Lord Nevill's family the manor continued till the reign of Elizabeth, when just before the forfeiture, Charles, Earl of Westmorland, 19th July, 1569, conveyed his manor of East and West Winlaton—which included Blaydon, Bates Houses, Thornley, Spen, Smailes, Sherburn, Lintz-ford, and Berley, and free fishery in the Tyne—for £2000, to Richard Hodgson and William Selby, in equal moieties. In 1613 William Selby died seized of half the manor, leaving George Selby his son and heir; which Sir George Selby died in 1625, and left six daughters, married to Belasyse, Delaval, Curwen, Conyers, Fenwick, and Delaval. The estate seems to have descended to Sir William Selby (brother and heir-male of Sir George), sometimes styled of Shortflat, county of Northumberland; and in 1633, John Hodgson, Esq., and William Fenwick, Gent., had pardon for purchasing without licence the same moiety from Sir William Selby, Knt., and William Selby, Esq. The alienation was probably on trust, for Sir George Selby of Whitehouse is sometimes styled of Winlaton. As to Hodgson's share, 8th August, 1631, George Hodgson, Esq., acquired three-eights of the manor of Sir Robert Hodgson, Knt. William Hodgson, Esq. (brother and heir-male of Sir Robert), is described of Winlaton, in 1661; his daughter and co-heir Alice, became the wife of Sir Thomas Tempest of Stella, whose representatives held a portion of the manor. The Andersons also retained some share of the purchase; for 14th April, 1600, Robert Anderson, merchant, acquired one-fourth of the manor from his father, Robert Anderson, alderman of Newcastle. According to a plan of the lordship of Winlaton (1632), Sir William Hodgson's share is 1,601 acres, 2 roods, and 36 perches; Sir William Selby's, 2,121 acres, 3 roods, and 28 perches; and Robert Anderson's, 509 acres and 36 perches. In the *Newcastle Journal* of February 10th, 1753, Winlaton Hall is described as the house in which Sir Robert Hodgson formerly lived. Probably Sir Robert only made the Hall his summer residence, as he is usually described of Hebburn. A few years ago, during alterations at Hebburn Hall, the arms of Sir Robert Hodgson and his wife were found on one of the panels. He died 13th September, 1624, and was buried at Jarrow. William Hodgson, brother and heir-male of Sir Robert, is described of Winlaton, and seems to have been a parishioner of Ryton, for at his death, which took place on the 14th January, 1661-2, he is not buried in the family vault at Jarrow, but at Ryton. This is the only member of the family buried at Ryton. Probably on Sir Ambrose Crowley founding his colony at Winlaton in 1690, the Hall would be deserted by the Hodgsons; although Surtees records the interesting circumstance of Mary Hodgson, daughter of Philip Hodgson, who resided in Lincolnshire, being married privately at Winlaton chapel to Shaftoe. Surtees does not mention to which family of Shaftoe the husband of Mary Hodgson belonged, neither does he give the date of the marriage. Philip Hodgson, Mary's father, was buried at St. Nicholas, on 11th of March, 1730, and as the chapel at Winlaton was not erected till 1705, the marriage must have taken place about the first quarter of the eighteenth century.

In the month of April, 1638, there is a petition to the king from Sir William Selby. He was disposing of property in Winlaton, and most of his money (said he) being to arise out of the sale of coal mines. No man could make any gain of them but a free Hostman of Newcastle, and there being very few of that Company that could dispend so much money, he was like to receive no fruit, and the debts must remain unpaid, and his friends who stood engaged for the same be undone. Sir William therefore prayed that such persons as should buy the coal mines should be admitted to trade as Free Hostmen of Newcastle, as he himself was: by this means he would soon find chapmen for his mines. Sir William Selby afterwards sold his unprofitable lands and coal mines in Winlaton to Sir William Blackett, who was a member of the Incorporated Company of Hostmen.

Lord Keeper Guilford who visited the North of England in 1676, relates the story that Sir William Blackett "cut into a hill in order to drain the water, and conquered all difficulties of such and the like until he came to clay, and that was too hard for him; for no means of timber and walls would resist, and all was crowded together; and this was by the weight of the hill bearing upon clay that yielded. In this work he lost £20,000." It is a pity the Lord Keeper does not mention the name of the hill; but in all probability it was Winlaton. At the time of Sir William Blackett's death, in 1680, he held the manor of Winlaton and the coal mines there.

In the year 1604, Winlaton was visited by the plague. The following entry appears in the Ryton register:—"1604. 35 persons died of ye plague between June and November out of the township of Winlington." It was not uncommon at that time for the people to leave the infected villages and erect huts for themselves on the fells, where they lived until the plague disappeared. The author of "England in the Fifteenth Century" states that "the disease was mostly of a typhoid character. The undrained, neglected soil; the shallow stagnant waters which lay on the surface of the ground; the narrow, unhealthy homes of all classes of the people; the filthy, neglected streets of the towns; the insufficient and unwholesome food; the abundance of stale fish which was eaten; the scant variety of vegetables which were consumed; the miserable wages of labourers and artisans, predisposed the agricultural and town populations alike to typhoid diseases, and left them little chance of recovery when stricken down with pestilence."

In the year 1690, Sir Ambrose Crowley removed his ironworks from Sunderland to Winlaton, which, says Surtees, "consisted of a few deserted cottages." It is said that the people of Sunderland regarded the ironworks of Crowley with disfavour; but probably a stronger reason for the removal of the factory to Winlaton was that the coal found in the neighbourhood was peculiarly adapted for smith work.

The following advertisement from the "Post Boy," No. 510 (published about 1697 or 1699), gives a detailed account of the iron-work Mr. Crowley dealt in at that time:—" Mr. Crowley, at the Doublet in Thames-street, London, Ironmonger, doth hereby give Notice, that at his works at Winlaton, near Newcastle-upon-Tyne, any good Workmen that can make the following Goods, shall have constant employment, and their wages every week punctually paid, viz:—Augers, Bed-screws, Box and Sad-Irons, Chains, Edge-Tools, Files, Hammers, Hinges, Hows for the Plantations, Locks, especially Ho-locks, Nails, Patten-rings, and almost all other sorts of Smiths' Work."

The ironworks, or factory as it was usually called, was extended in 1691 to Winlaton Mill, and afterwards to Swalwell, Dunston, and the Teams. The smaller ware was made at Winlaton, and the larger, including the hows for the plantations, harpoons for the Greenland whale-fisheries, artillery for the Government, as well as the larger chains and anchors, were made at Swalwell and Winlaton Mill.

A great number of workmen were brought from Liege, considered at that time the best place in Europe for smiths, who taught the Englishmen to make nails for sheathing ships. In the best days of the factory, 1,500 men are said to have been employed, using 7,000 bolls of coal per annum. Winlaton, which "consisted of a few deserted cottages" before the advent of Crowley, afterwards became a village of great dimensions and considerable social importance. Shops in which nail-makers, smiths, chain-makers, hinge-makers, and patten-ring makers made their respective wares, were erected in every part of the village; and at a census of the parish of Ryton, taken in 1788, by Jonathan Mirehouse, curate, Winlaton consisted of 617 families. The iron-work made at Winlaton was sent to Blaydon, where it was conveyed to the New Quay at Newcastle. The tolls of the Newcastle Corporation seem to have been considered by Crowley as exorbitant, which he refused to pay; for in July, 1694, arrears for three years, viz., from 5th March, 1691, to 25th March, 1694, were outstanding against him; and on October 12th, 1702, a complaint was made by Mr. Francis Johnson, the quay master, that Crowley, notwithstanding his agreement, paid no duty to the town, and loaded and unloaded his goods at Shields, and Blaydon, and other places, without licence of the Corporation.

From the year 1690 till 1815-16, nearly all the work for the Government was made by Crowley. The orders for iron-work were received at Winlaton every ten weeks; sometimes the orders were inadequate to keep the workmen employed for more than two or three weeks out of the ten, when they were obliged to seek work elsewhere.

The working hours of the establishment were from five in the morning till eight at night; and during the early years of the community little time seems to have been allowed for recreation and mental improvement; for the factory bell, which was a kind of curfew, rung every night at nine o'clock, when the workmen were expected to retire to rest. The curfew seems to have been occasionally disregarded, for the following entry appears in the Ryton church books:—"1745. Paid to the constable of Winlaton for giving notice to people not to keep late hours. 4d."

Sir Ambrose Crowley paid great attention to the religious welfare of his workmen. Winlaton Hall, which belonged to Sir William Blackett, was licenced for preaching in 1703. On April 17th, 1705, a subscription was commenced for building a chapel, which was finished and regularly pewed in the following January. It had a gallery at the west end, with a turret and a clock, and afforded accommodation for three hundred persons. The workmen chose a minister of their own, and contributed to his support from their wages, one half-farthing in the shilling. To the sum so raised the proprietors added an annual gift of £10. Afterwards a fixed stipend of £50 per annum was settled on the minister, and the workmen's contributions amounting to more than that, the surplus was devoted to the maintenance of a public school. The chapel was built on the foundation of St. Anne's Chapel, destroyed in the Rebellion of the Earls in 1569. An account of the re-building of Winlaton Chapel was printed in London in 1711, to which is prefixed a letter of Lord Crewe's (September 23rd, 1710), stating that Mr. Jonathan Story had been very instrumental in the good work. Hutchinson says that human bones have been frequently dug up, when there was occasion to break up the soil to any depth. In recent years excavations have several times been made in the grounds adjoining the chapel, under the direction of Mr. T. C. Nicholson, architect, of Blaydon, but no human bones have been found.

Among the chaplains appointed to Winlaton chapel were— Edmund Lodge, 1705 (Master of Haydon Bridge); Watson James Mear, 1706.

The following entry appears in the Ryton parish register:— "1721, Aug. 9th. Eleanor, —— of Mr. James Meier, late chaplain to ye factory at Winlaton (bur.)." "Affabel Battel (buried 26th March, 1723). Ions —— Robert Wright, died 1768; Thomas Spooner, T. Carr."

Daily service was performed in the chapel. In 1703 Sir

Ambrose also provided a gallery in Ryton church, for the accommodation of his workmen.

Winlaton chapel having been abandoned by the Company, it fell into decay. In 1816 a large school-room was erected upon the same site, by subscription, aided by gifts from the National and the Diocesan School Societies, and from Lord Crewe's trustees. On a stone inserted in the west end was inscribed:—
CURA CAROLI THORP, M.A., Ryton, 1816, but the hand of time has erased the inscription.

Sir Ambrose Crowley was knighted January 1st, 1706; served as sheriff of London in 1707; and died in 1713, being then one of the aldermen of that city, and M.P. for Andover. The sign of the Doublet, both at the Company's wharfs at Greenwich, and the warehouses in Lower Thames-street, is said to have been a picture of the identical leather jerkin in which he worked when a common smith. Surtees says:—"By Mary, daughter and co-heir of Charles Owen of London, gentleman, he had one son and five daughters. Mary, the eldest, was married before 1707, to James Hallet, citizen and goldsmith, of London; and Lettice, Sarah, Anne, and Elizabeth were under age at the time of his decease. Lettice married afterwards Sir John Hinde Cotton, Bart.; Sarah became the wife of Humphry Parsons, Esq. (Lord Mayor of London 1707); and Elizabeth married John, 10th Lord St. John. John Crowley, Esq., only son of Sir Ambrose, born in 1689, married Theodosia, daughter of the Rev. Joseph Gascoigne, S T.P., vicar of Enfield, Co. Middlesex, and by her had John and Ambrose, who died without issue, and four daughters: Mary, second wife to Sir William Stanhope, K.B.; Elizabeth, married to John, 2nd Earl of Ashburnham; Theodosia, married to Charles Boone, Esq., M.P. for Castle Rising; and a posthumous daughter who died under age. Theodosia, the widow of John Crowley, Esq., died in 1782, and devised the bulk of her property to the Earl of Ashburnham, her son-in-law, and to George, Viscount St. Asaph, his only son, and the ladies Henrietta, Jemima, Elizabeth, and Theodosia, his daughters, then her only surviving grand-children."

The firm was afterwards known as "Crowley, Millington & Co." In the year 1816 the establishment was removed from Winlaton, after which the greater part of Crowley's iron-work was made at Swalwell and Winlaton Mill.

The workmen employed by Crowley were governed by a code of laws instituted by the worthy founder, and put in execution by a Court of Arbitrators, held in Winlaton every ten weeks, for hearing and determining cases among the workmen, by which their differences or claims to justice were settled in an easy and expeditious manner, and they were secured from the expense of law-suits, the fees being fixed at a moderate rate. The compulsory power consisted in expulsion, which included a forfeiture of the claim on the fund to which they had been contributing while in the society. One regulation particularly merits notice: no publican could sue in the courts for debts contracted for drink. "Crowley's Court" was the chief tribunal of the factory, and from which there was no appeal. At the "Court" a tradesman might sue a workman at the factory for debt; and if he sustained his claim, the debtor had no other choice than to submit to a regular deduction from his wages. If he questioned the ruling of the "Court," and rebelled against its authority, he sacrificed his employment. The "Court" was held in the office at Winlaton.

The social arrangements of this community deserve the highest commendation, especially their scheme of old-age pensions. When any workman was ill, he sent a note to the Court, and, after being considered by the Arbitrators, and found to be a deserving case for assistance, a sum of money was lent to him until he recovered. When disabled, or unable to work through old age, the workmen received from the Court the sum of five shillings—and in some cases seven shillings—weekly. The superannuated were known as "Crowley's Poor," and wore a badge with "Crowley's Poor" on the left shoulder. On the death of a workman, the widow either received a weekly allowance of 2s. 6d. from the Court, or was provided with employment in the factory, usually to make nail bags.

From the following entry in one of the books of the Court, we ascertain how the money for the use of the "Poor" was provided:—
"17th January, 1810. Ordered—That all workmen in the service may be allowed the privilege of the Court. All workmen employed in the service as non-domestics, but paying 5d. per pound, are allowed the benefit of the Court and school for their children. All workmen employed in the service paying 8d. per pound, after a year's service, are considered as domestics in every sense of the

word." A surgeon was appointed to attend the whole body of workmen.

From the following entries in the books of the Court, it will be seen that all complaints, disputes, and misdemeanours of the workmen were dealt with by that Tribunal. "March 11th, 1807. John Ayre, being 63 yeare old, a report being prevalent that he is going to marry a foreigner, it is ordered that in the event of his superannuation, this committee consider nothing for his wife, or in the event of his death, the widow so left will not be entitled to relief from the poor box." "April 22nd, 1807. Jos. Smith's note requests to have his son bound apprentice." "John Whitfield requests to make the poors' clothes." " Decr. 7th, 1807. Stephen Hobbner's note to have his grand-daughter educated at the Free School." "June 8th, 1808. Jos. Greenfield not being able to work any longer, humbly requests the full allowance." "August 15th, 1810. Jos. Greenfield to be allowed a coffin." "October 3rd, 1810. Thos. Moralee requests a superannuation allowance for himself and wife (7s.), granted." "March 4th, 1812. Margaret Ayre having been put into the Court for scandal, it was agreed to by the Arbitrators that in all such cases, provided a mulct be awarded the plaintiff, the defendant, although a widow, must pay the Court charges." This Margaret Ayre was probably the foreigner married to the John Ayre mentioned above. "March 3rd, 1813. William Rippith requests the following pay for Edward Cowen, viz., repairs his shoes, 1s.; also a piece of cloth to make him a waistcoat breest, and an allowance of 6d. to pay for buttons and thread for the same." "John Lee requests a loan of 4s. (granted)." "August 11th, 1813. John Passmore requests a coat." "April 6th, 1814. The workmen who attend the poor's funerals kindly request an allowance of one pennyworth of bread each man. This may be allowed to twelve men only." "September 29th, 1813. Thos. Biggins, Robt. Parker, information being made against these persons by Jacob Bolt, for trespassing in the Company's turnip field, and taking from thence sundry turnips. We have examined the parties and find it to be fact, we therefore mulct them 2s. 6d., one half to the informer and the other to Winlaton Poor." "January 15th, 1814. John Sinart's salary to be stopped till he appears to Arbitrator's Court for going a begging." "July 6th, 1814. Thomas Biggins, Thomas Jobling. These persons having been detected in borrowing and lending iron, contrary to law 51 and verse 1 and 2, they are therefore mulcted 8s. each, to be collected at 6d. per week, for the benefit of Winlaton Poor." Bastardy cases were also settled at the Court.

In the factory the most rigid system of registration was carried out. When a workman secured employment, his name, place of birth, place of residence, height, religion, and complexion were tabulated.

On the 17th October, 1704, Mr. Crowley, who was in London, received information from Mr. Jonathan Story of Winlaton, that "many of his (Mr. Crowley's) nailors and patten-ring makers had left his service at Winlaton and gone to work for Mr. Edward Harrison, at Swalwell, after their passage money had been paid."

Afterwards every workman in the service of Mr. Crowley had to sign an agreement similar to the following:—"2nd May, 1720. Articles of Agreement between John Crowley, Esq., London, Merchant, and the workmen engaged in his service at Winlaton, Winlaton Mill, Swalwell, and other places, in the Parish of Ryton, in the County of Durham. I agree to give six month's notice before leaving my employment, and also agree not to work at any other place within forty miles of Newcastle. Penalty £50."

It was probably to secure his runaway workmen that so minute a description of them was registered by Mr. Crowley, at Winlaton.

The business of the firm was transacted by the head agent and two surveyors, called the "Committee of Survey." In the year 1704, Mr. Jonathan Story was the head agent, and William Wright and Henry Stafford were the surveyors.

In all communications relating to business between the firm and their customers, the number of weeks that had elapsed since the beginning of the firm was specified, as the following memorandum will show:—"Coales led from North Banks Pitts to Winlaton Mill, for use of the Executors of the late Alderman Crowley, defunct, in the following weeks. Week 2230, ending Thursday August ye 8th, 1728. 130 fothers."

Crowley's workmen were known far and wide as "Crowley's Crew," and formed a compact and independent body. Sometimes, when trade was depressed, or the price of provisions high, they were not particular about the rights of property.

From the following interesting letter to the Magistrates at

Gateshead, we learn that the people of Winlaton, in 1767, were on the verge of revolution, on account of the high price demanded for provisions.

"To the Worshipful the Justices of the Peace for the County of Durham, assembled at Gateshead.

"We, the inhabitants and workmen of Winlaton, in the Parish of Ryton, humbly beg leave to represent to your Worships that formerly we used to have butter, eggs, poultry, potatoes, and many other articles of life brought into town by ye farmers and country people adjacent and exposed to open sale and sold to the highest bidder, but that now we are come to that unhappy situation that we are forced to buy all our butter, &c., of hucksters, at the price they please to impose, who make a practice of meeting the country people at a distance from the town and buying up what they bring for sale, if they be not such people as they have already engaged to bring all they have to sell to their own houses, which is ye case of many farmers. But what we principally beg your Worships' advice about is concerning a very necessary article of life at this time when bread-corn is so dear that it is even beyond the ability of ye poorer sort to purchase a sufficiency of it, and that is the potatoes, which, throughout the whole parish (we believe) are already engrossed into a few hands as they are now growing, and some of these bargains transferred twice over at ye monstrous profits of five pounds each time. Now, as this is the case, and as there are many hundreds of ye inferior class of people here who are all murmuring at these impositions, and the cries of the poor are so intolerable that we are very apprehensive that if these grievances are not remedied, they will in a short time make a riot, in which some innocent person may suffer. Therefore we humbly beg your Worships will take the affair into your own hands, or else point out to us a method how these grievances may be redressed at the easiest expense, which will greatly oblige, gentlemen, your most obedient and very humble servants.

"Winlaton, September ye 4th, 1767."

In the above letter reference is made to the market which was held weekly at Winlaton, when articles of food were exposed for sale on the Sandhill. But what we wish to point out is, that after the magistrates had refused to interfere with the way in which the farmers sold their produce, self-preservation on the part of "Crowley's Crew," compelled them to set the "rights of property" at defiance, by stopping the carts of the farmers on the way to Newcastle market, and selling their produce at prices which the Winlaton people considered reasonable. This conduct would naturally evoke protests and grumbling from the farmers, but any active opposition on their part to the course adopted by "Crowley's Crew," would have been both useless and dangerous.

On August 18th, 1790, John Brown of Winlaton, and two of his companions, were executed at Morpeth for horse-stealing. The execution of three criminals at one time drew an immense concourse of spectators.

Some of the amusements and pastimes of "Crowley's Crew" were cruel and demoralising. Poaching was carried on to an alarming extent. Sometimes a gang of poachers would number twenty or thirty men, who naturally produced terror wherever they went. A desperate affair took place at Alston Moor on August 13th, 1839, between a number of men from Winlaton and the neighbourhood, and the gamekeepers connected with an estate at Alston. Among the poachers was Will Renwick, a well-known Winlaton man, and an ardent sportsman. The poachers having secured their booty, retired to a public-house for refreshment, when the house was surrounded by the keepers, who satisfied themselves with watching till the poachers made their appearance. The Winlaton men understanding the state of affairs, on leaving the house made a tremendous rush, Renwick taking the lead and felling several of the keepers with his gun, thus enabling his companions to reach the outside, where a long and terrible conflict took place, in which one of the keepers was so badly injured that he afterwards died. All the poachers escaped.

Cock-fighting did not prevail to the same extent at Winlaton as it did at Swalwell and Whickham, on account of the sport in the last-named villages receiving support from men of wealth and social influence; yet Barlow Fell, which was the usual resort of the sporting fraternity in the neighbourhood, has been the scene of many a hard-contested main.

Bull-baiting was a form of sport highly relished by crowds of people who assembled to witness it. Bulldogs were kept in great numbers by the iron-workers and pitmen. The bulls were generally brought from Newcastle or Sunderland. A shilling was paid by the owner of a dog for a run at the bull, which was fastened to a ring fixed in a heavy stone in the ground. If the dog seized the bull by the nose, and pinned it, as the act was termed, the owner of the dog was complimented on its strength and courage; but if the bull was attacked in any other part than the nose, the dog was considered cowardly and ill-bred. Frequently the dogs were tossed into the air, and sometimess killed by the bull, when the excited multitude cheered vociferously. Bulls were baited on a piece of ground called the bull-ring, on which Winlaton church now stands, and which at that day formed part of the common lands of Winlaton. The last bull baited on that spot was in the year 1826 or 1827. Bulls were also baited on Barlow Fell. An old man named James Massey, of Winlaton Mill, and another named Robert Brooks of Winlaton, both eighty-five years of age, have seen bulls baited on "the fell" about the year 1828.

The men of Winlaton were ardent and active politicians. Under the old *regime*, the iron-workers were noted for their strong *high-tory* principles, and any meeting held in the village calling for reform in Church or State, would have been for the promoters a dangerous proceeding. But about the beginning of the present century a change seems to have taken place in the political sentiments of the iron-workers of Winlaton; for at the first public meeting held in the open air at Newcastle, on the Parade Ground in Percy-street, October 11th, 1819, "Crowley's Crew" were present in great numbers, and Mr. Thomas Hodgson of Winlaton was one of the speakers. "Crowley's Crew" on that occasion seems to have spread terror through the town; for in a letter from the Mayor of Newcastle to the then Home Secretary, he states that "seven hundred men who came from a village about three miles distant were prepared with arms to resist the civil power." It matters little whether the village referred to by the Mayor was Winlaton or Swalwell, for at both of these villages arms were manufactured by the workmen, to protect themselves against what they considered to be the actions of a despotic government.

In the year 1839, Winlaton was the head quarters of Chartism in the North of England. Almost all the leaders of the movement, including George Julian Harney, Dr. Taylor, Dr. (afterwards Sir)

John Fife, Samuel Kydd, and John Emerson, visited Winlaton, and addressed public meetings on the Sandhill.

The authorities were made acquainted with all the proceedings of the Winlaton Chartists, for Colonel Campbell—afterwards Lord Clyde—who commanded a regiment of dragoons at Newcastle, frequently visited Mr. G. H. Ramsay, J.P., at his residence at Winlaton, for that purpose; so that when he had to disperse the Chartists at the Battle of the Forth, July 30th, 1839, their numbers and their peculiar method of warfare were well known to him.

The Winlaton Chartists, more active and daring than their brethren, were active in preparing for ulterior measures, and occupied every leisure moment in the manufacture of thousands of "caltrops," an iron-pronged instrument for the annoyance of cavalry. The "caltrop" was better known among the workmen as the "craa-foot." Pike-heads were made in great numbers, and sold to the Chartists in other places for 1s. 6d. a piece. On the 15th of July, 1839, a man named Jacob Robinson, belonging to Winlaton, was brought up at the police-office, Newcastle, and charged with being disorderly, and on being searched, two pike-heads, each eighteen inches in length, were found on him; he was immediately imprisoned. On the 2nd of August, 1839, a considerable number of special constables were sworn in, in the neighbourhood of Winlaton. During that year (1839) great excitement prevailed in the north of England, it being feared that the Chartists would come into collision with the forces of the Government. So bitter was the feeling of the Chartists against the reigning powers, that many of them began to smoke herbs instead of tobacco to reduce the revenue, and thus "bring the Government to its senses." The "sacred month" (August, 1839) was perhaps better observed by the Chartists of Winlaton than by those of any other village in England. At the "Battle of the Forth," "Crowley's Crew," attended by the Winlaton Brass Band, was there in strong force; and whatever may be said about the humiliating part played by some of Crowley's workmen who lived at other villages, in the memorable "battle"—perhaps "rout" would be the better word to use—during the same month (August) an event occurred at Winlaton which shows that the preparations made by the Chartists to oppose any hostile force were both extensive and dangerous. A report reached Winlaton that a number of dragoons intended visiting the village to search for arms. Previous to this startling announcement, large quantities of hand-grenades, pikes, spears, and caltrops had been made. Hand-grenades were bottles filled with gunpowder, in which a fuse was inserted, and the bottles placed in bags containing pieces of iron. After the report was made to the Chartist leaders, a number of men—one with a gun—were placed at every available entrance to the village; as soon as the soldiers were seen, the gun had to be fired, to apprise the villagers of their approach. Two men, one named John Mc.Pherson, better known as Jackey the Glazier, with a fife, and George Burrell with a drum, had to make known to the people the expected visit of the dragoons.

Fourteen cannons were placed on the Sandhill, opposite the principal entrance to the village. Scores of men were ready to scatter caltrops on the principal thoroughfare, while several with hand-grenades were secreted in a yard on the south side of the Sandhill, ready to throw them among the soldiers on their arrival. All superfluous pikes and spears were concealed, and the arrival of the soldiers was expected in breathless excitement. Fortunately the report was false, and the soldiers never appeared. We will not anticipate what the consequences would have been had the soldiers arrived, but the courage and daring of the Winlaton Chartists at that time is beyond dispute.

Few men are living now who can really claim to have belonged to "Crowley's Crew" in their palmy days, but episodes of the Chartist movement are still related by the old people with enthusiasm.

FREEMASONRY AT WINLATON.

Freemasonry in the north of England probably owes its existence to Crowley's workmen. A tradition existed among the older workmen, that a Lodge was founded by the operative masons brought from London by Sir Ambrose Crowley. From the records of the Lodge of Industry, No 48, we know that the Lodge was held at Winlaton in 1725. There is another tradition, that on the introduction of Freemasonry into the village the meetings were held in a field, and the entrance guarded by armed men. In 1735 the Lodge was removed to Swalwell, where it was held until 1845, when it was removed to Gateshead.

The iron-work made at Winlaton and Swalwell was carried from Shields to London by two vessels belonging to Crowley, viz., the *Crowley* and the *Theodosia*, and by means of these vessels communication was kept up between the Lodge at Winlaton and the Grand Lodge. Mr. Joseph Laycock was Provincial Grand Master in 1734. Among the Worshipful Masters of the Lodge are found the names of William Dalton, 1737; William Hawdon, 1740; and John Rayne, 1747; who lived at Winlaton and Blaydon.

WINLATON SUBSCRIPTION LIBRARY.

On July 19th, 1819, a Subscription Library was established at Winlaton. In 1828, it consisted of 340 volumes, and 55 members; in 1895, it consists of 2,549 volumes, and only 17 members. The library was originally held in a room on the west side of the Sandhill; and from the stairs which led from the street to the library the Chartist lecturers addressed the people. The library is now held in a room on the east side of St. Paul's School.

A Mechanics' Institution was established in 1847, but it was abandoned a few years ago. After the removal of Crowley's establishment from Winlaton to Swalwell in 1816, a great number of the workmen left Winlaton for other places.

We cannot do better than sum up the history of this remarkable colony of workmen than by quoting from Mr. Joseph Cowen's interesting address to the Blaydon Burn Lodge of the Durham Miners' Union, on the 7th October, 1883. Mr. Cowen says:—
"When many busy centres of industry in Durham were moorland and forest, Winlaton was the seat of a vigorous industry. The semi-socialistic experiment of Crowley was interesting both politically and industrially. It got together a body of workmen who gave a distinctive character to the village, who afterwards acted as pioneers in the special trades in other districts. They lived largely in community; they began their work with prayer; they ate together; they adjusted their differences by voluntary courts; they had a church and a school, a cock-pit and a bull-ring. They were stout church and king men, rough, but loyal."

Although the establishment of Crowley was removed from Winlaton to Swalwell, still the Winlaton smiths maintained their ancient fame, and for the description of articles they manufactured, were unequalled by any in the kingdom. A number of men who had worked under Crowley, now began business on their own account, and nails, hinges, patten-rings, chains, etc., were manufactured the same as under the old firm.

Early in the 18th century, Mr. Joseph Laycock came from Wetherby, in Yorkshire, to manage the factory at Winlaton. Afterwards the factory passed into the hands of the family, in which it remained till the beginning of the present century. In 1828, John Cowen, Charles Dixon, James Hurst, Robert Laycock and Sons, Richard Parker, Robert Ramsay, William Renwick, and George, Cuthbert, and Andrew Thompson, are described as manufacturers at Winlaton. These firms were all offshoots from Crowley, Millington and Company, the members of which represented the oldest families in the village. Afterwards a great many of the Winlaton smiths and nailors obtained shops of their own, and worked for other manufacturers. They received from their employers iron, and orders as to the kind of ware required. After being made, the goods were conveyed in panniers over the backs of donkeys, to their destination.

Many of the nailmakers, with donkeys and carts, travelled through Durham and Northumberland, and hawked their ware. The nailmakers and patten-ring makers, in their best days, could earn no more than 3s. a day; bed-screw makers and ladle makers, 4s.; makers of small chain, 4s.; and large chain, 5s. When we consider that the day's work commenced at five in the morning and lasted till eight o'clock at night, there was little chance of the workmen becoming millionaires. Females were employed in nailmaking; the last two girls worked in a shop near to Amen Corner, in 1835. It is worthy of remark that one of the girls afterwards was married to one of the most successful manufacturers on the south side of the Tyne.

Winlaton, as a manufacturing place, has seen its best days. At present there is not a man engaged in nailmaking or in making patten-rings. Smithwork and chains are still manufactured at the engineering establishment of Messrs. Thompson, at the east end of the village; chains by Messrs. Bagnall; and at the west end are the shops belonging to the "Nut and Bolt Company, Limited," but these establishments only remind us of the world-famed factory of Sir Ambrose Crowley.

WINLATON IN 1895.

WINLATON Bank commences at Shibdon, and leads to Winlaton. The route is both long and steep. At the foot of the bank, on the right hand side, are the Blaydon Board Schools, opened in 1889. They are built after the design of Mr. T. C. Nicholson, of Blaydon; they are large, commodious, and handsome, and occupy a commanding view northward. Half-a-mile away from the Schools, towards Winlaton, on the right hand, is the Bleach Green, or Ladywell Bleachery. In the year 1830, the place was used as a bleachery by Mr. Robert Belt of Winlaton, whose mills were situate at the foot of Pandon Dene, Newcastle-upon-Tyne. Mr. Belt's garden was at the high side of the Green, in which there was a fish-pond, supplied with water from the Ladies' well, or Ladywell, at the south side. The Bleachgreen now consists of about twenty old-fashioned houses huddled together, surrounded by a number of neat and well-kept gardens. A quarter of a mile further, on the left hand, stands Winlaton Cottage, formerly the residence of Mr. Robert Belt, a gentleman once well known and highly respected in the neighbourhood. On the south side of the road, and nearly opposite to this cottage, there are a number of allotments, comprising about three acres of land, purchased from W. B. Beaumont, Esq., M.P., in 1851. On the right hand there is a road called Litchfield Lane, which leads to Blaydon.

The Wesleyan Methodists have a handsome chapel on the east side of the lane. In the year 1836 they commenced to worship in the chapel in Front-street. In the year 1828, services were held in the long room of the "Oak Tree" public-house. Hodgson Casson frequently visited Winlaton, and preached in the "Oak Tree." On one occasion, when preaching from the words, "It is easier for a camel to pass through the eye of a needle, than for a rich man to enter the kingdom of heaven," he exclaimed: "It would be easier for a pig to flee up an apple-tree and whistle like a blackbird, than for a rich man to enter the kingdom of heaven!" This kind of language used to-day in a Methodist chapel, would be a glaring violation of good taste, and preaching in the long room of a public-house would not be allowed, yet the result of Casson's preaching in the long room was the opening of a chapel in 1836, which was used until the erection of the present building in Litchfield Lane in 1868. The chapel is built of stone, and will seat one hundred and eighty. The chapel was destroyed by fire on February 24th, and re-opened November 13th, 1895.

Striking to the left after reaching Litchfield Lane, and passing the Commercial Hotel, you reach Corner Houses and Commercial-street, chiefly occupied by miners. Southward there is a pleasant footpath through the gardens and fields to Park Gate, one of the entrances to Axwell Park.

Returning to the main street of the village, you have on your right hand "The Square," consisting of a number of very old shops, which were probably the first built by Ambrose Crowley in 1690. On the north side of the Square is Oldwell Lane. Formerly there was a well in the lane for public use, but it is now covered up. A stone inserted in the well bears the inscription: A. C. D. 1747, the letter C being the initial of Crowley.

Oldwell House, formerly the residence of the Laycock family, stands at the foot of Oldwell Lane. Early in the eighteenth century Mr. Joseph Laycock came from Wetherby, in Yorkshire, to Winlaton to take the management of the factory. He was succeeded by Robert Laycock, born in 1763. This gentleman had three sons—Joseph, Richard, and Robert Laycock. Joseph was born November 24th, 1798. About the year 1835 he built the present Winlaton Hall, the residence of H. W. Grace, Esq. Mr. Laycock was engaged in the iron trade at Winlaton, and in the manufacture of railway waggons at Stella, by which he became a wealthy man. He was Mayor of Newcastle in 1858, and was a Justice of the Peace for Durham and Northumberland, and for many years Chairman of the Blyth and Tyne Railway. Mr. Laycock bought the Low Gosforth estate, and built Low Gosforth House, where he resided until his death on August 2nd, 1881. His only son, Robert Laycock, Esq., born in 1833, married Anne, daughter of Christine Allhusen, Esq. He was M.P. for North Lincolnshire. His principal seat was Wiseton Hall, Nottinghamshire. He died August 14th, 1881.

Returned by Oldwell Lane to the main street, Winlaton Hall is seen on the west side of The Square. As already stated, the Hall was the seat of the Hodgsons, and in 1753 was tenanted by Ambrose and John Crowley, Esquires. Part of the old mansion is supported at the east side by strong buttresses. On a stone in the gable is inscribed—"Crowley and Belt's Castle, 1864." Sixty years ago, two sisters of Mr. Robert Belt sold provisions in a part of the building, which is the only claim the Belts have to be noticed in connection with it. The Primitive Methodists, previous to the year 1850, conducted religious services in part of the building, but in the above year a chapel was built on the east side, to seat one hundred and ten persons. On the west side of the Hall is the school, and behind the school is a lane leading to Golden Hill, where the shop stood in which Blythe Hurst worked before he became a clergyman.

This remarkable man was born on the 6th July, 1806. The Hursts came originally from the neighbourhood of Manchester, and settled at Winlaton about the closing years of the seventeenth century. Robert, the father of Blythe Hurst, married Susannah Gibson, who belonged to one of the old families of Swalwell.

Blythe was sent to school when four years of age, where he learned to read the New Testament; and at seven he was sent to work in one of the smiths' shops at Winlaton. Until he was fifteen, he attended the Sabbath-school established by the Venerable Archdeacon Thorp. When about eighteen he was seriously afflicted, which led him to think seriously about religion, and to surrender his heart to God. He soon after joined the Wesleyan Methodist body, and became an acceptable local preacher. He says: "On particular occasions I have addressed upwards of eight hundred people at once." When about nineteen, he began the pursuit of knowledge under difficulties of the most arduous character. In his daily labour he was employed from six o'clock in the morning till eight in the evening, with only an interval of two-and-a-half hours for rest and refreshment. His wages were small, and few books were at his command. Having determined to master the Greek language, and being possessed of one shilling and sixpence, he set off to Newcastle, and purchased a Greek Grammar at a second-hand book-stall. Having little time to spare, he wrote the declensions of nouns, and the conjugations of the verbs, upon the flame-stone which hung before the smith's fire to preserve his face from the heat; and by this means he got them off by heart. He afterwards purchased a Greek Testament, and, at the age of twenty-one being in possession of a pound-note, he secured "Parkhurst's Greek Lexicon" at E. Charnley's shop in Newcastle. Mr. Hurst subsequently became an adept in Latin, Hebrew, and Syriac. When about thirty years of age he left the Wesleyan Methodist body, and joined the Methodist New Connexion, still labouring as a local preacher. In the latter end of 1839 and the beginning of 1840, Alexander Campbell, one of Robert Owen's socialist missionaries, visited Winlaton, and lectured in the village. Mr. Hurst wrote a pamphlet entitled, "Christianity No Priestcraft," in reply to Mr. Campbell's lectures. Unfortunately for the writer, he was unable to sell his pamphlet, which brought to his assistance the Rev. H. Wardell, rector of Winlaton, who took all the remaining copies off his hands. Mr. Wardell sent a copy of the pamphlet to the Rev. Dr. Maltby, Bishop of Durham, who, after reading it, requested Mr. Wardell to supply him with particulars of the author's life. The bishop wrote next to Mr. Douglas, rector of Whickham, to ascertain Mr. Hurst's ability to make ready application of his acquirements.

Mr. Hurst had previously severed himself from the New Connexion body, and on the suggestion of Dr. Maltby, he determined to enter the Church of England. The bishop had an interview with him in Newcastle, and made arrangements for his ordination. On the 9th of July, 1842, the Winlaton blacksmith proceeded to Auckland, where, after passing the necessary examination, he was in due course ordained a clergyman of the Church of England. In a short time he was appointed curate of Garrigill, near Alston. On leaving Winlaton, Mr. Hurst was presented with a purse of gold as a mark of the esteem and respect in which he was held in the village. He was afterwards appointed to the living of Slaley, near Hexham; and in the year 1854 he was promoted to the vicarage of Collierly. After Mr. Hurst became a clergyman, and had at his command time for study, he became a linguist of the highest order. In addition to his complete acquaintance with the modern European languages, he was master of the Hebrew, Syriac, Sanscrit, Chaldaic, Persian, Arabic, and other languages of antiquity. Mr. Hurst delivered several lectures in the Church of England Institute, and in the Blaydon Literary Institute, on Semitic Inscriptions, and on Egyptian Hieroglyphics, displaying great information on those abstruse and difficult questions. In recognition of his scholarly attainments, the degree of Ph.D. (Doctor in Philosophy) was conferred on him by the University of Rostock, in Germany. After a long life of usefulness, the Rev. Blythe Hurst, one of the most distinguished men of his day, died on June 24th, 1882. His remains rest in the cemetery at Winlaton, where a handsome granite tombstone is erected to his memory, bearing the inscription—

In
Affectionate Remembrance
of the
Rev. BLYTHE HURST, M.A., PH.D.,
Vicar of Collierly,
In the County of Durham,
Who died June 24th, 1882,
Aged 76 Years.

A little westward is Jobling's Garth, in which stand the Congregational Chapel and Hall. In the year 1732, a number of people belonging to different churches in Newcastle, but unable to attend them regularly, owing to the distance, united and met in a dwelling house at Woodside, near Ryton. They were soon formed into a congregation, and placed under the care of the Rev. J. Crossland. In 1750, the society removed to Swalwell, and, after many changes, during a period of nearly eighty years, the church became connected with the Secession body on the 1st of April, 1827. At that time the preacher sent by the Presbytery divided his services between Winlaton and Swalwell, preaching at the latter place in the forenoon, and at the former place in the afternoon. For some reason or other, the Presbytery came to the resolution of discouraging the services at Winlaton, and confining them exclusively to Swalwell. The members from Winlaton, fourteen in number, applied to the Presbytery to be separated from the Swalwell congregation, and to have a distinct supply of sermons for themselves. The Presbytery granted their request, and the consequence was the withdrawal of many of their members, and the formation of an Independent congregation at Winlaton. The Congregational Chapel was built in 1829, and accommodates about 200 people. A little westward, and on the south side of the village, is Parliament Corner and Street. The "Corner," at one time, was the resort of the village politicians. Parliament-street contains a number of old smiths' shops, and the street leads to California, which comprises about three acres of land, purchased by a number of working men from the Hon. H. T. Liddell, in 1848, and laid out for gardens, which have been very successful. A number of excellent houses were afterwards built, and altogether California is one of the prettiest and healthiest parts of Winlaton. On the north side of Front-street is the Sandhill, which has always been a convenient place for holding public meetings, and where the Hopping is annually held. Formerly the Sandhill used to be illuminated by a large bonfire on Royal Oak Day (29th May). Previous to the illumination, a great number of the villagers repaired to the woods and returned with branches of the oak tree. Twigs were displayed in the button-holes of their coats, which were known as "bate wood," and if any unfortunate man was seen without the "sprig," or "bate wood," he was immediately "bated," which often meant rather severe treatment.

Behind Church-street is the Salt Market, which contains several very old houses, in one of which William (Will) Renwick was born, and in which he died. William Renwick was well-known in the North of England as a crack shot with the gun, and as a pugilist. Strong, active, and daring, he was a terrible antagonist in the usual pugilistic encounters at hoppings, hirings, and pigeon matches; and woe to the unfortunate gladiator who opposed Renwick without measuring his man. On October 31st, 1837, a pugilistic encounter between a negro, known as "Young Molyneux," and William Renwick, took place at Middleton, near Cambo, for £25 a-side. The battle, after lasting for an hour and a half, during which eighty-seven rounds were fought (forty in the dark), was won by Molyneux, who butted his antagonist with his head so severely and continuously as at length to render Renwick incapable of further resistance. Another battle between Molyneux and Renwick was fought on Shap Fell, Cumberland, in June, 1839, for £100 a-side, when Molyneux was again the victor. William Renwick was also defeated by John Oliver (Coffee Johnny), a well-known Winlaton character, in a pitched battle on Hedley Fell, 20th May, 1850.

North-street is a continuation of Church street, which leads *via* Blaydon Bank to Blaydon. On the west side of North-street is Cromwell Place, from which a field path leads to Blaydon.

The field in which the Hall Farm stands, and known as the Hall-Garth, was formerly the Winlaton Race-course. In 1839, on May 20th and 21st (Whit-Monday and Tuesday), a Sweepstakes of 3 sovs. each p.p., with 20 added by the Town, free for all horses, was won by Mr. R. F. Johnson's "Nancy Banks."

The Hack Stakes of £1 each, with £10 added from the Racing Fund, for horses not thorough-bred, 2 miles, was won by Mr. Humble's "Black Heddon."

The Town's Plate, for Ponies not exceeding 14 hands high, given by the Racing Fund, was won by Mr. Ogle's "Lady Mary."

A Sweepstakes of £2 each, p.p., with £10 added by the Town, for horses that never won in Plate or Stake before the day of running, was won by Mr. Hudson's b g by "Waverley."

A Handicap of £1 each, with £10 added from the Racing Fund, was won by Mr. M. Robson's "Ingo."

. Mr. William N. Cowen was Clerk of the Course. The Races shortly after that date were discontinued at the Hall Garth. They were subsequently held on Barlow Fell, and the last races were run on May 23rd, 1854.

Returned to Church Street, you have on your right hand the old disused Pinfold and the Drill Hall. The Drill Hall is used by the "Tyne and Derwent Volunteers." This popular Volunteer Corps was formed in 1860. The Volunteers appointed their officers in the Winlaton School, on March 5th, and on March 31st, the Volunteers received their rifles. Mr. (afterwards Sir Joseph) Cowen, was the first captain. The first inspection of the corps was held in Stella Park, on July 22nd, 1861.

These Volunteers are now known as the "Fifth Volunteer Battalion of the Durham Light Infantry." There are two companies at Winlaton, the I and K, 142 strong, under Captains T. W. Bagnall and J. W. Thompson. There is also a detachment at Blaydon, the H Company, 112 strong, under the command of Hon. Major William J. Douglas. The late John Anthony Cowen, Esq., of Blaydon Burn, became Colonel of the Volunteers on July 5th, 1875, a position which he retained until his death. Winlaton Brass Band, which usually accompanies the Volunteers, is one of the oldest, if not the oldest country band in England. It was formed about the year 1801, and attended the Gibside Cavalry until the troop was disbanded. It always accompanied "Crowley's Crew" to political demonstrations at Newcastle and other places of meeting. Mr. Henry Mc.Pherson, who was buried May 2nd, 1860, was connected with the band for 59 years, and for the greater part of the time was bandmaster. Altogether the Winlaton Band has an interesting history.

Before arriving at the Church, "Amen Corner" is seen on the east side of Church-street. A lane leads from this spot to Park Gate; and just at the commencement of the road, on the east side, there is a blacksmith's shop, which was formerly a dwelling house and the residence of Thomas Hodgson, weaver, who was one of the speakers at the great political meeting, held on the Parade Ground, Newcastle, on October 11th, 1819. Mr. Hodgson, shortly after this meeting, settled in Newcastle. He afterwards removed to Gateshead, where he died on the 2nd of November, 1827, aged 48 years.

At the east side of the Church is the house which the Rev. Mr. Kitchen used as a private school fifty years ago, and at which Mr. Joseph Cowen, Mr. John Anthony Cowen, Mr. William Cowen, Mr. Robert Laycock, Mr. Thomas Thompson, and other gentlemen of the neighbourhood, received a share of their education.

St. Paul's Church.

The Church was consecrated on September 9th, 1828, by the Bishop of Durham. The building is in the Gothic style, by I. Bonomi, Esq., and cost £2,500. It consists of nave, side aisles, chancel, and square western tower. The latter is embattled, and adorned with corner spires. The side aisles are each formed by three octagonal pillars, supporting obtusely-pointed arches, and a similar arch is over the chancel. There is a gallery at the west end of the church which contains the organ. The font is handsomely sculptured. A fine painting of Christ taken down from the Cross, presented by Charles James Clavering, Esq., is placed against the north wall. The east window, which is large and handsome, is in five compartments, and filled with stained glass, representing our Saviour, the Evangelists, and other saints. In the south aisle, at the east end, there is a window of three lights, dedicated to St. Paul, and containing passages from his life, which bears the following inscription:—"To the honour and glory of God, in memory of Robert Belt, Esq., of Winlaton Cottage, who died December 3rd, 1855, aged 70 years. Jane, his wife, died 8th February, 1840, aged 31 years. Sarah Belt, his sister, died February 28th, 1841, aged 66 years. Barbara Whitfield, his sister, died 11th March, 1862, aged 89 years."

A second window, dedicated to St. Mary, contains the following inscription:—"To the Glory of God and memory of Mary Wardell, at rest on St. Andrew's Day, 1868."

At the west end of the aisle is another, dedicated to John the Baptist, with the inscription:—"To the honour of God and memory of Philip Smith, O.B.; May 24th, 1837. Judith, his widow, O.B.; April 23rd, 1840. Henry, their son, June 19th, 1833. Also of Jane, wife of Philip Smith, jun., O.B.; December 10th, 1846. Philip, their son, O.B.; September 19th, 1853; and of Philip, Judith, and Thomas Smith, grandchildren of the above Philip and Judith Smith, who died in childhood."

In the north aisle, at the west end, is a window of three lights, with only one-half of the middle light stained. It is dedicated to

St. Philip, and bears the inscription :—" Dedicated to the honour of God and the beautifying of His Church, by certain poor Brethren and Sisters in Christ. Blessed be ye poor."

The second window represents Mary sitting at the feet of the Saviour, and bears the following :—" In affectionate remembrance of Mary, wife of George Heppel Ramsay, of Derwent Villa, Parish of Winlaton, County of Durham; died February 1st, 1869, aged 73. Also of George Heppel, their youngest son, who died September 14th, 1860, aged 31."

At the east end of the aisle, the window is dedicated to St. Barnabas, with the inscription :—"In memory of John Nixon, died August 22nd, 1839. In affectionate remembrance of Mary, relict of the late John Nixon of Barlow, died June 20th, 1869, aged 90 years. Interred at Ryton. Also of Mary Louisa Bell, died June 22nd, 1855, aged 32 ; and Jane Grey, who died March 30th, 1863, aged 50 years ; daughters of the aforesaid John and Mary Nixon."

The Church contains several tablets. One of white marble, on the south side of the chancel, bears the inscription :—" In a vault beneath are deposited the remains of Charles John Clavering, Esq., of the County of Northumberland. He successively and honourably sustained the important offices of High Sheriff of the Town of Newcastle-on-Tyne, and of the Counties of Northumberland and Durham, and constable of the Castle of Durham. An affectionate husband, an indulgent master, a warm and steady friend, an upright and independent magistrate. Liberal, but unostentatious in his charities. His loss was deeply felt, and universally lamented. He died on the 20th day of June, 1888, aged 77, in the faith and hope of a true christian. This tablet was erected to his memory by his sorrowing widow, Diana Clavering."

There is in the south aisle a marble tablet :—" To the memory of Robert Laycock, of Winlaton, who died August 18th, 1828, aged 65 years. Also Mary, his wife, who died January 21st, 1854, aged 92 years."

Another tablet bears the inscription :—"In loving memory of John Foster, of Winlaton, who died January 28th, 1873, aged 50 years. Isabella Barbara, his wife, who died November 18th 1877, aged 40."

On a tablet near the entrance is the following information :—

"This Chapel was erected in the year 1828. It contains sittings for 800 persons. And in consequence of a grant from the Society for Promoting the Enlargement and Building of Churches and Chapels, 400 of that number are hereby declared to be free and unappropriated for ever.

    CHARLES THORP, Rector,
    HENRY SANDERSON, } Churchwardens."
    JOHN FENWICK,

The tower contains six bells; on the tenor is inscribed :—" This peal of five bells was presented to the Church of St. Paul by Robert Belt, Esq., Winlaton, Anno Dom., 1828;" and on the reverse :—" Charles Thorp, B.D., rector of Ryton; Henry Wardell, M.A., John Reed, B.A., curates; Robert Watson, Newcastle-on-Tyne, founder."

At the time of the foundation of the parish, November 6th, 1832, the Rev. John Reed, A.B., officiated as curate; the presentation to the living was vested in the Bishop of Durham. The Rev. Henry Wardell was appointed in 1833, and remained rector of the parish until his death in 1884.

The living is a rectory valued at £275, and the Bishop of Chester is the patron. The gross annual value of the living was stated in 1835 at £356, subject to permanent payments amounting to £9.

The parsonage adjoins the churchyard on the south side, and is pleasantly situated.

THE CHURCHYARD.

The churchyard wall encloses an area of an acre and a half of ground, lying mostly on the north side. Alongside of the walk on the south side are the burial places of several of the old families of Winlaton.

A granite tombstone marks the resting place of the Rev. Henry Wardell, bearing the inscription :—

  MARY, wife of the Rev. Henry Wardell, M.A.,
    First Rector of this Parish,
      At Rest,
    St. Andrew's Day, 1868,
     Aged 64 years.

The above-named HENRY WARDELL,
At Rest,
October 3rd, 1884,
Aged 84 years.
Jesu Mercy.

On the left of the late rector's stone, is the burial place of the Ramsay's of Derwent Villa. A vault-stone bears the following :—

The family vault of George Heppel,
and Mary Ramsay of Derwent Villa,
Parish of Winlaton, County of Durham.
In Memory of GEORGE HEPPEL RAMSAY,
Their youngest and beloved Son ;
Who died September 14th, 1860, aged 31 years.
MARY, the beloved Wife of
George Heppel Ramsay,
Died February 1st, 1869, aged 73 years.
The above GEORGE HEPPEL RAMSAY, J.P.
Departed this life, November 27th, 1879, aged 88 years.

On a stone at the east end of the church is the following :—

The family Vault
of
Joseph Cowen,
Blaydon Burn House.
MARY, Wife of Joseph Cowen,
Born June 8th, 1795; died July 30th, 1851.
ELIZABETH, daughter of the above,
Born 27th October, 1823; died 21st May, 1853.
EDWARD, youngest son of the above,
Died in Octago, New Zealand, 3rd June, 1867,
Aged 31 Years.
The above JOSEPH COWEN, Knight, M.P.,
Died at Stella Hall, 19th December, 1873,
Aged 73 Years.
WILLIAM, Third Son of the above,
Died at Capheaton, 14th March, 1875,
Aged 42 Years.
MARY CARR, Daughter of the above,
Who died 4th December, 1891,
Aged 69 Years.

A Cemetery on the west side of the church was consecrated by the Bishop of Durham, June 16th, 1879.

Charles Clavering Wardell, better known in the dramatic profession as Charles Kelly, was born at Winlaton on January 4th, 1839, and was the son of the Rev. Henry Wardell, M.A., rector of Winlaton, He became an officer in the English army, but quitted it for the theatrical profession. He made his first appearance at the Theatre Royal, Hull, in 1868, in the character of Montano in "Othello." In London he played at the Surrey, Holborn, Globe, Queen's, Royal, Court, St. James's, Adelphi, and Haymarket theatres in many parts. In October, 1873, at the Globe Theatre, Mr. Kelly sustained his "original" part of Richard Arkwright, in the drama of "Arkwright's Wife," by the late Tom Taylor, first performed at the Leeds Theatre Royal, his acting on this occasion being highly praised. Having previously appeared in Charles Reade's plays of "Rachel the Reaper" and "Griffith Gaunt" at the Queen's Theatre in Long Acre in 1875, Mr. Kelly accepted an engagement at the Court Theatre under the management of Mr. Hare. On Saturday, March 13th of that year, Mr. Kelly appeared there as Lord Melton in an original comedy by Charles F. Coghlan, entitled "Lady Flora," in which he won high honours. In January, 1876, at the same theatre, in the first performance of "A Quiet Rubber" (C. F. Coghlan) adapted from the French "La Partie de Piquet," Mr. Kelly played Mr. Sullivan. In December of the same year, at the same theatre, in a revival of "New Men and Old Acres" (Tom Taylor and A. Dubourg), the part of Mr. Samuel Brown was sustained by Mr. Kelly. The revival of this play was very successful, and remained on the "bills" of the Court Theatre for 250 consecutive nights. At the same house Mr. Kelly appeared as Darnley in "The House of Darnley." At St. James's Theatre, in "Such is the Law," he gained further reputation by his careful acting of Tom Goacher. At the Adelphi Theatre, in 1878, he played for a time the part of Pierre Lorance, in "Proof." The same year, on Monday, December 2nd, at the Haymarket Theatre, in the first performance of "The Crisis" (James Alberry), adapted from M. Emile Augier's "Les Fourchambault," Mr. Kelly presented in a remarkably able and finished way the character of John Goring. On April 14th, 1879, at the same theatre, in an original comedy-drama in five acts, by W. G. Wills, entitled "Ellen; or Love's Cunning," he played the part of Thomas Pye with admirable earnestness. This character and that of Lady Breezy, (sustained by Miss Blanche Henri), and the excellent acting that was displayed in their presentation, probably suggested to Mr. Wills to reconstruct his play, and reproduce his "comedy" scenes under the title of "Boag," Mr. Kelly playing his "original" character. Mr. Kelly married Miss Ellen Terry, the celebrated actress. Miss Terry has visited Winlaton several times, on one occasion placing a wreath on the grave of the Rev. Henry Wardell, M.A., the father of her husband. Mr. Charles C. Wardell died on April 17th, 1885.

PARK HEAD HALL.

This fine modern mansion, which is the seat of John Ramsay, Esq., was built in 1836, by the late George Heppel Ramsay, Esq., J.P. The house stands on the north side of the Derwent, and the view from the front is one of striking beauty, possessing the charm of breadth and distance, a soft sweep of undulating country, with an occasional glimpse of the Derwent gleaming here and there out of its covert of crags and trees. The Hall is surrounded by a small park, and the farm connected with the Hall comprises about 200 acres of land.

Mr. George Heppel Ramsay was the son of Thomas Ramsay and Mary Heppel. Mary Heppel was the daughter of George Heppel of Swalwell, who was connected with the ironworks of Messrs. Crowley, Millington & Co. The Heppels came originally from Saxony, about the beginning of the 17th century, and were steel makers on the banks of the Derwent. On a plan of Winlaton, dated 1632, there is a forge on the east side of the present station at Rowland's Gill. Tradition states that at this forge the Heppels manufactured their steel. They afterwards removed to Derwent Cote, higher up the Derwent, with which forge the father of Mr. G. H. Ramsay was connected. Mr. G. H. Ramsay was born at Park Gate Farm, in the year 1790. In his tenth year he was sent to Tanfield, to be educated under the Rev. R. Simpson, vicar of Tanfield. As soon as his education was finished, he returned to Park Gate and learned farming. But his mind was not content with farming alone, he therefore joined his grandfather in the

Derwent Haugh brickworks, collieries, and ammonia works, and, under his direction, the works were vastly increased, to which were added coke-making, malt houses, manure works, and bone mills. Mr. Ramsay still devoted part of his time to farming, and it was on the Park Gate Farm, in 1859, that oxen were last used in the North of England for agricultural purposes. In 1853, Blaydon Main Colliery was sunk by Mr. Ramsay, which turned out to be an advantageous adventure. The ordinary coal obtained from this colliery was celebrated for the valuable coke it yielded, commanding the highest price in every market in the world. It is known as the "Ramsay Condensed Coke," and its chief markets are Spain, Russia, and Italy. In 1878, Mr. Ramsay was awarded ths Gold Medal at the Paris International Exhibition of Industries for the products of his mines and manufactures. In addition to the ordinary coal and fire-clay seams of Mr. Ramsay's Colliery, a valuable seam of cannel coal was deposited throughout a portion of his royalties. This coal is well-known for its high illuminating qualities and freedom from sulphur, and is extensively used in the lead-mining districts of Spain and other countries where silver is found co-mingled with other geological products. Mr. Ramsay was fond of field sports, and was a reputed shot in his earlier years, and even at the advanced age of 78, brought down his black game at eighty yards distance, in the presence of the Duke of Northumberland and other sportsmen, the bird being preserved to this day at Kielder Castle. Mr. Ramsay was a Magistrate for the County of Durham. In every respect he was a fine specimen of the old English gentleman. He died on November 28th, 1879, at the advanced age of 89 years, and was buried at Winlaton. Mr. G. R. Ramsay, the well-known colliery owner and brick manufacturer of Swalwell, is the son of the present owner of Park Head Hall.

In 1875, a School Board was formed for the Township of Winlaton, comprising seven members, the first election taking place on April 21st.

In 1875, a Local Board, which was formed at Blaydon in 1861, was extended to Winlaton.

Formerly the boundaries of the Parish were perambulated, the last time being on October 22nd, 1850. "Riding the Boundaries" was an interesting event fifty years ago. The officials represented the lords of the manor, who were usually accompanied by the

Steward and the Bailiff. They assembled at Derwenthaugh, after which they advanced westward along the river side as far as Blaydon Burn foot, they next went southward *via* Blaydon Burn to Winlaton. Here they advanced westward, following the Burn as far as the road on the north side of the Spen; after which they took a south-westerly direction past Bede Lodge to the Derwent, near to Lintz Ford. They then retraced their steps to Swalwell Bridge, which concluded the day's proceedings. The Bailiff carried a small red flag, and preceded the company on horseback. The cavalcade was always accompanied by great numbers of the parishioners on foot, who took the liveliest interest in guarding the boundaries of the parish. A number of medals were generally distributed to the young people as a memento of the occasion. The medal struck in 1850 bore the following inscription:—
"Winlaton Lordship, Durham. John Clayton, Esq., Steward. Boundaries Perambulated October 22nd, 1850. On the obverse side:—Charles Towneley, Esq.; Hon. H. T. Liddell; W. B. Beaumont, Esq.; John Bowes, Esq.; Marquis of Bute; Joseph Cowen, Esq., Lords of the Manor of Winlaton."

[handwritten notes:] + The Claverings bought the Liddell interest in the Lordship of Winlaton. & are now included in the list of Lords of the manor + have 27/96ths Share of all Minerals found there —

+ Lord R

WINLATON MILL.

"Again the bordering woods, aroma'd fill
With blending balms the chalice of the dews;
Charm laughs on charm, and hill sweet smiles on hill
Till beauty bids us pause at old Winlaton Mill."
—*Barras.*

WINLATON MILL is an old-fashioned little village seated on the north side of the Derwent, one mile and a quarter west of Swalwell Bridge, and a similar distance south of Winlaton. The most of the houses are old, and *after* being whitewashed, give to the village a picturesque appearance. Before the advent of Sir Ambrose Crowley, the hamlet was called Huntlayshaugh.

In 1361, Agnes, widow of John Menevylle, held of Ralph Nevill, the hamlet of Huntlayshaugh, in Wynlawton, by 2s. rent. The old public-house (Golden Lion) is still called Huntlay's Hall; the well at the east end of the village Huntlay's Well; and the burn, which runs down the wood on the north side, Huntlay's Burn, by the old people.

Sir Ambrose Crowley after establishing his ironworks at Winlaton in 1690, extended them to Winlaton Mill in 1691. There is on a stone in the mill dam, on the west side of the village, the inscription "Sir Ambrose Crowley, Anno 16—." As Sir Ambrose was not knighted until the year 1706, the inscription must have been made after that date (1706), or *Sir* added to it. The inscription is formed on two stones, and the figures after 16 have been effaced from one of the stones. In the *Universal Magazine* for 1782, there is an account of Crowley's ironworks, in which it is stated that the date on the mill dam was 1691; so that we may conclude that the ironworks were commenced at that date, or immediately after.

The Derwent, at the west side of Winlaton Mill, after passing through the viaduct at Lockhaugh, makes a circuit of about half a mile round the base of a steep and lofty bank, after which it flows southward. It was at this point that Crowley commenced operations for the making of the mill-race. A water-course was made on the west side of the stream to carry off the superfluous water; and on the east side was formed the dam, through which passes the water required for the ironworks, the water not required falling over the "steps," and forming a junction with the water which disappears on the west side, continues its course eastward. The visitor to this romantic situation should follow the footpath from the dam to what is known as the "Scaur Head," and obtain a view of the country south and west of the "Scaur." The scenery is wild and romantic in the highest degree. Away in the distance, westward, rising above the surrounding woods is the column of "Liberty" at Gibside, while immediately before you is the Lockhaugh Viaduct, rising seventy feet above the Derwent. On the north side of the river is an immense sweep of hill, rising one hundred and fifty feet above the water, and completely wooded; at the south side, on a steep and commanding position, are the ruins of Hollingside Manor House, formerly the seat of the giant race of Hardings. The mill-race pursues its course from the dam to the ironworks, after leaving which it empties itself into the Derwent.

The ironworks of Crowley comprised rolling mills, slitting mill, file-cutting and chain shops. The mills, forge-hammers, and shears were kept in motion by nine water-wheels. Only one water-wheel now remains, which assists in propelling the machinery of the present rolling mills. The ironwork after being forged, was carted to Swalwell. After the ironworks had remained in the hands of Sir Ambrose Crowley, and Crowley, Millington & Co., for nearly one hundred and seventy years, on February 10th, 1863, the whole of the fixed stock, plant, rolling mill, houses, watercourses, &c., were bought by Messrs. Pow and Fawcus of North Shields, for the sum of £780. But the factory did not flourish in their hands; and, fortunately for Winlaton Mill, Messrs. Raine took possession in 1885, and since that time the mills have been as busy as ever they were in the palmy days of Crowley. Nearly everything about Winlaton Mill bears traces of old age. The walls around the factory; the bell, with the date 1791; the clock underneath the bell, with its brass face ornamented with angels at the corners, bearing the inscription, "Thomas Pare, Londini fecit," said by the oldest inhabitants to be as old as the mill itself; the old houses and their primitive arrangements; all strike the observer as belonging to a generation far remote from our day.

Formerly the factory bell was used as a "Curfew," and was rung every night at eight o'clock, when the workmen were expected to retire for rest. This interesting custom, after existing for nearly two hundred years, was discontinued in April, 1860.

There is at the west side of the village and the north side of the mill-race, an old road which leads to the "Scaur" wood. In 1632, this was the only road which led through Winlaton Mill. After passing through the wood, it crossed the land on the north side, again passing through a wood which formerly filled the Shotley Bridge turnpike, and entered the "Birk-gate," the way to the Birks and Winlaton. This was the road taken by part of Cromwell's army with his artillery, after passing down Clockburn Lane, and fording the Derwent. After reaching Stella, the army forded the river Tyne, and proceeded to Dunbar, in 1650. Old men are still living who remember this road, but a considerable part has now been effaced from the topography of the neighbourhood. The Derwent is crossed by a bridge of primitive construction; it is formed of one beam of timber, resting on stone pillars. The pillars were built by the well-known "Lang Jack," the Samson of the locality. Previous to the erection of the bridge, the Derwent was crossed on stepping-stones. On the west side of the middle pillar is the inscription, "John English, Mason, Anno 1842." On the south side of the bridge begins Clockburn Lane. The burn here empties itself into the Derwent. Formerly there stood on the south side of the stream a flour mill, with a water-wheel propelled by the water which ran down Clockburn Dene. The miller's house still stands on the west side of the bridge. The scenery on the north side of the village is uncommonly fine. The visitor will be amply repaid by stopping for a few minutes at a point near to the Spa Well, and looking up the Derwent towards Winlaton Mill. A prettier scene is not to be imagined. It is one deep mass of wood and lawn, the woods having the appearance of dipping in the water, and this without a break until the water seems to lose itself in the forest.

It is needless to say that every part of this charming neighbourhood has been reproduced on canvas by the artist. Otters are sometimes captured in the Derwent; bird-life is plentiful; and the botanist will find the valley a successful hunting ground.

On the west side of Winlaton Mill, and just where the Derwent makes a bend after passing through Lockhaugh Viaduct, there once stood a flour mill, which, according to tradition, belonged to Messrs. Sharp and Walker of Lumley. An old wall, said to belong to the mill, and the remains of the dam can still be seen. Walker had another mill at Lumley. Sharp and Walker were tried at Durham in the year 1631, for the murder of a young woman of the name of Anne Walker, a niece of John Walker, the owner of the mill. The young woman had gone to the house of her uncle to act as his housekeeper. She is described as a pleasing woman of twenty-five, and her appearance handsome. Unfortunately, after staying some time at her uncle's house, she found she was to become a mother. Anne disappeared, nobody knew where. It is said that the spirit of Anne appeared to John Grahame, miller, at Lumley, and revealed to him the circumstances of the murder. Her uncle had sent her away with Mark Sharp, who had to take her to some place where she was to be taken care of until her trouble was over. Sharp murdered her with a pick, making five wounds in her head, afterwards throwing her down a pit. The ghost of Anne made known these circumstances to Grahame; the pit was examined and the body found. The evidence against Sharp and Walker must have been convincing, as they were afterwards executed at Durham in 1631-32. This murder created an immense sensation at that time in the County of Durham. The appearance of Anne Walker's "ghost," no doubt, adding to the excitement. The flour mill at Lockhaugh was worked until the middle of the last century, and retained the name of Sharp and Walker's Mill.

From the following account of a robbery which appeared in the *Newcastle Courant*, May 7th, 1814, Winlaton Mill appears to have been a rather unsafe route for travellers to take on their way home:—" Fifty Pounds Reward—Whereas last night between the hours of ten and eleven o'clock, as Mr. John March of Greenside, cattle dealer, was returning from Darlington Market, he was attacked by two men in the lane leading from Winlaton Mill to Winlaton, one of them middle-sized, the other stout made, who struck him with a bludgeon on the left arm and head, which unhorsed him, and after receiving several bruises, was robbed of £340, principally £5 Darlington and Durham Bank Notes. A reward of £30 is hereby offered by the Stella and Winlaton Association for the Prosecution of Felons; also a further reward of £20 by the said Mr. John March, to any person or persons giving such information as may lead to the conviction of the offender or offenders. Stella, April 27th, 1814."

Formerly, the men of Winlaton Mill had a strong propensity for poaching. In the time of Sir Ambrose Crowley, bitter complaints were made to him by the surrounding landowners about his workmen capturing salmon, and after his time; many sanguinary conflicts have taken place between "Crowley's Crew" and the gamekeepers in the preserves of Gibside and Chopwell. Cock-fighting was carried on to a great extent on the "Scaur Head," especially at Easter time, when "Crowdy Mains" were fought by "Hamey" cocks. It is said the ironworkers were not very particular about the way they secured the cocks; after being killed, they were eaten at a supper the same day, at one of the public-houses in the village.

The Primitive Methodists have a neat chapel, which stands on the side of the Shotley Bridge turnpike, erected in 1870, and capable of seating 150.

A delightful walk for about two miles brings the visitor to Rowland's Gill Station.

> "In summer time maw heart dis yorn
> Te hev a range throo Blaydon Burn;
> Thy rocky banks, se jagged and torn,
> Aw'm fond o' climbing Blaydon Burn."
>
> —*Horsley.*

THE Burn commences at the north side of Coalburn's farm, and runs down between the hills on the north side of Barlow, keeping a westerly course until it reaches the north side of Winlaton, where the stream makes a bend and takes a northward direction through a deep valley a mile and a quarter long, when it empties itself into the Tyne at Blaydon. In a plan of the Winlaton lordship dated 1632, the burn for half way down the valley is named Winlaton, in the other half of its course it is called Blaydon. At the present time the stream in the whole of its course down the valley has Blaydon applied to it. About a quarter of a mile before the Burn enters the valley, it is known as the Brockwell, from the Saxon word *Brock* = a badger, and *well*, which sometimes means a stream as well as a spring of water.

The following entry in the Ryton parish register shows that formerly the "brocke" was taken in the parish :—" 1667.—Chopwell, thirty-six foxes heads and one brocke head." The Brockwell has undoubtedly taken its name from the circumstance of brocks, or badgers, frequenting the burn at that part. At the head of the burn is Blaydon Burn House, the residence of the late John A. Cowen, Esq., one of the best known men in the North of England. The late Sir Joseph Cowen made this mansion his residence after he entered into the brick making business at Blaydon Burn. After

[handwritten annotation: The Brockwell Seam of Coal outcrops here hence its name. In a similar manner further up the Derwent Valley. The Busty seam outcrops on Busty Bank Farm — hence the name of the seam.]

his removal to Stella Hall, his son, Colonel Cowen, became the occupant of the hall. It was here that Mr. Joseph Cowen of Stella Hall, was born. The house has been considerably enlarged since it became the property of the Cowen family, and now it is one of the best in the neighbourhood. It is surrounded by a small but beautiful park, which is entered by a drive from the north side. Mr. Cowen was a Justice of the Peace for the County of Durham, also Colonel of the Tyne and Derwent Rifle Volunteers, Chairman of the Blaydon Local Board, and Master of the Braes of Derwent Foxhounds. This pack of hounds is one of the oldest in England. Nearly sixty years ago, they were known as the Prudhoe and Derwent Foxhounds, but in 1841 they were taken to the kennels at Coalburns, when Mr. Thomas Ramsay became master of the hounds. Afterwards the pack was sent back to Prudhoe. Again it was brought to Coalburns, when Mr. William Cowen was appointed master, a position he held until his death in 1875. At that time Mr. John A. Cowen became master of the hounds and removed them to Blaydon Burn. Mr. Cowen remained master until his death on April 14th, 1895. He was buried in the family vault at Winlaton. His funeral—which was a military one—was the largest ever known in the village.

At the top of Blaydon Burn are Messrs. Joseph Cowen & Co.'s brickworks, where are also made their celebrated retorts. These brickworks were established about the year 1730. Seventy years before that date, fireclay was worked at Blaydon Burn, and manufactured into bricks at Paridise, on the north side of the Tyne. The clay manufactured at present at the Burn makes about six million bricks a year. The major portion of the trade of the firm is foreign and colonial. At the west side of the brickworks are the remains of a flour mill, which formerly belonged to Mr. Anthony Foster. According to the plan of Winlaton, 1632, a Foster had a mill there at that time, so that for 2co years there have been millers in the family. Adjoining the mill there once stood a forge, which belonged to Mr. Clark Foster, but all traces have disappeared. On the south side of the brickworks stands Messrs. Belt and Whitfield's disused corn-mill. The water-wheel still rests on the east side of the building. Messrs. Cowen have lately erected, a little eastward of Belt's mill, substantial screens. Underground communication has been made between the Lily Drift at Rowland's Gill and Blaydon Burn, so that the coals are now brought to the staiths at Stella. This part of Blaydon Burn is a hive of industry, but we are not sure whether Mr. Ruskin would not deplore the changes that have been made in this pretty valley. Proceeding down the Burn, with steep banks on either side, the visitor sees a chimney emerging from the trees on the east side. This is the only remaining part of what was known as Robinson's Flour Mill. It was sometimes called Shipping's Mill, from a man named Shipping, who was the miller. After passing a small pit belonging to Messrs. Joseph Cowen & Co., the remains of Wintrip's Flint Mill are seen standing on the left of the waggon-way. The mill-race is now filled up, and the arms of the water-wheel are at rest. The miller's house is still standing, and along with the rich and varied scenery which surrounds it, forms one of the delightful spots on the burn. The ruins of Fenwick's Flour Mill are next seen on the burn side. The mill was used last by Messrs. Bagnall as a file-cutting establishment. Hobby's dam is soon reached, which forms a sheet of water both broad and deep. The burn, after winding round the bank on the south side, appears again emerging from the clumps of brushwood and trees on either side, and presents a pretty scene. All around, the banks are clothed with trees, and in summer are studded with a rich profusion of flowers, which makes the spot extremely attractive. No one is able to tell who the Hobby was whose name is connected with the dam. On a plan of Blaydon Burn, dated 1775, the mill on the north side belonged to a person whose name was Hoplyh. The dam at that time would be Hoplyh's, and Hobby's is evidently a corruption of Hoplyh. On September 8th, 1869, Robert Foster of Winlaton, nailmaker, committed suicide by drowning himself in the dam; and on May 10th, 1875, Robert Prudhoe, nailmaker, also committed suicide by drowning himself in the same place. The remains of a waggon-way may be seen on the east side of the dam, by which coals were brought from Barlow to Stella staiths. A little further down the burn is another flour mill. This mill, in 1775, was called Hoplyh's Mill. Thirty years ago it was called Burn's Mill, on account of William Burn, who occupied the adjoining farm, using the mill to grind his corn. At present it is worked by Mr. Edward Gibson, and is known as Gibson's Mill. The water-wheel is confined within the walls of the mill. This is the only one among all the mills standing on the burn that has not fallen into disuse. A pleasant walk down a footpath with delightful scenery on the east side, brings you to another mill, which was formerly used by Messrs. Joseph Cowen & Co. for grinding clay. The water-wheel is hidden by a picturesque little cottage standing by the side of the path; the wheel is silent, and only the murmuring of the stream is heard as it proceeds in its course down the valley. A few minutes' walk brings the visitor to Massey's Forge, which are in ruins. The water passed from the dam through large pipes on to the wheel, by which it was set in motion. The building was afterwards used as a foundry by Messrs. Smith, Patterson & Co. of Blaydon. On the north side of the old forge is the Milner Pit. The Hodge, or Cannel Seam, is being wrought at this pit, and is 3 feet 2 inches, including 22 inches of cannel coal, the depth being 14 fathoms. Another mill, known as Haggerston's Mill, stood below the site of the old forge in 1775, but all traces of it are gone. At the bottom of the burn stand the brickworks, No. 2, of Messrs. Joseph Cowen & Co.

THORNLEY.

AFTER leaving Winlaton by Scotland Head at the west end, and proceeding southward for about half a mile, the pedestrian reaches Snooks Hill farm. In the "survey" of 1632, this house and land are described as belonging to one Snurke. Snooks is really a corruption of Snurke, the name of the man who two hundred years ago farmed the land. The land was subsequently occupied for two or three generations by members of the Hancock family, a branch of the Hancocks of Friarside. At this farm, a road known as the Birkgate, leads to Winlaton Mill; and another road, a little lower down than the farm, branches to Thornley.

Thornley is described by Surtees as a single tenement to the west of Winlaton, nearly opposite to Gibside. In 1361, Agnes, widow of John Menevylle of Hardon, held the manor of Thornelly, in Wynlaton, of Ralph Neville, by 40s. rent. In 1368, Thornley is mentioned in the inquisition on the death of Ralph de Nevill, and it probably rested in the family till the sale of Winlaton in 1569. Thornley was the seat of a branch of the Tempests from 1565 to 1709. By fine, 8th August, 12 car. 1636, William Tempest acquired from Sir William Selby, Knt., and Elizabeth and William Selby, half of a messuage, toft, and garden, two hundred acres of meadow, as many of pasture, a hundred acres of arable land, and as much of moor and whin in Thornley, in the parish of Ryton.

On the 4th December, 1636—the year in which William Tempest obtained from the Selbys the lands in Thornley—William, son of Sir William Selby, was killed in a duel by John Trollop of Thornley.

The land is now owned by the Marquis of Bute.

The district extends from the Birk-gate to The Spen, and from the north side of Barlow to the Derwent, and is exclusively agricultural. It comprises High and Low Thornley; High Thornley lying westward, and Low Thornley eastward. At Low Thornley there are two farm houses; one of them evidently has not been built for a farm, but has been quite a superior mansion. It is of two storeys, and so old that the front of the house is considerably out of plumb. At the east side there has been an arched doorway about ten feet high, which is now built up. There is evidence of several alterations having been made to the house, at different dates. As this house is only a mile from Winlaton, and the Tempests of Thornley are nearly always described as of Winlaton— for instance: "Dec. 26th, 1613. Mary, daughter to Mr. William Tempest of Winlawton [bur.]" this house in all probability was the seat of the Tempest family at Thornley. The farm on the south side of the turnpike is modern.

About half a mile west of Low Thornley farms, there is a secluded glen known as Lily Crook. Fifty years ago there were two coal-pits at this romantic spot, one of which was known as the Lily Crook Pit, which belonged to the Garesfield Company, the other was worked by Mr. Daniel Elliot, and used for Land sale. Both these pits have been abandoned; and now there is nothing to disturb the silence which prevails from one end of Thornley to the other, except the noise of the waggons as they run down the High Thornley waggon-way to Derwenthaugh.

A pleasant road leads from Low to High Thornley, which comprises about a dozen houses. On the west side of the waggon-way, in a most delightful situation, stands Thornley House, the residence of Mr. Thomas Bagnall, formerly of Winlaton. At the top of the bank there is a large house, now falling into a state of decay, but which still bears traces of former grandeur. At one time the agents of the Marquis of Bute lived here; but at present it is let to several tenants. A footpath leads from High Thornley for about half a mile to the Shotley Bridge turnpike, from which there is a commanding view of Gibside and its picturesque surroundings.

On the west side of Winlaton, and the north of the church, there is a turnpike leading to the villages of Barlow and Spen. Not far from the entrance to the road are the Winlaton Board Schools, built in 1877, after designs by Mr. John C. Nicholson of

Blaydon. The schools comprise boys', girls', and infants' departments, having in all accommodation for 500. The cost of the schools was £5,000.

Half a mile from Winlaton there is a place called The Nobbys, or Nobbies, where there is a large stone quarry. Previous to the erection of Winlaton church, the people of Winlaton Mill were compelled to travel to Ryton church. They left Winlaton Mill by the Birk-gate, and walked to Snooks Hill farm, when a road on the south side of the farm house led to The Nobbys, down to Blaydon Burn, and met the old Hexham turnpike. At The Nobbys, the road crossed the Barlow turnpike, and made four lane ends. Tradition says that in the corner of the present field, at the north side of the turnpike, a man who committed suicide was buried, and a stake driven through his body. This tradition is supported by the fact that formerly every pedestrian who passed the spot threw three stones on the grave; and old people are still living who have seen the stake or stob which marked his place of burial. Formerly a *felo de se*, or one who committed a felony by laying violent hands upon himself, was denied Christian burial, and usually buried at midnight, at a place where four roads met. In the township of Cornforth, in Durham, there is a place called Stobcross, which derives its name from being the burial place of a man who committed suicide. The fixing of the body by a stake or stob was thought to get rid of corpse and ghost together. Stones were thrown on the grave as a token of abhorrence, common to most nations. The burial place of the suicide at The Nobbys has always been called "Selby's grave;" but who Selby was is uncertain. Sykes gives the following account of a suicide at Winlaton in 1660. He says: "It is related that in the spring of this year, an unknown gentleman came to reside at Winlaton, near Newcastle, living very privately, and daily more and more inquisitive after news and every circumstance of the Restoration. Upon understanding the passing of the act of indemnity, together with the exception of the murderers of King Charles I., he went into an adjoining wood and hanged himself." Tradition mentions "Lands Wood," on the south side of Winlaton, as that in which the "unknown gentleman" hanged himself. Not only does Sykes mention the fact of the suicide's name being unknown, but unfortunately the Ryton register is silent in regard to the event; so that we have nothing more than tradition affirming that the name of the suicide was Selby.

Advancing westward, in half an hour the visitor reaches

BARLOW.

BARLOW, Barley, from *bare*, and *ley* = ground lying uncultivated, lea land meant the land lying idle. This little village or hamlet lies one and a quarter miles west of Winlaton, and is composed chiefly of workmen's houses. There are also several farms in the neighbourhood. In the year 1632, a great part of the land lying south of the present village was known as Gair's Field. A "field" was originally so called, as being a piece of land on which the trees had been *felled*, and it is spelled *feld* in old authors, and opposed to woods or uncleared land.

Garesfield Colliery, which stood on the south side of Barlow Fell, was commenced in the year 1800, by the Marquis of Bute and Mrs. Simpson of Bradley. The depth of the shaft was 25 fathoms, and there was a day-level at the eastern part of the workings. Two other pits stood on the north side of the "Garesfield" pit on the "fell," all of which were abandoned on the opening of the Spen (Garesfield) Colliery in 1837. The coals were led in waggons to Derwenthaugh.

Barlow Fell, Blaydon Green, Beda Hills, and the other waste lands in the manor or township of Winlaton, were divided and enclosed in pursuance of an Act of Parliament passed in 1823, Thomas Bell of Newcastle being the sole commissioner employed, who made his award of the division, June 29th, 1829. The lands divided, exclusive of that portion allotted for roads, quarries, wells, watering-places, &c., were declared by this award to contain 394 acres, 1 rood, 13 perches; of which 3 roods 26 perches was allotted to the rector of Ryton for a churchyard or cemetery, for the use of the township of Winlaton. Winlaton church was built on that part of the "fell" allotted to the rector of Ryton. Formerly the sports connected with Winlaton Hoppin—which included cock-fighting, bull-baiting, and horse-racing—were held on Barlow Fell. Horse-racing was last held there in 1854.

The workmen living at Barlow to-day are chiefly employed at the Lily Drift and the Spen Colliery.

The "Fell" was also frequented by the "boxing" fraternity of the neighbourhood. On 25th October, 1824, a pitched battle was fought by James Wallace and Thomas Dunn, for £40, when Wallace was the victor.

On the north side of the village stands the Methodist Free Church, rebuilt in 1870. Early in the history of Methodism, John Wesley had a good number of followers in this wild and uninviting district. Christopher Hopper, who was both schoolmaster and local preacher, tells us of some of the difficulties he experienced in prosecuting his work at Barlow one hundred and sixty years ago. He says:—"In the year 1744, I taught a school at Barlow, in the parish of Ryton. My time was employed six days in teaching the children under my care the branches of learning I professed, and the first principles of Christianity. But Satan did not like this work; therefore he stirred up the rector of Ryton and his curate, with those under their influence, to prevent me. They gave first hard words, and then hard blows. In a little time I was summoned to appear in the Spiritual Court at Durham, to answer for my conduct. I did not know what I had done; but was soon informed that I was impeached for teaching a school without a licence; and what was still worse, for calling sinners to repentance, and warning the wicked to flee from the wrath to come—an offence that cannot be overlooked by men who know not God! But God raised me up friends, who stood by me, and defended my cause against all my adversaries." Notwithstanding the assistance which Christopher Hopper received from several of the farmers in the neighbourhood, his labours did not secure the success they deserved, and in 1746 he removed from Barlow to Sheephill, on Derwentside.

John Nixon of Barlow was a devoted member of the Methodist society. He frequently entertained John Wesley, and opened his house for religious services. His daughter, Miss Nixon, was united in marriage with a member of the Stephenson family of Throckley. The eldest son of the marriage was Alderman William E. Stephenson of Throckley House, and a grandson, Alderman William Haswell Stephenson, is now (1895) for the third time Mayor of Newcastle.

THE SPEN (High.)

This village, which is three miles distant from Winlaton, is inhabited almost exclusively by the workmen of the colliery.

In the year 1370, Katherine, widow of Hugh de Fery, held four messuages and a hundred acres in Berley and Spen, of John de Nevill, Knt., by 3s. rent, and suit at the Manor Court of Winlaton. The Spen is included in the general alienation from Nevill in 1569. William Shafto, gent., who died in 1631, held lands here; and James Wild, who lived at the Spen about the same time as Shafto, and married a lady of the name of Barloe, also possessed lands, but afterwards sold them to William Tempest of Thornley.

The locality has been extensively worked for coal, which in the early period of the coal trade was carried by wains down the "Smeales Lane" to Derwenthaugh. The present colliery (known as Garesfield) was opened in 1838. At the depth of 30 fathoms the Brockwell seam is worked. About 200 men and boys are employed. The workmen live in houses formed of streets, and are known as East Street, West Street, Glossop Street, Cardiff Square, and Howard Terrace. One of the streets is known as the "Jawblades" cottages, from two jawblades of a whale which at one time formed a gateway near the cottages.

On the north side of the colliery, and separated by a field used as a "Recreation ground," are a number of streets, known as "Ramsay's cottages," which are modern erections for the use of the miners. At the west end of East Street the Primitive Methodists have a handsome chapel, erected in 1884, upon their removal from an older building erected in 1867.

On December 17th, 1865, Matthew Atkinson murdered his wife Ellen, at The Spen, for which he was afterwards executed at Durham.

On the south side of the village are the commodious Board Schools, opened in 1894, to supply a lack of accommodation in the old Primitive Methodist Chapel, in which the school was held.

THE SPEN (Low).

THIS little hamlet lies about half-a-mile south of High Spen. It consists of a farm house and a number of cottages. In the spring of 1743, John Brown, a plain farmer, removed from Tanfield Leigh to the above-mentioned farm house, and invited John Wesley to his house. Christopher Hopper, in referring to this time, and having in his mind John Brown's house at the Low Spen, says:— "I then heard occasionally those preachers who I thought could tell their story well, without stammering; but still found much fault with this strange method of proceeding." "The Sabbath-day following," he says:—"Mr. Reeves (one of the earliest of the Methodist local preachers) preached at the Low Spen at one o'clock in the afternoon, and in the evening again, on these words: 'And now abideth faith, hope, and charity, these three; but the greatest of these is charity.'" He further says:—"My mouth was stopped. I stood guilty before God. He discovered to me the blessed plan of man's redemption through the blood of a crucified Saviour." And thus commenced, in the house of John Brown, the religious life of Christopher Hopper, one of the most remarkable men in Methodist history. Soon after, John Wesley visited Low Spen, formed a little society there, and made Christopher Hopper a leader. The society held their religious services in John Brown's house, and under his roof the preachers, often weather-beaten and weary, received a welcome and found a home. For sixty-four years John Brown continued a devoted member of the Methodist society. St. Patrick's Church stands about half-a-mile south of High Spen, and on the east side of Huger-gate. It is built of red bricks, and covered with red tiles; internally, the arrangements are neat and unpretending, and capable of seating 200 people. A grave-yard surrounds the edifice. The church was built in 1889, and cost about £500. Huger-gate leads from Beda Lodge to the Lintz Green Station. A branch road near the church enters Smailes' Lane, which terminates near to Rowlands Gill Station.

It was at the bottom of Smailes' Lane, after crossing the Shotley Bridge turnpike, that Mr. Robert Stirling, assistant to Dr. Watson of Burnopfield, was murdered on the 1st of November, 1855. He had been little more than a week in the service of Mr. Watson, and was returning from visiting the patients of that gentleman, when he was shot by some persons lurking near the road, his throat cut, and his head and face frightfully injured, apparently by the butt end of a gun. His watch, money, and lancets were taken from his pockets, and the body was dragged through a fence and deposited among the bushes in a plantation which covered a steep declivity, where it was not discovered till about a week afterwards. A considerable sensation was excited throughout the county by this atrocious deed, and large rewards were offered for the discovery of the perpetrators. Two men, named John Cain, the proprietor of an illicit still in the neighbourhood, and Richard Rayne, a blacksmith at Winlaton, were apprehended on suspicion, and brought up at the Durham Spring Assizes in 1856, but the evidence not being complete, they were remanded to the Summer Assizes in July of that year. After a prolonged trial, in which a variety of circumstantial evidence was adduced on behalf of the prosecution, a verdict of Not Guilty was returned.

Rowland Gill derives its name from Robert Rowland, who possessed lands there in 1621, and Gill, a north-country word for rivulet.

About a quarter of a mile eastward of Rowlands Gill Station is the Lily Drift, belonging to Messrs. Joseph Cowen & Co. The workmen live in a row of houses at the west side, at the end of which there is a neat Primitive Methodist Chapel, erected in 1883, and capable of seating 200. The coals are now drawn by an endless rope to the screens at Blaydon Burn, after which they are sent to Blaydon and conveyed by wherries to their destination.

CHOPWELL TOWNSHIP.

This township comprises an extensive district, lying immediately west of the High Spen and Low Spen, and stretching to Milkwell Burn. It also extends from the Derwent on the south to the Leadgate on the north, and contains about 3,850 acres. Population in 1801, 348; 1811, 291; 1821, 237; 1831, 254; 1841, 320; 1851, 458; 1861, 563; 1871, 788; 1881, 1,614; 1891, 2,193. Rateable value—In 1821, £2,120; and in 1893, £9,323.

Chopwell, eleven miles W.S.W. from Newcastle, anciently comprised the south-western angle of the parish of Ryton, but the estate has now been divided into several distinct portions.

Bishop Hugh gave Chopwell to Newminster Abbey, in exchange for Wolsingham. Surtees conjectures that the Swinburns, who were already tenants of Chopwell under the Abbey, obtained at the dissolution the fee-simple of the Crown or its grantees. In 1562, John Swinburne, Esq., was litigating his boundaries betwixt the manors of Ryton and Chopwell, with Pilkington, Bishop of Durham. In 1569, he was deeply engaged in the great northern rebellion, fled under attainder to Fernicherst in Scotland, escaped from thence into Flanders, was afterwards a pensioner at Madrid, and probably died in exile. The manor of Chopwell, thus vested in the Crown, was granted by the Queen to Sir Robert Constable, of Flamborough, in recompense of his services as a spy and informer. Sir William Constable, son and heir of Sir Robert, sold the manor of Chopwell to Anthony Archer; and he immediately conveyed to Ambrose Dudley, alderman of Newcastle, who, son and heir, Toby Dudley, Esq., left an only daughter, Jane Dudley, wife of Robert Clavering, a younger brother of the first Sir James

Clavering, of Axwell. The male issue of Clavering failed in his grandchildren, and Sarah, the sister and eventual heir of John and Dudley Clavering, became the wife of the Lord Chancellor, William, Earl Cowper. Earl Cowper sold Chopwell Hall, Horsegate, and Broomfield House to Dr. Thorp, rector of Ryton, and to his son, Robert Thorp, of Alnwick, Esq. West Chopwell and Greenhead were purchased by Mr. John Taylor, of Swalwell; Leadgate and Ravenside, by Anthony Surtees of Hamsterley, Esq.; and other portions by William Surtees, Esq., Mr. Miller, and Mr. Robert Waugh. The mines of coal were reserved by Earl Cowper.

In the reign of James I., John Lyons of Bradley, Esq., receiver of the revenues, being a defaulter to the Crown, an extent was issued against his estate in Chopwell, "the East Wood, Moor Close, Deane, and the Carres." When Chopwell was granted to Sir Robert Constable, this portion, which is of considerable extent, was reserved. The present landowners are J. C. F. Cookson, Esq., William Tudor Thorp, Esq., Miss Surtees, Mrs. Liddle, Consett Iron Company, and the Commissioners of Woods and Forests.

After leaving Rowlands Gill Station, on the Consett branch of the North-Eastern Railway, and advancing westward for about a mile, Chopwell Woods are reached. These woods are what remain of the ancient forest which extended from Axwell Park to Allenheads. About a mile north-west of Rowlands Gill is Victoria Garesfield, a modern colliery village, surrounded by woods and charming scenery. Large quantities of coke are also produced there by Messrs. Priestman. The seams of coal worked are the Brockwell and Three-Quarter. A pleasant walk of a mile-and-a-half on the Shotley Bridge turnpike, through the forest, brings the visitor to Lintz Ford. A road branching northward, known as Huger Gate, leads to Bede Lodge and the Spen. Half a mile southward is the Lintz Green Station. Branching off the Shotley Bridge turnpike, past the houses occupied by the workmen at Lintz Ford Paper Mills, you are in the heart of the forest. The scenery is of a quiet and gentle character. The Derwent flows through the woods on the south side, and occasionally the banks of the channel rise precipitously, which darken the otherwise crystal waters. Walking in a north-westerly direction for a mile and a half, the Tongue Burn is reached before it meets the Derwent. Alongside of the burn stands the Carr farm, which in the time of James I. formed that part of the Chopwell estate known as "The Carrs." Advancing northward about a mile through the forest, you reach Heavy Gate and Horse Gate, two old roads which, in the 17th century, were used as "coalways" to Stella. At the west side of Horsegate is Horsegate farm, which is an old building with a horse-shoe nailed to every door. If the existence of horse-shoes affixed to the doors of farms and cottages in this thinly-populated district be evidence of the belief in witchcraft, that belief must have prevailed extensively in former times, as nearly every door you see is guarded by a horse-shoe. A pleasant walk from Horse Gate, through the woods, brings you to Chopwell Church, which is a small edifice standing on the north side of the road, near to Chopwell Hall. The church was erected in 1843. On the south side is Chopwell Hall, which is to-day what it always has been—a large farm-house. On the west side of Chopwell Hall is Chopwell Wood farm, and in the distance westward are the Broomfield, Greenhead, and Ashtree farms. Chopwell Mill, which lies south of Chopwell Wood farm, is an old-fashioned building; the water mill has disappeared, and only the mill-race, on the west side of the farm, is now to be seen. Westward from the "Mill" is Newhouse farm, near to Milkwell Burn, the birthplace of Joseph Bulman, a well-known local poet.

Joseph Bulman, son of Thomas Bulman, was born June 11th, 1833. His father was farm bailiff for R. Surtees, Esq., and also rented Newhouse farm under the same gentleman for a great number of years. He had a family of ten children, of whom Joseph was the youngest, and who, in early life, exhibited signs of a delicate constitution, and not being likely to obtain his livelihood by hard work, was put to school until he became a very good scholar, and was very expert in land surveying, in which employment he had a good deal of practice in assisting his father on Mr. Surtees' estates. On March 5th, 1852, he obtained a situation on the Newcastle and Carlisle Railway, at Hexham station. After spending a few years at Hexham, he was removed, by the wish of the directors, to the audit office at Newcastle, and subsequently from that to the manager's office, and was entrusted with the collection of the Company's accounts, a situation of some trust. At length he had an offer of a situation in the Union Bank at

Newcastle, and from thence to their office at Sunderland, to which place he removed. About this time his health began to give way, and no sooner had he removed to Sunderland, than evident symptoms of a disease set in which compelled him to give up his situation at the bank. He removed to Ryton for a suitable residence, as he thought, where he began to sink fast under the unmitigated effects of consumption, and died on 5th April, 1861. His poems were published in 1861. Several of them were produced while following his regular duties, and others were only written during his illness, and finished while he had very little strength.

His poem, "On Passing Newhouse," his birthplace, is a charming description of the old homestead :—

>Once more I climb the old oak stile,
>　And tread the grassy green,
>Where first the gazing sun on me
>　Did cast his radiant beam.
>I pass the well-remembered cot,
>　My first, bright sunny home,
>Where life's rough tempest harm'd me not,
>　Nor care could near me come ;
>Where all was innocence, joy, and mirth :
>The dearest, choicest spot on earth
>
>Yonder stands the Scotch fir clump,
>　Beneath whose ample shade
>Old Nanny's lambs did racing jump,
>　And judding, gambolling, play'd.
>The old pit-hole with rashes grown ;
>　The well so cooling, clear ;
>The hurdle gate and grassy lawn,
>　Yes, all these yet are here :
>To each some story does belong,
>Of deeds performed in days byegone.

There is at Newhouse a commanding view of the country south of the Derwent, which Bulman describes in picturesque language :—

>The eye can wander far from here,
>　Can view the stretching plain,
>The pretty hamlets far and near,
>　And fields of waving grain.

> Wild Derwent's waters, shining bright,
>   Like glittering silver lies;
> While Pontop's tree-capp'd towering height
>   Seems propping up the skies:
> Frowning at its neighbour still,
> The sunny, airy, Ash-tree hill.

The following verse has reference to Chopwell woods:—

> O how I love that wild, wild wood,
>   It's shaggy, briary glens:
> It's nut-bush hills, where secret brood,
>   The robins, tits, and wrens.
> Where woodcock, wild duck, and heron,
>   Haunt the lonely dells;
> Adown yon holly banks whereon
>   The blackbird's music swells,
> Where songbirds make the welkin ring,
> And squirrels high, so fearless spring.

Bulman's poems, "On Leaving Milkwell Burn," and "Sighing of the Breezes," are worthy of high praise. They were published in 1861.

On the south side of Newhouse farm is

BLACKHALL MILL.

THIS hamlet is situated on the south-west of Chopwell, and alongside of the Derwent. Nearly the whole of the village has been erected during the last thirty years. The estate of Blackhall was held under the Crown grantees by the Rutherford family, when the Dudleys of Newcastle purchased Chopwell. A feud took place between these two families in 1615, and which probably arose from some contention respecting rents and boundaries. The consequences were "John Rutheforth, or Rudderford, Gent., of Wren's Nest; Charles Rutheforth, of the Blackhall; Hugh and Gaven Rutheforth, and William Shafto, were outlawed for forcibly entering into the manor of Chopwell, with intention to kill Ambrose Dudley, Esq., George Gifford, and others, at a place called Westwood, in which affray William Shafto struck George Gifford a mortal wound in the thigh, of which he soon died, with an iron lance." The Rutherfords fled from the face of the law. The Bishop, to whom the forfeiture accrued, granted their interest in the Blackhall to Sir Philip Constable of Everingham (15th April, 1615), who in the same year conveyed it to William Carr of Cocken. The above Charles Rutherford married Margaret, daughter of Thomas Swinburn of Capheaton; but from an entry in the Ryton register, it would seem that he had returned when the storm was over, and died in his old habitation. Blackhall and Milkwell Burn were purchased, in 1626, by Anthony Surtees.

Anthony Surtees was the son of Cuthbert Surtees of Ebchester. Robert, son of Anthony, married, in 1663, Isabella Newton, from whom descended the family of Surtees of Hamsterly Hall.

Although Blackhall Mill is on the north side of the Derwent, only a part of the village is in Chopwell. The Derwent is the boundary until it reaches "The Ship" public-house, when an imaginary line runs along the west side of the house to a hedge about forty yards on the north side. From this point the line runs westward till it reaches the old Smelt Mill, where the Derwent is again the boundary. Several old houses, and one of the old Smelt Mills arrest the attention of the visitor. Seventy years ago, Isaac Cookson, Esq., employed a number of workmen in the manufacture of German steel. Forges and smelt mills have existed on the Derwent, at Blackhall Mill, from an early period. There is a tradition that the colonists came from Solingen, a small city on the Wiffer, in the Duchy of Berg, which had long been noted for its fine elastic sword blades. At the present time Derwent Cote and Swalwell are the only places on the Derwent where steel is forged.

About a quarter of a mile west of Blackhall Mill, is the Milkwell Burn, which flows into the Derwent, and which is the south-western boundary of the old parish of Ryton.

Half a mile north of the Derwent, on the side of the Burn, is Blackhall, at one time the seat of the Rutherfords. Blackhall probably obtained its name from its situation on the edge of what was anciently the Black Moor, on the west side. The Hall is an old stone building, bearing traces of former elegance and importance. At present it is occupied by several tenants. On the east side of the Hall is Blackhall farm, formerly connected with the Hall.

On the north of Blackhall is Ravenside, and north of Ravenside is Ash Tree, both of which are agricultural districts.

AXWELL PARK, 1894.
Photo by R. Barrass.

AXWELL PARK.

THIS beautiful modern seat of the Claverings lies in Winlaton township, and north of the Derwent. It stands open, but not unsheltered, in the midst of a soft wooded park, which slopes gently to the Derwent, and is diversified by beautiful swells and undulations of ground. A number of deer add to the simple and rural beauties of the scene. The southern view overlooks the rich enclosures and hanging woods of Gibside. The east front commands a prospect of Derwent Bridge, and extends over part of the Vale of Tyne, the shipping at Newcastle quay, and the heights of Gateshead.

The name Axwell is probably derived from ak = oak, and $sheals$ = sheds; sheds made from branches of oak trees. The Claverings transferred the name from their estate on the south side of the Derwent, to the park which now surrounds their present beautiful residence. On the plan of the Winlaton lordship (dated 1632), there is a mansion on Springhill, which is about one hundred yards west of the present hall. Surtees states that Whitehouse, the former seat of the Claverings, stood about half a mile west of Axwell Hall. Surtees was evidently mistaken in the site of Whitehouse, as the house on Springhill was undoubtedly the Whitehouse of the Claverings. The father of Mr. Ralph Norton, the late agent to the Axwell estate, was present at the demolition of the old hall, after which the site was planted with trees. Whitehouse was surrounded by a small park comprising 30 acres. On the north side of the park was Newfield, 53 acres; on the west the Hagg, 150 acres; on the east Lady Close, 6 acres; and the Black Meres—lakes or ponds—24 acres; and on the south Broom Close, 40 acres. On the erection of Axwell Hall, all the above-mentioned parcels of land were enclosed in the new park.

Axwell Hall was built by Sir Thomas Clavering, from the designs of Payne, and is considered by professional men to be one of that eminent architect's happiest efforts. Bishop Pococke, who visited Gibside in the year 1760, says:—"We came about two miles to Whickham, and saw on the left Sir Thomas Clavering's fine large house, the shell of which is just finished in hewn freestone." From what the bishop says, we may conclude that the Claverings made Axwell Hall their residence about the year 1761. The entrance into the mansion is by a hall, on the right of which, to the east, is the ante-chamber, or common dining-room; in the centre of the east front is the best dining-room; in the south-west angle, and on the left of the hall, is the withdrawing room; and in the centre of the building are the staircases; in the north-east angle is a small study; beyond that, and on one side of the common passage, is a small room or office for business; and on the opposite side of the same passage is the steward's office; in the north-west angle, is the housekeeper's room, which serves also as a dining-room for the upper domestics; in the intermediate part of the west front is the kitchen, taking in a part of the subterraneous storey, and rising as high as the mezzanine, the roof being substantially arched to prevent any disagreeable smells. The mezzanine storey is continued over the before-mentioned part of the building and through the north front, in the centre of which is a passage to the laundry, and other subordinate offices, which, on account of the natural situation of the ground, are built above the level of the house, but entirely out of sight. This mezzanine affords six good rooms for the upper servants of the family and those belonging to visitors. In the centre of the upper landing of the great stairs is the entrance to the ante-chamber; in the south-east angle is Lady Clavering's dressing room, which commands most beautiful views of Newcastle and the village of Whickham; in the centre of the east front, are the principal family apartments, including two dressing-rooms; a bed-room and dressing-room occupy the south-west angle; in the intermediate part of the west front is another bedroom and a dressing-room; and in the north-west angle is a single bedchamber. The attic storey contains four bedrooms, with dressing-rooms to each, and three single bedrooms. The Hall is roofed with slates. The handsome porch, which forms the principal entrance, was built about twenty years after the erection of the mansion. Previous to that time the principal entrance was on the east side. A flight of steps leads to the porch, and on each side there stands a small brass mounted cannon, placed there by the late Sir Henry A. Clavering. Above the porch, on the third storey, are the family arms—Quarterly : Or and Gules, a bend Sable. On the south side, and at the termination of the carriage drive, the entrance is formed by a terrace, which runs along the south and east sides of the house, from which there is a commanding view of the wooded banks on the south of the Derwent.

The Hall contains some interesting and valuable pictures, amongst which may be enumerated "The Raising of Lazarus," and "The Inauguration of a Bishop," by Paul Veronese; "The Holy Family," by Carracci; "The Passover," by Le Seur; "Bentivoglio," by Titian; "Interior of a Cathedral," by Neep and Tenier; "Sacking a Village," by Vander Malin; "Skating," by Bout; and several family portraits. The park, which comprises 270 acres, is enclosed by a wall. The house is approached by two carriage drives—one at Shibdon, on the north side of the park, the other at Derwent Bridge, on the east side. The drive from the direction of Swalwell (*via* Derwent Bridge) is especially worthy of notice. From the entrance gates to the house it winds under the branches of ancestral trees, through the vistas of which the deer may be seen bounding over velvety turf or bushes, or among the tall brackens, where they often seek refuge from the burning rays of the sun. After passing an ornamental bridge and turning a gentle curve, a splendid view of the house is obtained, which, from the gentle style of its architecture, has a very imposing effect. On the west side of the house are the stables, neatly and compactly built, terminating at each end by a lower tower; in the centre is a high tower, in which is placed a clock. A gentle drive from the north side leads to the large and beautiful gardens and greenhouses, which have always been a great attraction to those living in the neighbourhood privileged to visit them. West of the gardens is the "Home" farm and the old joiner's shop. Formerly there stood on the north side of the lake a house covered with shells, and known as the "Shell House," which, having fallen into a state of decay, was set on fire by the late Sir H. A. Clavering, and burnt to the ground 22nd March, 1876.

At the west end of the park is "Park Villa," formerly the residence of the steward of the estate, and at present occupied by Mr. Thomas Metcalfe. On a hill, hidden by trees, about two hundred yards south-west of the hall, there are the remains of a building known as "The Temple," built by Lady Clavering during her husband's detention in France by Napoleon, at the beginning of the century. The structure is semi-circular in form, its height about 16 feet and diameter inside 20 feet. At the entrance stand three polished pillars. Whatever the building may have been intended for, it was never finished, and to-day lies in ruins. The park contains several very fine trees, including a Sycamore four hundred yards N.E. of Hall, girth at a height of 5 feet, 15 feet 4 inches, spread of branches 28 yards, height 65 feet; a Lime, near to joiner's shop, girth at a height of 5 feet, 13 feet, height 101 feet; an Oak, two hundred yards west of Hall, girth at a height of 4 feet, 17 feet, spread of branches 22 yards, height 44 feet; an Oak, four hundred yards S.W. of Hall, girth at a height of 5 feet, 14 feet 5 inches, spread of branches 34 yards, height 59 feet 6 inches; a Beech, three hundred yards E. of Hall, girth at a height of 5 feet, 13 feet, height 55 feet; Beech, one yard W. of Park Wall on the west side, girth at a height of 5 feet, 13 feet 10 inches, height 55 feet; Ash, three hundred and thirty yards N.E. of Hall, girth at a height of 5 feet, 13 feet 10 inches, spread of branches 18 yards, height 60 feet; Sycamore, about four hundred and seventy yards S.E. of Hall, girth at a height of 5 feet, 13 feet 7 inches, spread of branches 20 yards, height 65 feet. Several large trees have lately been destroyed by storms. In the year 1763, March 11th, as some men were digging in the park, they discovered an urn with a little dust in it, and by going further they found a large stone coffin, in which was a skull with the teeth very fresh, and several bones of a great size. It is not known in what part of the grounds the coffin was found, and it is uncertain what became of it. Axwell Park contains within its area the old Whitehouse Park, the seat of the Selbys and the Claverings, until the present Hall was built.

The Selbys, as already noticed, were extensive landowners in Winlaton. A branch of this influential family settled at Old

Axwell, on the south side of the Derwent, as early as the middle of the 16th century, afterwards removing to Whitehouse, on the north side.

Sir William Selby, sometimes described of Bolam and Shortflatt Tower, County of Northumberland, is also described of Winlaton. He was buried at Ryton, 3rd April, 1649.

Sir George Selby, created a baronet 3rd March, 1664, and buried at St. Nicholas, 16th September, 1668, is described of Whitehouse and sometimes Winlaton.

Mr. Charles Selby of Winlaton, was buried at Ryton, 29th May, 1668.

Thomas Selby of Winlaton, was married to Susan Heslerigg, in March, 1670.

Five individuals of the Selby family obtained the honour of knighthood from King James. Sir William Selby of Biddlestone; Sir George, the King's host; Sir William of Winlaton; another Sir William of the Mote, Ightham, Kent; and Sir John Selby of Twizel.

The Whitehouse Estate was probably considered too small to give a name to it, hence the residence of the Selbys is described as Winlaton.

In the year 1749, Whitehouse Park still retained the old name, and it was not until the erection of the present hall that the old park disappeared in the newer and larger one, Axwell.

The Claverings.

The family of Clavering derive their descent in the male line from Charlemagne. The original family name is De Burgh, which was resumed by the Marquis of Clanricarde in 1752. Eustace de Burgh, a noble Norman, had two sons, who came over with William the Conquerer. Serlo, who built Knaresborough Castle, died without issue; but his brother, John, had three sons, whose descendants became connected with the noblest houses in England. One branch of the family became barons of Warkworth, of whom Eustace de Vescy was one of the competitors for the Crown of Scotland. The surname of Clavering was given by King Edward I. from Clavering in Essex, which was the chief estate of

Robert Fitz Roger, Lord Clavering, Baron of Warkworth and Clavering. Robert Clavering, son and heir of John Clavering and Elizabeth Fenwick, married Ann, daughter of Sir Thomas Grey of Horton Castle, Northumberland, from which last are descended the family of Clavering of Axwell Park. James, son of Robert Clavering and Ann Grey, was sheriff of Newcastle in 1599, and mayor in 1607 and 1618. His son, John Clavering, Esq., of Axwell, also served the offices of sheriff and mayor of Newcastle. He married Ann, daughter of Robert Shafto, alderman of New-

SIR HENRY A. CLAVERING, BART.

castle, widow of Robert Tempest. He was buried 6th of May, 1648. This John Clavering seems to have been the first member of the family to make (Old) Axwell, in the parish of Whickham, his residence. James, the eldest son of John Clavering, married Jane, daughter and heiress of Charles Maddison, Esq., of Saltwellside. He was high sheriff of the County of Durham in 1650; but in 1656 it would seem that he was an object of suspicion to the government, for in the information of Lady Hall, dated 7th November, 1656, it is stated that one Mr. Clavering of Axwell, in the County of Durham, who was chosen a member of this present parliament, but not admitted, did lend to Charles Stuart £4,000, since March last. In the following year, however, the church-wardens' book of Gateshead shows that he had at least set out for the purpose of attending his public duty, as one of the charges to the parish is for one gallon of mulled sack, had of Mr. Watson, bestowed on Mr. James Clavering, Justice of Peace, at his taking journey to parliament. He was created a baronet 5th June, 1661, and stood an unsuccessful contest for the county in 1675. He was buried at Whickham 24th March, 1701-2, aged 82 years.

About the year 1670, the Greencroft estate came into the possession of the Claverings. James Clavering was succeeded by his grandson James, in 1702, and at his death, in 1707, his brother, John Clavering, became the third baronet. He died in 1714. In 1735, under date February 22nd, Sykes says:—" Died at Newcastle, Dame Jane Clavering, widow and relict of Sir John Clavering of Axwell Park, aged 66 years; a lady of most exemplary life and unbounded charity. Her ladyship left by will £50 to the poor of each of the four parishes in Newcastle, and £60 to the charity school in St. John's parish. The residue of her estate, amounting to £120,000 and upwards, devolved upon her ladyship's two daughters. Her corpse was interred in St. Nicholas' church, upon which occasion, pursuant to her own directions, an excellent sermon was preached by the Rev. Mr. John Ellison. The funeral procession was very magnificent, the pall being supported by eight gentlemen of distinction. Before the corpse went the master and charity boys of St. John's, followed by the beadles, several mourners with cloaks, and eight of her ladyship's servants in full mourning, without cloaks; next after the corpse went a great number of gentlemen and clergy, as mourners; then walked the mayor and aldermen with their regalia and ensigns of honour and after them most of the gentlemen in the town and adjacent country with scarfs, &c.; after which followed her lady-ship's coach, in deep mourning, succeeded by many others."

John Clavering was succeeded by his son, Sir James Clavering; baptized August 3rd, 1708, and died May 18th, 1726. The title next devolved on his uncle, Francis Clavering, who died without issue in 1738, and was succeeded by his cousin, Sir James, sixth baronet. He died May 12th, 1748. Although the Claverings had been active and distinguished partisans of the Stuarts during the great Civil War, they were strong and vigilant supporters of the Government in the Rebellions of 1715 and 1745; in fact, it was chiefly due to their watchfulness that the Government was apprised of the proceedings of the Northern Jacobites. In the "Rising of 1745," Sir Thomas Clavering raised a troop of horse militia at his own expense. Sir James Clavering had by his first wife, Catherine, daughter of Thomas York, Esq., one son, Thomas, by whom he was succeeded. He was baptized June 19th, 1718. He was M.P for Shaftesbury in 1754, and for the County of Durham in 1768, 1774, 1780, and 1784. He unsuccessfully contested the county in 1760, when John Wesley used his influence in Sir Thomas' favour, by writing the following letter to his friends :—" 20th November, 1760.—I desire earnestly all who love me to assist him, to use the utmost of their power; what they do, let them do it with all their might; let not sloth nor indolence hurt a good cause, only let them not rail at the other candidates. They may act earnestly, yet civilly. Let all your doings be done in charity ; and at the peril of your souls receive no bribe ; do your duty without being tired. God will repay you both in this world and to come." Sir Thomas Clavering married Martha, daughter of Joshua Douglas of Newcastle, and died without issue October 14th, 1794. 2. George Clavering, Esq., of Greencroft, who by Mary, daughter of the Rev. Mr. Palmer of Comb, Rawleigh, Devonshire, and relict of Sir John Home, Bart., left a son, eighth baronet. 3. Sir John Clavering, K.B., Major-General in the Army, Commander-in-Chief in the East Indies, Governor of Berwick, and Colonel of the 52nd Foot. He began his career in the Coldstream Guards, and was sent with General Barrington to take the French island of Guadaloupe. He is said to have displayed great skill and bravery on the occasion of taking the island, which elicited the highest admiration from his friends in the North of England in learning the news. The local papers of June 17th, 1759, contain the following account of the reception of the news :—" On the arrival of the agreeable and welcome news at Newcastle of the reduction of Guadaloupe, on the 21st of the preceding April, the bells were immediately rung, and the day was concluded with every demonstration of joy. The news was particularly pleasing at Newcastle, as the brave Colonel Clavering, who brought home the dispatches was of that neighbourhood, and whose relatives were complimented on his account. The colonel had greatly distinguished himself on the occasion."

On the appointment of Warren Hastings as Governor-General of Bengal, Sir John Clavering was one of the four persons appointed to constitute a Council to act with him. He received as a councillor £10,000 a year, He was to command the Bengal army, and to be next in rank to Hastings; but the Governor-General and the Council could not agree. Sir John Clavering fought a duel with one Barwell, a friend of Hastings; and he and Hastings nearly came to grief in a similar manner.

Sir John was a man of great ability and sterling integrity. He undoubtedly was the most distinguished member of the family of Claverings of Axwell and Greencroft; but his abilities seem not to have been appraised at their true value in India, and after much worry and many disappointments, he died at Calcutta, August 30th, 1777, aged 55 years.

Sir Thomas John Clavering of Axwell Park, son of George Clavering and Mary Palmer, born April 6th, 1771, married August 21st, 1791, Clara, daughter of John de Gallais, Count-de la-Sable of Anjou, by whom he had issue William Aloysius, born January 21st, 1800; Clara Ann Martha, married February 8th, 1826, to General Baron de Knyff of Brussels; and Agatha Catherine, married February 12th, 1821, to the Baron de Montfaucon of Avignon.

In 1798, Sir Thomas Clavering raised, at his own expense, a troop of yeomanry known as the Tyne Hussars. Sir Thomas Burdon was colonel, and Mr. William Lockey, land agent to Sir Thomas Clavering, was captain of the troop. The cavalry was composed of men who lived at Swalwell, Whickham, Winlaton Mill, and Sir Thomas's tenantry at Axwell Park. The regiment was extremely popular in the neighbourhood, which in a great measure was due to the geniality and the commanding presence of its captain. His sword, and a handsome silver cup, presented to him, are still preserved by one of his descendants at Whickham. The cup bears the following inscription :—

Presented to
CAPT. WILLM. LOCKEY,
by the Axwell Park Troop of Volunteer Cavalry,
1815.

At the time of the "False Alarm" (January 31st, 1803), when it was reported that Buonaparte was ready to invade England, the people of Blaydon, Swalwell, &c., had a great many carts and rolleys to carry their furniture and goods to Alston Moor for safety; but Captain Lockey, at the head of his gallant cavalry, disarmed their fears, and they returned to their respective homes.

Sir Thomas lived chiefly at Greencroft, devoting his time to the improvement of his estates. He was held in high esteem by his tenantry. On the 20th October, 1845, the tenants met him at Greencroft and presented him with a full-length portrait of himself, executed by Hastings of Durham, as a token of their respect. The painting is now among the family pictures at Axwell Park. Sir Thomas died at Clifton, on November 4th, 1853, at the ripe age of 83 years, and was buried at Greencroft.

Having paid a visit to France soon after the peace of Amiens, Sir Thomas was detained by Buonaparte from the rupture of that treaty until 1814, and a singular dispute arose in 1854 as to whether his children born in that country were entitled to a share in the property left by his father, George Clavering, that gentleman having expressly excluded any descendants of his son that should not be members of the Church of England or that might be born or educated abroad. William, the only surviving son of Sir Thomas, was the sole person entitled to claim under the strict letter of the will. Lengthened litigation ensued as to whether the terms of the will had been broken by the heir having been born abroad, but, ultimately, the son of Sir Thomas was adjudged the legal claimant to the title and estates of the family.

Sir William Aloysius Clavering seldom visited Axwell Park, the most of his time being spent in London and on the continent, He died unmarried in 1872, and was buried at Greencroft. He was succeeded by his cousin, Sir Henry Augustus Clavering, son of Rawdon Clavering, Esq., born 30th August, 1824, and was educated at the Royal Naval College. He was with Sir Charles Napier on the coast of Syria in 1840, was present at the siege of

Jean D'Acre, and held a medal for the gallant part he took in those events. He married a daughter of the late Andrew Alexander, LL.D., Professor of Greek at St. Andrew's University, who survives him. Sir Henry made Axwell his residence, and during the latter years of his life was never away from it. He took no part in national or public affairs, but devoted his time to the beautifying of his charming residence. He died on the 9th of November, 1893, aged 69 years, and was interred at Blaydon Cemetery in a new vault built by Sir Henry during his lifetime. He was the tenth and last baronet, and his death terminated the male line of one of the oldest, most influential, and far-branching of the county families in England.

The Rev. John Warren Napier, Vicar of Stretton, South Staffordshire, third son of the Hon. Charles Napier, and grandson of Frances, Baron Napier, in the peerage of Scotland, succeeded to the estates in 1893, on which he assumed the name of Clavering, in accordance with the will of Sir William Aloysius Clavering. This gentleman now lives at Axwell Park.

On the north side of Axwell Park there is an extensive tract of land bordering the river Tyne. Part of it is a marsh or swamp called the Strothers, and as the bog produces nothing but rushes, it is the resort of water-fowl, among which may be mentioned the Snipe, Golden Plover, Water Hen, Red Shank, and Water Rail. The last Water Rail was shot in 1892.

On the west side of Axwell Park is the Hagg, which signifies the broken ground in a bog.

> "He led a small and shaggy nag,
> That through a bog from hag to hag."
> —*Lay of the Last Minstrel.*

There is at the Hagg a neat house, the residence of Mr. Thomas Battensby, one of the agents of the Axwell estate. A pleasant path from the house leads to the Shotley Bridge turnpike at the foot of the hill. Formerly there was at this spot a well-known sulphur spring, known as the "Spa Well," but unfortunately the water disappeared a few years ago, to the regret of the multitude of visitors to the Derwent. A short walk along the south side of Axwell Park brings the visitor to Derwent Bridge. On the north side of the bridge, and the east side of the Blaydon turnpike, is "Bates' House." On the plan of the Winlaton lordship (1632) there is a mansion which stood on the east side of the present farm-house, with a park on the south side stretching to the Derwent. Bates lived in the house at that time. It is uncertain what social position Bates occupied in the world, but an old woman who died some years ago remembered the ruins of the old hall, which were of considerable dimensions, and had been the residence of a man of wealth and influence.

Two old white-washed cottages stand on the west side of the farm, and were probably connected with Bates' House in the olden time. It was here that Cuthbert Houston lived. He was a cripple from his birth, and notwithstanding his infirmities he was a frequent contributor to the *Newcastle Weekly Chronicle*. Being unable to walk, he was wheeled in a perambulator along the side of the Derwent, where he enjoyed the sunshine, the flowers, and the music of the birds. But his life was short; he died on February 15th, 1877, aged 19 years. He rests in Whickham churchyard. A neat stone, subscribed for by Mr. Joseph Cowen and other friends, including many of the contributors to the *Weekly Chronicle*, marks his resting-place.

From Derwent Bridge a commanding view of the Derwent and Axwell Park is obtained, and in the moonlight the scene is delightful. The bridge, which was built of stone from a quarry belonging to Sir Thomas Clavering, was opened in 1760. After leaving the bridge you pass along an avenue of trees, at the end of which is the "Clavering Arms" public-house. Previous to the erection of the Scotswood Suspension Bridge, this avenue formed the carriage drive from Axwell, before reaching the Hexham turnpike, to Newcastle. The trees are sometimes called the "Crow Trees," on account of the crows formerly building their nests there. Swalwell Bridge is next reached, which formerly was the the south-east boundary of the township of Winlaton.

On the north side of the mill-race are the paper mills belonging to Messrs. Wm. Grace & Co., which occupy part of the site of the factory established by Sir Ambrose Crowley about the year 1700. On the west side of the paper mills are substantial houses, built for the workmen. They occupy the site of a row of very old houses once inhabited by Crowley's workmen, and known as "Cuckold's Raw." The word Cuckold, according to Bailey, formerly signified a man whose wife's adulterous conduct is said to have grafted horns on his head. From the name, evidently the place was one of evil repute. On the north side of the paper mill are the gardens cultivated by the working-men of Swalwell. Seventy years ago, the land was used as a cinder-heap for Crowley's factory, but since that time the workmen have made the spot to blossom as the rose. Formerly the boundary line between the Winlaton township and Whickham parish ran from the Stone Bridge along the Hexham turnpike to the Keelmen's Bridge, where it took the middle of the dam to the east side of Errington Terrace; it there made a northern course till it reached the north side of the field lying along the Derwent side, it then ran eastward to the east hedge, when it returned to the dam. On the 31st March, 1896, the boundary was altered. Now the line runs from the east side of the Railway Station to the Derwent, then proceeding eastward to the point where the Derwent and the Mill Race meet. The field known as the Preste's, or Priest's, field, although on the north side of the dam, is in Whickham parish, and is ecclesiastical property. A pleasant walk through the gardens to the Shotley Bridge turnpike, and proceeding northward, in a few minutes the visitor reaches Derwenthaugh.

This hamlet stands on the south bank of the Tyne and west of the Derwent, at the point where the tributary empties itself into the Tyne. The word Haugh signifies a meadow lying in a valley, and is a noted surname on the south side of the Tyne.

Derwent Haugh is one of the oldest villages in the North of England. In the year 1724 there were at this place staiths belonging to several coal-owners, namely, Sir James Clavering, George Pitt, Mr. Blakston, and Mr. Shafto. Stathe, stade, and steed, are Anglo-Saxon terms, formerly applied to single fixed dwellings, or to places on the banks of rivers where merchandise was stored up, and at which vessels could lie to receive it. These places were also formerly called dikes, probably on account of their being diked or defended from the river, for dike in the North of England has always a mixed meaning between defence and limit, but probably the word dike has reference only to those repositories for coal which were uncovered. The staiths were afterwards provided with roofs, under which coals were deposited in bad seasons of trade, and with stages and spouts from which they are poured into keels when the demand for them was immediate. Great quantities of coals were brought from Whickham, Spen, Thornley, and the neighbourhood of Pontop at the beginning of the eighteenth century, to the staiths. Before the introduction of waggon-ways, coals were conveyed in panniers hung over the backs of horses, and afterwards in wains or bulky carts. Several of the old coal-ways may still be seen on both sides of the Derwent. One may be traced on the south side of Landswood, on the north side of Winlaton Mill, which proceeded along the south side of the Hagg, through the low ground of Axwell Park, and afterwards to the staiths. A man named George Potts of Bates' House, was killed by the upsetting of a waggon or wain on this old coalway in 1710. Another commenced in the neighbourhood of Hollinside and proceeded by Old Axwell and Woodhouse to Swalwell and Derwenthaugh. When waggon-ways were adopted at the end of the 17th century, the line of way from Pontop to Derwenthaugh was called the Main Way, other smaller lines being connected with it. Hutchinson describes this waggon-way as the most expensive that had been made. The rails were of wood and the waggon wheels were of the same material. The following account furnishes us with the cost of the material for the construction of the old railways:—

PER MAIN WAY.
Received George Bowes, Esq.

	£	s.	d.
4917 Sleepers at 8d. ...	163	18	0
4282 Yards of Rails at 6d. ...	107	1	0
Totus ...	270	19	0

May 2nd, 1723.

According to Hutchinson—In the year 1794, about 62,000 Newcastle chaldrons of coals were yearly received at Derwenthaugh, to work, lead, and deliver, at which upwards of 600 men and boys were employed, and about 400 horses, together with 200 keelmen to navigate them down the river to the shipping below the bridge.

The cost of bringing a waggon of coals from Pontop to Derwenthaugh was 2s. 3d. Keels received the coals at the Staiths. Keels in bygone times were strong, oval, and clumsy-looking vessels. Probably the name is derived from the keles of the Greeks and the clax of the Romans, a small swift-sailing vessel. The keel was sometimes navigated by a square sail, but generally by two long oars. When by contrary winds neither sails nor oars could be used, the keel was pushed forward through the shallow parts of the river by a long pole called the pooey, fixed against the bed of the river and the keelman's shoulder, while they walked on each gunnel from head to stern, in a strong, stooping position. The keel was navigated by two men and a lad called the Pe-dee. The keelmen were a strong, hardy, and industrious class of men, but much given to indulge in the intoxicating cup; they earned their money with difficulty, and spent it with corresponding recklessness. Of late years, however, a considerable improvement has taken place in their modes of life, and many of them now are sober, active, and intelligent. A curious custom at one time prevailed among the keelmen. Every time they led a keel of coals from the staith or dike, they got a "can," or an allowance of ale, equal in value to 2s. 6d., and when the number of keelmen was considerable and trade flourished, the stormy scenes that took place in the "Skiff" public house at Derwenthaugh, may be more easily imagined than described; but the increased facilities offered by steam communication on both land and water have considerably injured their trade, and their numbers are consequently diminishing. Formerly the villages of Whickham, Swalwell, and Derwenthaugh were composed mostly of keelmen, to-day their number is not more than twenty. There are at the present time at Derwenthaugh, on the west side, coke ovens and a staith belonging to the Stella Coal Company, also a lofty building in a ruinous condition, at one time used as a malt house. There is also a large house used by Mr Joseph Cowen for an office, which fifty years ago was the residence of Mr. G. H. Ramsay; one of the old staiths is still used by the Consett Iron Company for the coals brought from the Spen (Garesfield) Colliery. There is a third staith belonging to Mr. Joseph Cowen, while eastward stands the disused bone mill and guano works which once flourished under the direction of Mr. Ramsay. On the east side are the coke ovens belonging to Mr. Joseph Cowen. On the west side of the Derwent may be seen the remains of some of the staiths of the 17th century.

At the end of a row of houses running in a line with the railway is a public house, the Skiff Inn, which fifty years ago was occupied by Harry (Henry) Clasper, the renowned oarsman, and in front of the house, alongside of a large pond, stood his boat-building establishment. "Harry" Clasper was born at Dunston, July 12th, 1812. When young, his parents removed to Jarrow, and Harry was sent to work in the pits. After a time he returned to Dunston and worked as a cinder-burner at Derwenthaugh; and when about twenty years of age he became a wherryman for the same firm (Garesfield), removed to the scene of his future triumphs, and became the host of the Skiff Inn. One of his earliest attempts at boat-building was the "Five Brothers," which he built at nights after his day's work was done. In this boat, the crew, consisting of Harry, Robert, William, Edward, and Richard, he was for years victorious at the annual gala on the Tyne, commonly known as "Barge Thursday." On the 16th June, 1842, the Clasper brothers were defeated on the Tyne by a London crew named Newall, Coombes, and J. and R. Doubledee. The Clasper brothers on this occasion rowed in the "St. Agnes" (No. 1), built by John Dobson of Hillgate, which was a clumsy and unwieldy boat, and no doubt contributed not a little to the defeat of the Clasper brothers. Harry, who had improved the shape of the skiff, and had built "The Hawk" in 1840, and "The Young Hawk" in 1841, with which he won at Durham Regatta in 1842, now set about improving the four-oared boat. On December 18th, 1844, he was defeated by Robert Coombes of London, in a skiff race on the Tyne for £100. In 1845, his new four-oared boat, named "The Lord Ravensworth," was finished, and on June 26th, at the Thames Regatta, Harry, with his brothers William and Robert, and his uncle Edward Hawks, won the champion prize of £100, and for the first time the championship of the world was wrested from the Thames. On the 29th of September, 1845, Harry defeated Thomas Carrol on the Mersey; and on November 25th, defeated W. Pocock of London on the Tyne, each match being for £200; in the same year he won the skiff race in "The Hornet," at Shields Regatta. Early in the following year, 1846, he was defeated on the Tyne by Robert Newall in a match for £200; and on the 2nd November, 1847, by Anthony Maddison, in a race for £200. In 1848, in the famous "St. Agnes" (No. 2), Harry and his brothers, with

J. Wilkinson, won the champion prize on the Thames. On July 2nd, 1849, at the Royal Thames Regatta, the champion prize for four-oared boats was again won by the "St. Agnes," the crew of which consisted of Robert and Harry Clasper, and R. and S. Coombes of London. In 1849 Harry removed from Derwenthaugh to The Close, Newcastle. On the 9th September, 1851, he and James Candlish rowed on the Tyne for £100 a side; a collision took place, when Candlish claimed and obtained the stakes. On the 1st January, 1853, "Harry," with his brothers, were defeated by the celebrated Elswick crew, namely, Oliver, Bruce, Winship, and Spoor. On the 8th August, 1854, at the Thames National Regatta, the champion four-oared race of £100, was won by the Elswick crew; the eight-oared race was won by a crew exclusively composed of Newcastle men; a match for £100, between Robert Newall and Harry Clasper, was won by the latter; the Clasper crew gained the landsmen's prize, and Harry Clasper, with Pocock of London, won the waterman's pair-oared match. This was the last time the Clasper brothers rowed together, the name of the boat being the "Lady Kilmorney." On July 22, 1858, Harry won the championship of Scotland, defeating Robert Campbell for £200, and again defeated him on October 6th, in another match for £200, on Loch Lomond; but on November 9th, 1858, he was beaten by Thomas White on the Thames, in a match for £200. He took part in several races afterwards, but age began to tell upon him, and meeting younger men, success did not crown his efforts. He was closely associated with the famous champion, Robert Chambers, in the early part of "Honest Bob's" career, and died on July 12th, 1870. On the Sunday following, his remains were brought by river to Derwenthaugh, after which they were conveyed to Whickham Churchyard, followed by a multitude of people such as has never been seen in the quiet village before or since. The boathouse at Derwenthaugh has been removed, and the pond filled up, and at the present time nothing remains to indicate the site of the once famous establishment.

Three hundred yards west of Derwenthaugh is the Suspension Bridge, connecting the township of Winlaton with Scotswood. Previous to the erection of the bridge, the old turnpike road through Swalwell, was the only way to Newcastle. The bridge was opened April 12th, 1831. It is 630 feet in length, the distance between the two points of suspension being 370 feet, with two half-arcs of 230 feet each; the roadway rises in the centre about eight feet, causing the bridge to assume a curved line of a graceful and pleasing effect; the carriage-way is 17½ feet. On July 21st, 1829, the first freight of stones for the masonry was conveyed to the site of the bridge, and the foundation stone laid on the 9th of February, 1830. The first chain was suspended across the river on the 23rd February, and the last on the 5th March, 1831.

INDEX.

Addison Colliery, 62
Amen Corner, 137
Armstrong, Charles, 104
Anderson, 49
Axwell Park, 171
Axwell, Old, 176
Bagnal, 129, 137
Barmoor, 43
Barlow, 159
Bates' House, 182
Battle of Stella Haughs, 74
Bede Lodge, 165
Belt, Robert, 130
Bells, 6, 103, 140
Birk Gate, 149
Blacket, Sir William, 115
Blackhall Mill, 168
Blaydon, 99
— Burn, 152
Bleachgreen, 130
Boxing, 160
Bradley, 48
— Hall, 48
Braes of Derwent, 153
Brockwell, 152
Broomfield, 166
Brown, Dr., 109
Brown, Rev. William, 104
Bucksnook, 58
Bues Hills, 52
Bullbaiting, 124

Bulman, Joseph, 166
Bunny, 18
Burn Hill, 60
Casson, Hodgson, 131
Castlehill, 47
Cave, 19
Chancer, Thomas, 28, 33
Chare, 47
Charities, 30
Chartists, 126
Chopwell, 164
Claraville, 47
Clasper, Henry, 186
Clavering, Family of, 175
Clavering Arms, 182
Coalburns, 57
Cockfighting, 124, 151
"Coffee Johnney," 136
Congregational Church, 134
Conway, Lord, 75
Cromwell, Oliver, 80, 149
Crowley, Sir Ambrose, 116
Crowley's Court, 120
— Crew, 124
— Poor, 120
Cowen, Jane, 96
— John, 137, 153
— Sir Joseph, 90
— Joseph, 2, 38, 52, 92, 128, 137
— William, 136, 153
Cross, 26, 33, 90

Cuckold's Raw, 182
Curfew, 118, 149
Daniel Farm, 48
Derwenthaugh, 183
Derwentwater, Lord, 66
Dockendale, 100
Dunn, Archibald, 47
— Sarah H, 47
— William M., 62
Easten, 9
Edington, Robert, 59, 81
Elliot, Sir George, 48
Elvaston Hall, 35
Emma Pit, 44
Emmerson, Edward, 82
— John, 126
— Thomas, 97
Eyre, 71, 89
Folly Pit, 54
Forts, 77
Foster, Anthony, 153
— Clark, 153
— General, 66
Freemasons, 127
Galley, 81, 98
Galloway, Robert L., 38
Game, J. O., 37
Gilpin, Bernard, 5
Glebe Pit, 60
Grace, H. W., 132
— William, 182
Greenside, 54
Hagg, 51, 181
Hall, James, 54
— Thomas Y., 55
Hassocks, 76
Haugh, 183
Hauxley, John, 36
Heavygate, 166
Hedgefield, 61
Hedley Fell, 136
Heppel, 143

Hindmarsh, James, 37
Hindhaugh, 36
Hirings, 33
Hodgson, Family of, 114
— Thomas, 91, 137
Holburn Dene, 38
Hopper, Christopher, 58
Horsecrofts, 100, 105
Horsegate, 166
Houston, Cuthbert, 182
Hugergate, 162
Image Hill, 74
Independents, 39
Jenison, Henry, 60
Keels, 185
Kenmure, Lord, 68
Kepyer, 47
Kielder Castle, 144
Kossuth, 73
Kyo, 57
Lamb, Humble, 39
— Joseph, 39
Lambton, 15, 64
Lang Jack, 149
Laurel Leaf, 98
Laycock, Joseph, 128, 132
Leadgate, 59
Lily Crook, 157
— Drift, 163
Lincoln, 73
Lockey, Capt., 179
Lockhaugh, 148
Market, 123
Marmion, 60
Martinson, 61
Mazzini, 73, 94
Milkwell Burn, 169
Mirehouse, 25
Napoleon, 82
Napier, Rev. J. W., 181
Newburn, 76
Newhouse, 166

Newton, Anthony, 90
Nicholson, T. C., 109, 118, 157
Neville's Cross, 33
Oldwell Lane, 131
Orsini, 73
Parish Hall, 35
Parkhead Hall, 143
Payne, 73
Penny Hill, 59
Pethhead, 52
Plague, The, 116
Post Boy, 116
Queen Elizabeth, 84
— Philippa, 33
Quern, 112
Races, 80, 136
Raine, 148
Ramsay, George H., 143
— George R., 144
— John, 143
— Thomas, 153
Ravenside, 169
Ravensworth, Lady, 48
— Lord, 48, 50
Realy-Mires, 60
Rectors, 17
Register, 20
Renwick, William, 135
Ricklis Farm, 60
Ritchie, Rev. Dr., 93
Rockwood, 60
Rotheram, John, 19
Rowlands Gill, 163
Runhead, 38
Rutherford, Dr., 73
Rutherford, Family of, 168
Ryton, 1
— Church, 3
— Cross, 33
— Ferry, 40
— House, 39
— Lawn, 38

Ryton Village, 35
Saltmarket, 135
Sandhill, 126
Saunders, 9, 43
Savings Bank, 38
Scaur Head, 148
Schmalz, Herbert, 39
Secker, Thomas, 19
Selby, 114, 174
Selby's Grave, 158
Simpson, John, 50
— John B., 50, 62
Silverhill, 101
Silvertop, 81
Smailes Lane, 163
Snooks Hill, 156
Sourmires, 50
Spen, High, 161
— Low, 162
Spencer, Thomas, 35
Spring Hill, 171
Square, 131
Staith, 183
Stanley Burn, 51
Stargate, 52
Stella, 63
— Chapel, 87
— Hall, 71
— House, 81
— Staiths, 85
Stephen's Hall, 52
Stints, 42
Stirling, Robert, 163
Stocks, 26
Strothers, 181
Summerhouse Hill, 74
Surtees, Anthony, 169
— Robert, 36
Suspension Bridge, 187
Tablets, Memorial, 9, 104, 139
Tapestry, 73
Terry, Ellen, 143

Thompson, Canon, 61
— Messrs., 129
— J. W., 137
Thornley, 156
Thorp, 9, 11, 14, 15
Tongue Burn, 165
Towneley, 71
Tumulus, 29
Volunteers, 137
Wallace, Sir William, 31
— Terrace, 37
Wallis, Owen, 50
Wardell, R. H., 140
— Charles C., 142
Weeks, Richard M., 38, 92
Wesley, Charles, 37
— John, 46, 56, 160, 162, 178
Westwood, 60
Whitefield, 59
Whitehouse, 38, 171, 175
Whitewell Lane, 35
Widdrington, Family of, 65
Winlaton, 111
— Cemetery, 142
— Church, 138
— Hall, 118, 132
Winlaton Mill, 147
Wood, Nicholas, 50
Woodside, 60
Young, Robert, 46

G. AND T. COWARD, PRINTERS, CARLISLE.

Lightning Source UK Ltd.
Milton Keynes UK
UKHW011031301018
331457UK00005B/783/P